THE RACIAL IMAGINARY
OF THE COLD WAR KITCHEN

RE-MAPPING THE TRANSNATIONAL
A Dartmouth Series in American Studies

SERIES EDITOR
Donald E. Pease
Avalon Foundation Chair of Humanities
Founding Director of the Futures of American Studies Institute
Dartmouth College

The emergence of Transnational American Studies in the wake of the Cold War marks the most significant reconfiguration of American Studies since its inception. The shock waves generated by a newly globalized world order demanded an understanding of America's embeddedness within global and local processes rather than scholarly reaffirmations of its splendid isolation. The series Re-Mapping the Transnational seeks to foster the cross-national dialogues needed to sustain the vitality of this emergent field. To advance a truly comparativist understanding of this scholarly endeavor, Dartmouth College Press welcomes monographs from scholars both inside and outside the United States.

For a complete list of books available in this series, see www.upne.com.

Kate A. Baldwin, *The Racial Imaginary of the Cold War Kitchen: From Sokol'niki Park to Chicago's South Side*

Yuan Shu and Donald E. Pease, *American Studies as Transnational Practice: Turning toward the Transpacific*

Melissa M. Adams-Campbell, *New World Courtships: Transatlantic Alternatives to Companionate Marriage*

David LaRocca and Ricardo Miguel-Alfonso, editors, *A Power to Translate the World: New Essays on Emerson and International Culture*

Elèna Mortara, *Writing for Justice: Victor Séjour, the Mortara Case, and the Age of Transatlantic Emancipations*

Rob Kroes, *Prison Area, Independence Valley: American Paradoxes in Political Life and Popular Culture*

Etsuko Taketani, *The Black Pacific Narrative: Geographic Imaginings of Race and Empire between the World Wars*

William V. Spanos, *Shock and Awe: American Exceptionalism and the Imperatives of the Spectacle in Mark Twain's* A Connecticut Yankee in King Arthur's Court

KATE A. BALDWIN

THE RACIAL IMAGINARY OF THE COLD WAR KITCHEN

From Sokol'niki Park to
Chicago's South Side

To Pamela #1
Forever yours,
Kate

DARTMOUTH COLLEGE PRESS
HANOVER, NEW HAMPSHIRE

Dartmouth College Press
An imprint of University Press of New England
www.upne.com
© 2016 Trustees of Dartmouth College
Manufactured in the United States of America
Typeset in Sabon by Integrated Publishing Solutions

For permission to reproduce any of the material in this book, contact Permissions, University Press of New England, One Court Street, Suite 250, Lebanon NH 03766; or visit www.upne.com

Hardcover ISBN: 978-1-61168-862-7
Paperback ISBN: 978-1-61168-863-4
Ebook ISBN: 978-1-61168-864-1

Library of Congress Cataloging-in-Publication Data available on request

5 4 3 2 1

For Brian, Oliver, Pia, Theo, and Charlotte

CONTENTS

Since first encountering it in a history textbook many years ago, I have been fascinated by the image of Vice President Richard Nixon and Soviet Premier Nikita Khrushchev going head to head in a modular suburban kitchen. The reason for my initial interest was probably irony—two of the most politically powerful men of the period thrashing it out in a space I associated with women. Having mulled it over for some time, what I now see as the most captivating part of this image is less the ideological noise created by the repartee of these political figureheads, but rather the radical silence of the space they occupied. Not so much what was said, but what was left unsaid. For all their messiness, kitchens served as a kind of ideological straightjacket for many of the women who inhabited them on a daily basis during the early Cold War. And a kitchen was equally a container for the structures of labor that these quotidian female rituals layered over. In other words, it was the figures that were not pictured in the iconic photo that spoke to me. As the years have gone on, I have continued to be struck by the absence of women—whose bourgeois subjectivity was named but not embodied in the reporting of this event—and even more so by the absence of women of color, whose labor haunts the postwar, middle-class U.S. kitchen.

This book is an attempt to excavate that absence, to understand it through an archive and prism of texts contemporary to the debate by scrutinizing the kitchen as a rhetorical conceit and as a space of lived realities. Not only is the kitchen everywhere in U.S. media and literature of the late 1950s, but its various logics also inform U.S. and Soviet cultural production of the period in ways that have been overlooked, misapprehended, and misread. In order to do justice to the comparative camber of the above scene, I am interested in puzzling out the Soviet side of this equation and the asymmetrical and yet vital ways black women and Soviet women were put on par with one another—marginalized, silenced, but also hovering at the frame of the bourgeois postwar U.S. housewife and her kitchen.

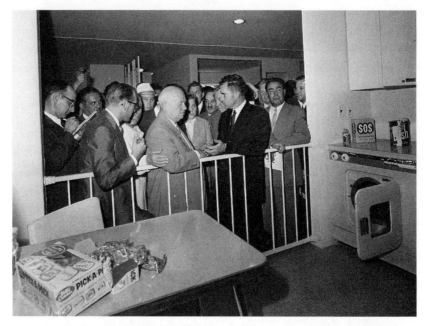

FIGURE P.1. Soviet premier Nikita Khrushchev and U.S. vice president Richard Nixon debate the kitchen at the American National Exhibition in Moscow's Sokol'niki Park, July 24, 1959. Getty Images

In order to reach these histories, this book looks back at the kitchen debate as a defining moment of early Cold War rhetoric. From a U.S. perspective, the debate set the terms and the tone for the ideological differences between the United States and the Soviet Union, and likewise the superiority of democracy over communism. The debate used the pretty persuasion of freedom as consumer plenty to equate market choice with democratic liberties. But the debate and its context also summoned serious questions about the limits of that appeal.

This book asks how the quiet figures of the kitchen—in Moscow and elsewhere—responded to the seductions of U.S. capitalism, how they were structured within its architectures, but also how they constructed alternative modes of inhabitation. I am interested in how the kitchen permeated both American and Soviet cultural production of the period, but also in how some of these nations' most ambitious literary and artistic thinkers of the period responded to the call of the Cold War kitchen.

This call has implications not only for comparative studies of the period, but also for more pointed debates within the fields of feminism and black transnationalism. While many scholars, including myself, have underscored the importance of transnational affiliations for establishing the solidarity of African America with the globally oppressed, the efficacy and afterlives of these connections, especially for women, have remained under-interrogated. In other words, we have yet to have a full conversation about the bonds—and the breaks—of the Soviet international. To a large extent, then, this book is motivated by two things: an interest in what happens when a cultural logic of democracy as consumer choice gets articulated in a site in which actual diversity has been silenced; and, relatedly, what transpires when this logic based in erasure then moves through various cultural sites—American and Soviet—including literature, architecture, film, photography, music, and advertising. The relationship between diversity and captivity is likewise taken up in what follows as a means for thinking through, on the one hand, the appeal of American pluralism and, on the other hand, the accusation of Soviet totalitarianism as the defining features of the West/East division. How might an exclusion of female bodies of color from this binary fracture the larger claims of liberal democracy versus Soviet internationalism?

Thinking this through requires recalling the historical links between Soviet ideology and African American radicalism. Throughout the first half of the twentieth century, Soviet internationalism offered African Americans a model for thinking of themselves as a coherent nation that had structural links to other nationally oppressed peoples. The "Black Belt" thesis, the idea that African America constituted a "community of culture" linked not only by territory but also by language, economics, and psychology, positioned blacks in the U.S. South as an oppressed nation.[1] The thesis came out of the Comintern's Third International in 1928, and was a response to "The Negro Question" that had been posed in 1922 and whose answer was shaped by an interracial group of contributors, including Claude McKay, Otto Huiswood, Harry Haywood, and Sen Katayama. Although the notion of a self-determined black nation in the United States was not a viable political alternative, the yoking of political enfranchisement to cultural autonomy carried a certain purchase with many leading African American artists and intellectuals through the 1950s, including Langston Hughes, Richard Wright, Chester Himes, W.E.B. Du Bois, Shirley Graham, Lorraine Hansberry, Alice Childress, Victoria Garvin, Claudia Jones, Paul Robeson, and Eslanda Robseon. Throughout this period these figures and others were intrigued by the idea of linking self-determination to the notion of a unique black cultural production concentrated within vernacular traditions, and capitalizing on this affiliation as key to black advancement and political action. As I discuss in *Beyond the Color Line and the Iron Curtain*, many of these figures traveled to the Soviet Union to test the waters of proclaimed solidarity with African America, and of Soviet support for racial equality more generally.[2] Yet as knowledgeable as these figures were about the U.S.S.R., they were not invited to participate in the American National Exhibition in Moscow (ANEM), the site of the kitchen debate in 1959. There were, however, African Americans at the exhibition.

"Early in 1958," writes William B. Davis, a U.S. treasury agent, "the U.S. Government was in need of young Russian-speaking Americans to serve as guides at the American National Exhibition in Moscow. Eight hundred young men and women applied; seventy-five were selected. Among this number were four Negroes. I was one of them."[3] Chosen along with Davis were Norris Garnett and Herb Miller; the name of the other black guide has not been identified.[4] Although African American women worked at the exhibition as models for the fashion show and the wedding scene (later cancelled), and black women of American descent were living in Moscow at the time, none were chosen as guides. This problematic performance of U.S. inclusion reflected some of the tensions between the ideals of liberal democracy as racially integrated and the appeal of Soviet internationalism as supportive of American blacks.[5] Before they were selected by the United States Information Agency (USIA), the black American guides were fully vetted, not only regarding their Russian fluency but also as to their ideological affiliations (they were not communist sympathizers).[6] Blacks of American descent who were either well-known in the U.S.S.R., such as Du Bois and Robeson, or living there—including Frank Goode (Eslanda Robeson's brother), George Tynes, Robert Ross, William Patterson, Lily Golden, Margaret Scott, Robert Robinson, and their families—were not called upon to participate. (Granted, there may have been good reason for this: these figures would have been unlikely champions of the American way of life.)

Yet even without the physical presence of Robeson and his more leftist colleagues, these figures were summoned by curious Soviet fairgoers. "Why don't you love Paul Robeson in America?" Davis recalls being asked. "Why didn't the U.S. give Robeson a passport?" Making his affiliations quite clear, Davis retorted, "we don't have *organized love* in America," and noted that most Russians "don't seem to realize . . . that Robeson earned thousands of dollars with his great singing voice in America and . . . is considered by most Americans a wealthy man."[7] Such a reply does not allow for anything other than empty speech: Davis's portrait of "how Negroes live in Russia" ultimately reveals that they do so by remaining out of touch with the world, lacking a true concept of life in the United States and suffering lack of personal freedom, including the freedom to travel at will. Davis's criticisms raise valid points, but they are also overly polemical: "what freedom does the Russian really have except the freedom to be kept in the dark by his government?" he asks. And "No Russian delegation of any kind to visit America has ever included a Russian of Negro extractions. This leaves room for considerable doubt about Russia's official attitude about her own Negroes."[8] Statements like these played into a polarized image of black Americans as either for or against the Soviet Union, leaving the more muddled, and more accurate, portrayal of African American ties to the Soviet Union and to communism more broadly unrehearsed.

Getting lost in an ideological battle between right and wrong is not my endeavor here. What interests me is the fact that political negation was presented as a kind of necessary corollary to the inclusion of racial others at ANEM. This kind of blacklisting of African Americans has been taken up by a rich historical scholarship that traces the political exclusions of the black left in the post–World War II era.[9] Later in the 1960s, a similar pattern would be repeated in U.S. immigration, as white, Eastern European emigrés took visible refuge in the West while Africans became more and more invisible. Just as the politics of liberal pluralism vs. socialist internationalism resulted in easing the immigration of Soviet Jews to the United States, so too would it bring about increased scrutiny of Jim Crow. While we could see this as a productive tension over the years, the limits of racial scrutiny were precisely the issue at the Moscow exhibition.

At the same time that Davis was deflecting questions about racism in the United States, others were decrying the exhibition's planned interracial wedding scene. South Carolina's U.S. senator, Strom Thurmond, objected vehemently to the idea of a racially mixed barbeque and marriage party at the exhibition's fashion show. In addition to Thurmond, forty-one fashion editors signed a letter protesting the mixing of blacks and whites at the staged wedding. Yielding to these collective objections, U.S. officials removed the integrated scenes from the fair.[10] Not before *Look* magazine photographer Paul Fusco, however, took several rolls of film at the wedding tableaux as well as the fashion show. These photos, stored deep within the archives of the Library of Congress, show the faux marriage of Norma and Gilbert Noble. Although *Look* put one image from Fusco's slides on the cover of its June 21, 1960, issue, there was no discussion either of the controversial wedding scene or of ANEM within the

magazine's pages. Fortunately for us, Fusco's photos of these scenes remain as historical documents. (Davis identifies the Nobles as two of the
four African Americans who worked as models at ANEM in his article,
"How Negroes Live in Russia." Although there appear to be more than
two other black models at the wedding party, Davis does not identify
them.) Historians Walter Hixson and Joy Carew both briefly mention
the wedding in footnotes, but neither remarks that the wedding party
was staged at least once while Soviet citizens observed the festivities from
behind glass-paned windows. The U.S. protests against these interracial
tableaux, and their subsequent removal from ANEM, would have undercut the image of racial integration posed by Davis and the other guides,
and given Soviet viewers even more reason to be skeptical of U.S. claims
of racial democracy.[11]

To be sure, the four black American guides would have received considerable pressure to act as native informants, and to "enlighten" Soviets
about racism in the United States. In a report on the exhibition for the
Rand Corporation, another guide, John R. Thomas, noted that, "There
was also significant difference in the questions asked by visitors of different nationalities. Nearly all asked about racial discrimination in the U.S.
But some non-Russian visitors, such as Kazakhs and Uzbeks, inquired
about domination of national minorities by the dominant group in the
U.S. . . . Without exception, Soviet citizens had difficulty comprehending
the fact that the nationality concept as such does not exist in the U.S.
Under the Soviet system, one is a Soviet citizen and then a member of a
nationality group stipulated in his passport. Consequently, after I identified myself as an American, I was inevitably asked about my nationality.
Our Negro guides had even more difficulty in answering the question."[12]
For a Soviet, it may have been hard to imagine that Negroes could have
diverse and even contrary political opinions, that William Davis was no
W.E.B. Du Bois. What is especially interesting, however, is when questions about U.S. racism came from Soviet ethnic minorities.[13]

While we don't have access to these exchanges verbatim, the fact of
their existence offers a moment for thinking about international, cross-
ethnic communications during the Cold War; the conflicts between inclusion and exclusion instantiated by the claims of democracy versus internationalism; and the pressure on race to act as the barometer of social
justice. While the Soviets may nominally have created a multicultural
nation, in which fifteen ethnically diverse republics were federated in a
Soviet state, there can be no denying that ethnic particularism and racism
against non-white minorities ran strong throughout the Soviet period. At

the same time, the United States did not express a particular interest in the peoples of the Soviet republics outside of Russia, but rather typified Soviets as Russians, which is to say ethnically white Russians. It is possible that the United States followed the claim of a unified Soviet people, but in turning a blind eye to the variations within the greater Soviet Union, U.S. observers blurred a fuller picture of diversity. What the record reveals, of course, is that Soviets were of many ethnic extractions. An eagerness to compare notes about racism against ethnic nationals suggests cracks in the ideological edifice of "national in form, socialist in content," as much as it suggests cracks in the sheen of democratic liberalism.[14]

As far as these conversations may take us, however, they still leave behind gender. When the USIA asked William Davis to raise the American flag with a white male guide from Boston, to the tune of "The Star Spangled Banner," as Nixon cut the opening ribbon for the fair, they were inviting racial difference into the picture. But beyond the racial tokenism of this performance, the exhibition's larger articulation of universal subjecthood elided the fact that a racial articulation of the subject is always present in the construction of the abstract individual as representatively male. When we think about Nixon and Khrushchev's exchange, then, we must see it as a performance in which both acknowledgment and expropriation take place, a kind of female minstrelsy in which lack of attribution sidelines all women but marginalizes women of color even more so. Although women of color were present at the exhibition, they have been almost completely removed from the historical record. The removal of black women, in particular, leads us back to a white, masculinist supremacy, gainsaying Nixon's claims of liberal pluralism and challenging the claims of black American guides, such as Davis, who were instructed to engage Soviet interlocutors but dismiss their challenges of U.S. racism. (Although Davis does not discuss the kitchen itself, others who attended the exhibition did, as we will see in the following introduction.) Just as we have failed to take note of the removed wedding scene, we have overlooked its quiet potentialities as a site for thinking through the dynamic intermixing of U.S. and Soviet bodies, desires, politics, and mood.

Not much is known about Norma and Gilbert Noble. They were a couple hired to get married in front of a Soviet audience, to perform at a wedding party that was to be staged and repeated numerous times over the course of the exhibition. The removal of this scene makes clear that key exclusions existed at the heart of the exhibition's structure. While Soviet internationalism hardly solved the problems of national oppression, it did create uneven spaces for imagining what a transnational collectivity might look like, a future yet to be discovered amid the scattered remains of a black Soviet archive. This book offers the Cold War kitchen as one of those spaces, one in which we might see the imperfect elision of Cold War women and their voices—taken up as a call to action.

THE RACIAL IMAGINARY
OF THE COLD WAR KITCHEN

INTRODUCTION: COLD WAR HOT KITCHEN

In the private space of domestic life, the Kitchen Woman Nation's voice murmurs that it is done this way because it has always been done more or less like that; however, it suffices to travel, to go elsewhere to notice that over there, with the same calm obviousness, they do it differently without seeking to explain further, without noticing the profound meaning of differences.

—Michel de Certeau, "Plat du Jour"[1]

IN JULY 1959 COUNTLESS examples of American consumer culture were sent to Moscow's Sokol'niki Park as part of a propaganda campaign known as "The American National Exhibition." Aimed at Soviet viewers, this exhibition was designed to display the splendors of American consumption, from Chevy trucks and the suburban home to cake mixes and cosmetics. In so doing the exhibition sought to stem Soviet anxieties about nuclear war through images and artifacts of a streamlined domestic environment that focused on the joys of living and not the perils of destruction. Masterminded by American architects hired by the United States Information Agency (USIA), the planned environment became a stage for the spectacle of everyday life in the United States. The goal was to showcase the "American Way of Life" as superior in every respect to Soviet living conditions, and thus lure Soviet viewers away from their entrenchment in socialism. The American way, according to the exhibition's planners, was not only better, it was also available to anyone who lived under the sway of democracy.

At this moment when geographic, military, economic, and diplomatic disputes characterized the tensions between the United States and the Soviet Union, a battle of ideas ran alongside these more heated struggles. In September 1958, with the aim of ameliorating tensions on all fronts, the two nations signed an agreement to bolster cultural, scientific, and technological exchange. Although the alleged goal of this pact was the sharing of ideas, it also provided platforms for grandstanding, framed within national exhibitions. The Soviets were the first to share the wealth of their nation's industry: on June 29, 1959, the Soviet trade and cultural exhibition opened at the Coliseum in New York City. Despite the fact that the exhibition featured the satellite *Sputnik* and the internationally revered Soviet space program, the event received only a lukewarm response.

About a month later, the American exhibition hit Moscow, where U.S. journalists dispatched to cover it declared the fair a major success for boldly displaying the bounty of American consumerism. If this was indeed a "cold war," one waged through ideas not bloodshed, then Soviet technological sophistication had been countered by a national ideology that celebrated the abundance of consumer choices and the productive capacity of the economy to please the buyer. Sidestepping the space race and military conflicts, the diversity of consumer goods at the American National Exhibition in Moscow (ANEM) was meant to represent ideals of democracy—difference, multiplicity, and freedom of choice.

The Moscow exhibition was staged by some of the era's most innovative thinkers. Soon after the U.S.-Soviet exchange agreement was reached, President Dwight Eisenhower appointed USIA director George Allen as the exhibition's chief coordinator and the prominent Republican Harold McClellan as general manager.[2] Jack Masey, head of the agency's exhibits division, was named director of design and construction. Masey turned to well-known architect George Nelson to come up with a development team, and Nelson suggested the West Coast designers Ray and Charles Eames as chief consultants. Although the Eameses were best known for their furniture—their plywood chair[3] was already an icon of mid-century design—they considered themselves technicians of communication. They leapt at the chance to put their theories of design and communication to the test in Moscow.

The Eameses' Venice, California, studio became command central for the Moscow exhibition. There they gathered friends including architect and inventor Buckminster Fuller and the film director Billy Wilder. Fuller agreed to construct a geodesic dome, similar to the one he had built for the much-heralded U.S. pavilion in Kabul in 1956. The first point of entry for visitors, the dome was to house the key orienting features that would set the tone for the visitor's experience: the Eameses' seven-screen film, *Glimpses of the USA*; graphic display panels on U.S. architecture, agriculture, science, and education; and an IBM RAMAC computer programmed to answer in Russian four hundred questions about the United States.[4] Adjacent to the dome, a smaller glass pavilion designed by architect Welton Becket would house a cornucopia of American consumerism—splayed out in a grid-like space called the "Jungle Gym," and designed by

Richard Barringer. Several hundred U.S. corporations and manufacturers signed on as financial backers, including Pepsi, American Airlines, Bon Ami, and Mattel, and representative products were to be on display both in the pavilion and around it. The USIA commissioned Disney's "Circarama" theater display; an architecture exhibit curated by Peter Blake; a fashion show directed by Eleanor Lambert; a cosmetology studio by Helena Rubenstein; an exhibit of art from the Whitney Museum of American Art; and Edward Steichen's touring photographic exhibit "The Family of Man"—all of which would be displayed beneath plastic umbrella structures in venues surrounding the central dome.[5]

Among all these stages, the American kitchen—of which there were four on display—would come to be the most historically salient. More than any other space, the kitchen brought together two key aspects of what American innovation had to offer: technology and style. This marriage of science and design was featured in the RCA/Whirlpool "miracle kitchen," the General Mills labor-saving kitchen, and the General Electric suburban home kitchen. But it was not only for these new styles and inventions that the kitchen took on such prominence in the American National Exhibition.

Instead, the kitchen became remembered as the setting of a diplomatic showdown between U.S. vice president Richard Nixon and Soviet premier Nikita Khrushchev. Held in the kitchen of a Long Island modular house that had been split in half—and thus dubbed "splitnik" by the Soviets—the exchange between Nixon and Khrushchev was dubbed by U.S. journalists the "kitchen debate."[6] Elsewhere in the exhibition, Eisenhower's "Atoms for Peace" campaign featured a model of an atom that some outsiders predicted would become the exhibition's feature attraction. But the atom was upstaged and superseded by the kitchen.[7] Nixon's handlers had chosen the kitchen as the backdrop for the leaders' exchange because they believed it best represented the triumphs of capitalism, showcasing the pleasures of consumer culture over and against the labor-weary backwardness of Soviet communism. So key was the staging for the showdown between Nixon and Khrushchev that, on the previous evening, U.S. planners had summoned photographers and journalists to the site to line up the best camera angles. Though chosen by Nixon's men as a ploy to advertise consumer culture to the Soviets, the kitchen proved to offer much more than a photo op.

As an historical place of women's labor, the kitchen has long been a feminist touchstone, a focus of women's thought and literature in addition to the space of their daily toil. How strange, then, to have two men waging ideological warfare in this prototypically private and female space. Yet the use of the kitchen to advertise the bounty of American consumerism underscored its political valences. The *New York Times* reported that, "the purpose was to show the American economy as it is broadly shared by all the people, the immense variety and great freedom of choice."[8] The kitchen encapsulated freedom American-style, and the U.S. press described it as a "little America in the heart of Moscow."[9] What could be more exemplary of an emancipated populace than their easy access to the appliances of the free market? Although the phrase "kitchen debate" never appeared in the Soviet coverage of the event and likewise does not serve as a reference point in the annals of Soviet history, the moment is clearly etched in U.S. popular consciousness. The debate was where Nixon faced down the belligerent Khrushchev, and as reported in the United States, it was a slam dunk for the West and its women.

As much as it helped to produce a dualism, the kitchen debate also reflected the binary logic typical of Cold War discourse in the United States. This discourse was characterized by central antagonisms between East and West, communism and capitalism, godlessness and god-fearing, evil and good. But on closer consideration, it quickly becomes apparent how radically unstable these oppositions were—even within the venue in which its distinctions should be most apparent. Nonetheless, the export of the U.S. kitchen to Moscow established an early example of the broadcasting of binary thinking as a hallmark of America's approach to the world: as if the world could be grasped from within two positions.

An idea of two-ness pervaded not only America's global understanding during the Cold War, but also the notion of its own exceptionalism.[10] A belief in the United States as an "exception" to the paradigms of self-government through which European nations understood themselves informs much of the foundational work in conceptualizing the United States, from John Winthrop's 1630 sermon, "City on a Hill," to Alexis de Tocqueville's 1835 account of the United States' egalitarianism, to Frederick Jackson Turner's 1893 "Frontier Thesis." The problematic conception of America as both exemplary to the rest of the world and exempt from critiques infused state thinking in the period after World War II, a period encapsulated for many by the visionary proclamations of Henry Luce in his famous essay, "The American Century." Written in 1941, this essay launched an understanding of the era to come as one in which the world would be led by American forms—political and cultural.[11] Following Luce, the architects of the exhibition understood America's voice as the preeminent one in the Cold War. As exemplified by the exhibition's planning and execution, this calling could be transmitted as one of connectivity, resonance, and understanding through empathy—a universalism that sought to establish not only norms of subjectivity but also ways of understanding otherness. In attempting to move American studies beyond exceptionalist frameworks, Brian Edwards and Dilip Gaonkar have argued that it is impossible to imagine from such a position "that the American voice could just be one among many, one that could easily not be heard or not resonate in certain parts of the world."[12] The planners of ANEM were unable to conceive of the possibility that the America they presented as both exemplary—an ideal—and as average—available to all—would not be universally appealing, nor could they understand that the logic of exceptionalism subtending their exhibition would not resonate with all Soviet visitors, not because they were locked in a binary system that opposed the West, but because their reactions were multiple, discontinuous with expectation.

Diversifying Captivity

The Cold War kitchen was a surprisingly frequent point of reference not only for architects and politicians, but also for writers, filmmakers, advertisers, and others for whom this dynamic space was both a place of departure and an end, both restrictive and inspiring. As such the kitchen offers a lens through which to interrogate the reigning ideals of postwar American exceptionalism and the broadcasting of this ideology, as well as Cold War rhetoric about women and minorities during the late 1950s and early 1960s. Tracing key facts and facets of the debate between Nixon and Khrushchev through each of its chapters, this book shows how the kitchen was, in fact, an organizing principle not only for contemporary designers and filmmakers, but also for literature by women. The kitchen informed both canonical texts and those that have been overlooked. *The Racial Imaginary of the Cold War Kitchen* demonstrates how the insights of these texts constellate around the kitchen and explains why the kitchen created lasting reverberations and resonances alongside deep political meanings. In so doing, this book maps the ways structures of feeling associated with domesticity in the United States were taken up, championed, reconstituted, and resisted in the Soviet Union, where American architects and cultural exchanges were, in architect Buckminster Fuller's words, turning "weaponry into livingry."[13]

If the kitchen debate announced the political uses of domestic spaces, it also revealed the complexly embedded logics of captivity buried within

American narratives of domesticity in general and in narratives of the kitchen in particular. U.S. press coverage affirmed that American superiority over the Soviets was lodged in freedom of consumer choice.[14] "Diversity," Nixon claimed, was synonymous with "the right to choose." Nixon's invocation of "diversity" as a matter of "choice" between abundant options was explicitly linked to gendered consumerism. After all, "Americans were interested in making life easier for their women." When Khrushchev replied that the Soviet Union "did not have the capitalist attitude towards women," Nixon's retort was even more compelling: "I think that this attitude toward women is *universal*. What we want to do is make easier the lives of our housewives."[15]

Nixon's confusion of "women" and "housewives" offered Khrushchev only a point of disjuncture: there were no housewives, per se, in Russia (or there were *only* housewives, though not the sort Nixon imagined— these housewives had day jobs outside the home).[16] Moreover, Nixon's unconscious collapsing of *woman* and *housewife* provided the ammunition for his pride in the United States as exemplary of universal attitudes towards housewives. In this account of democratic liberties, consumer choice begets human rights and an interest in female autonomy is submerged in the idealization of American domesticity as sacred. Yet the binary logic at work in Nixon's rhetoric erases not only the histories of gender inequity, but also those of racial subordination.

The gambit of this book is that we can understand the mid-twentieth-century kitchen as symptomatic of these erasures, and as a site for addressing these elisions. Doing so means bringing together two antagonistic understandings of the Cold War kitchen—Nixon's understanding and the one that informed its dynamic artifacts. In *The Racial Imaginary of the Cold War Kitchen*, these artifacts are understood as the political unconscious of Nixon's discourse. In order to get a fuller picture of these antagonisms, we must begin by addressing the slew of associations stirred up by the kitchen scene in Moscow. To be sure, Nixon deployed the housewife as a powerful ideological weapon. But in so doing he relied unwittingly on associations among domesticity, female sentiment, and American empire that had been previously established. At least as early as the nineteenth century, the term "domestic" had two simultaneous registers, gesturing at once to the home and to the homeland. These spheres were conventionally split through a division of labor: women occupied the home, men occupied the land. As Amy Kaplan has pointed out, however, if women and men were divided into private and public spheres during this period, they were at the same time aligned nationally against the foreign. Slippages between these various intonations of the domestic enabled domesticity to do the work of establishing the racial boundaries of the foreign, because a woman's sphere of sentiment was set up as the morally privileged site (however unstable) that condoned and authorized the expansion of American empire. Thus the image of social unity—of universal attitudes and emotions generated from the home kitchen—actually depends upon and sustains visions of domestic expansion. At the same time, these "universal" attitudes parse who and what can be accepted into the national space. What is so interesting then about Nixon's stance in Moscow is the way in which he unconsciously steps into the position of female authority at the heart of a sentimental ethos, proclaims this ethos universal, and in so doing abets the imperial expansion of the United States while implicitly proclaiming its internal limits. The authority of this stance relied on Nixon's ability to conceal the Cold War kitchen's political unconscious—its disavowals and erasures—from both Khrushchev and himself.

The ideological uses to which the kitchen was put occluded the histories (of slavery, colonialism, and racial genocide) upon which the claim of superiority was staked. And in order for the idea of "universalism" to ring true, there could be no particularized woman in this kitchen. In U.S. press coverage, Nixon and Khrushchev debated the relative merits of appliances and household gadgets in the kitchen of a tract house shipped from Brooklyn, but there was no American housewife anywhere to be seen.[17] Khrushchev shrewdly noted this absence when he asked an American guide to "Thank the housewife for letting us use her kitchen for our argument."[18] His invocation of the absent housewife underscored not only Soviet skepticism about U.S. technological feats, but also a constitutive ambivalence between presence and absence when it comes to the gendered and racialized terms of universal subjecthood in the American kitchen.

Nixon's declarations about housewifery also should be considered in the context of another event that caught Khrushchev's attention. Congress had declared "Captive Nations Week" just as Nixon was departing for Moscow; this measure called attention to the fate of nations oppressed by Communism and other non-democratic regimes.[19] In 1959, the declaration called for "a week of prayer for peoples enslaved by the Soviet Union." On the one hand then, Nixon's kitchen rhetoric declares support for diversity in the marketplace and for liberating women. On the other hand, his attitude also forces women into a position of captivity. (Nixon wasn't in Moscow promoting a wealth of new job opportunities for women, after all.) In this sense, the universalizing tendency of global democracy encourages ease for its women, so long as they stay within the domestic sphere.[20] To be sure, Nixon could not have been conscious of the foreclosures in his speech. In fact, it was his lack of recognition of racial subordination and sexual inequality that produced his ability to speak from the Cold War kitchen with authority. As demonstrated by the experimental novels *Like One of the Family*, by Alice Childress, and *A Week Like Any Other*, by Natalya Baranskaya, Nixon's proclamation that diversity in the marketplace liberates women necessarily highlights their captivity in the Cold War kitchen.

Never one to miss an opportunity for sarcasm, Khrushchev greeted Nixon by welcoming him to "the land of captive people." He went on, "Would that the Vice President who has just landed come and see these captive people who are present here."[21] Khrushchev wasn't the only Soviet aware of Nixon's slippery discourse. A visitor to the exhibition identified as an engineer, with the surname Yatsenko, commented that, "In the miracle kitchen a woman is just as free as a bird in a miracle cage. The miracle kitchen shown at the exhibition demonstrates America's last word in the field of perfecting obsolete forms of everyday living which stultify women."[22] Women were not only caged, however, but positioned in the proverbial kitchen, as part of an ideology that Amy Kaplan calls America's culture of "manifest domesticity."[23] It is this site of agency and influence that Nixon invoked by deploying the kitchen as a space of moral righteousness, a position he could take only through an ability to conceal—from himself and his audience—the Cold War kitchen's erasures.

While useful in this context, an internal/external framework of the domestic also occludes the particular subjectivities identified by the term. In the 1950s, the term "domestic" was not limited to the duality that Kaplan suggests: it also outlined a subjectivity, that of *the* domestic, frequently African American, who labored in the American kitchen. Kitchens in America had been segregated at least since the days of the plantation kitchen, which was physically separated from the rest of the house. As Trudier Harris has argued, a symbolic chasm between white and black spaces exists even after the kitchen becomes part of the house.[24] The middle-class American kitchen retains the remnants of this association— the kitchen as the place where cheap labor provides familial nourishment that is then consumed elsewhere. The constitutive ambivalence between presence and absence is already caught—captivated, as it were—by the larger, sedimented and racialized vectors of domesticity, diversity, and captivity within which the kitchen debate was staged.

The exclusion of women and minorities from the kitchen at ANEM—
that is, the occlusion of the material bodies who do the kitchen's work—
intensified the affective confusion between inside and outside, state and
self, public and private, on display in Moscow. The binary logic suggested
by Nixon's discourse in the kitchen enabled the disavowal not only of
their presence, but also of the breach created by the fiction of this absence.
The Racial Imaginary of the Cold War Kitchen takes up the kitchen as
symptomatic of such a fissure, disclosing it as a site for addressing the
ruptures inherent to Nixon's kitchen logic. When read in the context of
archival sources—including the U.S. and Soviet press, USIA records, and
the comments of Soviet visitors—the kitchen can be seen not only as a
central conceit for the alleged ideological superiority of U.S. capitalism,
but also as a central affective site in the circuitry of U.S. domesticity during the period. The occlusions of the Cold War kitchen presented a kind
of affective conditioning, a way of being in the world. Most crucial to the
study of the Cold War kitchen, therefore, is this book's focus on the erasure of racial and sexual inequalities, not only in Nixon's assessment, but
also from subsequent accounts of what happened in Sokol'niki Park.[25]

If You Can't Stand the Heat

The kitchen debate has become a key reference point for acknowledging the problematic claims of Eisenhower's administration regarding U.S.
consumer culture in the 1950s. For example, historian Elaine Tyler May
points out that Nixon exaggerated the liberating features of the kitch-
en's so-called labor-saving devices, while Beatriz Colomina describes how
many of the technologies on display in the kitchen came directly from
those developed by the military during World War II. Borrowing from
Joseph Nye's idea of "soft power," Victoria De Grazia and Gregory Castillo use the debate as a prime example of the opening of a third front
on which to wage the Cold War—that of culture. And in her articles
on Soviet domesticity, Susan Reid emphasizes the ambivalence many Soviet visitors expressed when asked to describe their reactions to ANEM.[26]
Ruth Oldenziel and Karin Zachmann's important collection, *Cold War
Kitchen: Americanization, Technology, and European Users,* investigates
the American kitchen through its international circulation as ideological
construct and material space. As the editors point out, both Nixon and
Khrushchev recognized the political symbolism of the modern kitchen
and the fact that "the kind of technological innovation represented in this
everyday context spoke to the political system that produced it."[27]

While indebted to these studies and the critical research they have amassed, *The Racial Imaginary of the Cold War Kitchen* offers a different lens through which to investigate the Cold War kitchen. When Nixon walked into the General Electric kitchen in Moscow, he entered a space that was far from neutral. Long before ANEM's design team was formed, the American kitchen was already a key part of Cold War consciousness, replete with material histories and a highly politicized interior. Through the kitchen's various appearances and articulations in literature, film, design, and advertising—in both the United States and the Soviet Union—I show how Nixon's promotion of the kitchen as the best representative of freedom and democracy actually helped to make the social ties between Americans and their kitchens more systematically invisible. In fact, the ideological and material realities of the kitchen as a site of female domestic toil, racial segregation, and critical "feeling states" were all present in Moscow, although the exhibition's designers did their best to hide them. In his 1957 *Problems of Design,* George Nelson wrote, "What I dislike very much is the visual evidence of the machine—I would greatly prefer having it out of sight."[28] Following this preference for hiding the machinery through innovative design, the exhibition presented a kind of science fiction of technological advancement. In the presence of automated appliances, labor became a kind of clutter to be expunged from the scene. This paradox of presence and absence is central to the Cold War kitchen: like the new technological innovations, women also are present there. But their work can be hidden behind labor-saving devices and, to a large extent, women and minorities were the "machines" removed from sight in the Moscow kitchen.

Only two years before the kitchen debate, the Soviets had demonstrated their technological prowess with the launch of *Sputnik* (thus motivating the formation of NASA). Many of the previously mentioned studies focus primarily on how Nixon placed his emphasis on consumer goods in Moscow, a calculated shift away from space and nuclear technologies. But Nixon could not advance any agenda without a means to communicate it.

The American exhibition was not only broadcasting a new vision for the world, it was also creating a newly prioritized place for communications within that world.[29] Thus the exhibition marked a key moment in the histories of both the design and the communications industries. When Luce proclaimed the twentieth century as the American Century, he inaugurated a forward-thrusting mandate of U.S. cultural hegemony. ANEM brought some of this mandate to fruition with the dome and the jungle gym, with computer and television technology. With these new advances at the forefront, ANEM marked the debuts of, among other things, the televisual image as public stage; what Paul Edwards identifies as the "closed world" of data-driven, computational understandings of modern life; and the multimedia installation—all wrapped into one experiential and sensorial environment. One of the key contributions of the Eameses, who went on to partner with IBM after Moscow, was their belief that the world could be modernized by communication. Echoing both Luce and the directives of USIA, the Eameses' work supported a notion of globally converging subjectivities. Their notes make clear that they sought to win over the Soviets and change the way they thought—all under the guise of universalism.[30] Relying on a set of tools rooted in sentiment, the Eameses used the technologies at hand to relay notions of continuity between "us" and "them." Rather than deploying mathematical formulas or computer algorithms, the Eameses worked with aesthetic and affective processes, employing empathy and envy to demonstrate how personhood could be worked into products.[31] The Eameses set out to demonstrate how a communications-based global democracy could be the new force of good in the world, as opposed to the backwards totalitarianism of the Soviets.

How Soviet citizens would respond to these attempts at winning them over—how they would answer back—was not really an issue. For the Eameses, the United States was not one of many nodal points with which foreign peoples might engage; it was both the image and the end. According to this logic, a person must become—must see, feel, and respond—like an American in order to understand the world. The Eameses' film *Glimpses of the USA* became a gateway for such attunement. Through the logic of exceptionalism advocated in Moscow, America became the more universal universal, wherein, as Donald Pease has elegantly argued, U.S. ideals were limited in order to protect the idea of these ideals.[32]

If the communications industry represented the perfect instrument for propounding American exceptionalism, then the kitchen became its mouthpiece. We witness this in diverse readings of the kitchen in the years before and after the Moscow moment, including those in Sylvia Plath's *The Bell Jar*, Natalya Baranskaya's *Nedelia kak nedelia* (*A Week Like Any Other*), Lorraine Hansberry's *A Raisin in the Sun*, and Rouben Mamoulian's *Silk Stockings*, along with those of the countercultural Soviet youth known as the *stilyagi*, to name just a few. As these examples demonstrate, the kitchen is not only a physical space; it also travels (as Certeau remarks in the epigraph to the chapter). By going elsewhere with these wayward kitchens, we can latch onto the discontinuities they summon; this book is, in part, an attempt to provide a roadmap for those differences—and for contemplating their profundity. Along the way, the discussion will reconfigure the binaries used to read global polarity, racial hegemony, and the sexual division of labor—all of which are typically taken as axiomatic narratives of the postwar era and its kitchen.

While the Moscow iteration of the U.S. kitchen may have reproduced the logic of American exceptionalism, it also offers an opportunity to observe instances of this idea's undoing. The texts discussed in *The Racial Imaginary of the Cold War Kitchen* offer opportunities to understand how this universal space was not only resisted, but refused and returned in ways that did not correlate with U.S. expectations. Taken together, they bear witness that the mechanisms through which people understood themselves to be American—or un-American—in the mid-twentieth century were intimately linked to the kitchen as a space of exception.

Communications Breakdown

The American National Exhibition in Moscow defined a particular moment in consumer culture and helped to launch a communications industry that subtended the discourse of American exceptionalism through—and perhaps beyond—Luce's century. Defining a "communication unit" as "one person hearing one question put by a member of the crowd and answered by a guide," the organizers originally estimated that ANEM would involve 30 to 40 million such units, or about 15 to 20 for each person attending the exhibit, which the report described as "a record of some kind in the history of international communication."[33] Reports from the *New York Times* spread the word of this achievement: "The U.S. Government has given itself an A+ in communicating ideas at the American National Exhibition in Moscow," opened one dispatch.[34] But if the exhibition actually set a "record of some kind," the particularities and implications of this record have been largely overlooked. Relying on a triangulated system of anecdotal reporting, in which overheard conversations were the principal source of data, the USIA supported a unidirectional kind of information flow. The relationships among question, crowd, and answer are important here. Although this system acknowledged the function of the individual as both an independent shaper of the question and as part of a larger group, the process for determining its rate of success stopped at the guide's answer. The scattershot nature of this approach did not listen for crowd response or account for crowd noise. It assumed each answer was heard and absorbed as intended.[35]

Nonetheless, it was the communications success of ANEM that vivid journalistic accounts projected back home, accompanied by photos boasting of Soviets spellbound by U.S. consumer goods. The Soviet response beyond these reports—the reverberation of individual accounts through Soviet cultural production—has received much less attention. Although the USIA acknowledged a discrepancy between American press reports on the exhibition and Soviet reactions on the ground, that discrepancy has faded from memory.[36] As with other American texts from the same period that lodged logics discontinuous with the narratives of American exceptionalism, the Soviet reception of ANEM goes to the heart of the kitchen, though in divergent ways.

Although the USIA report cast the exhibition as a watershed moment in international communications, we can never know precisely what that meant. Nor can we ever know what, exactly, was communicated to Soviet citizens. Some vestiges of Soviet reaction exist: polls were taken at voting machines stationed throughout the exhibit; U.S. guides replied to a questionnaire in August 1959; and some visitors left intriguing comments in the exhibition's "guest books." More than 2.7 million Soviets visited the exhibition over five weeks, well over the allotted quota of 50,000 per day. Given that figure, the database of reactions seems scant in comparison. About 15,000 people used the voting machines; only about 2000 signed the guest books.[37] Although the guest books may not reveal what people honestly thought about the exhibition, the reactions recorded in them are worth considering, especially as they help to shed light on Soviet impressions of the ideological differences between the two state systems, and on the kitchen as central to these differences.[38]

In his recent book, *The Democratic Surround*, Fred Turner provides an historical background for the tendency in media studies to rely too glibly on the utopian possibilities of technology to democratize the world. To excavate the connections among democracy, liberalism, and technology, Turner turns to the intellectual milieu surrounding new media during and just after World War II. Here Turner locates compelling links between anti-fascism and the development of democratic uses for media by those seeking to avoid the "one to many" paradigm of Nazi propaganda. Turner describes how "multi-image, multi-sound-source media environments" were developed in order to counter the threat of fascism. He argues that psychologists of the 1940s—seeking to oppose the controlling psychology of Nazism—endeavored to create a new, anti-totalitarian state of mind. To this end they "developed a theory of what I will call *surrounds*." These psychologists (and, later, other intellectuals and artists) believed that experiencing such surrounds would enable individuals to make rational choices based on the available range of options, thereby paving the way for democratic decision-making and a democratic personality.[39] Turner uses ANEM as one of his many examples of this attempt at democratic personality-shaping, seeing in the Moscow surround a version of how "political choices and consumer choices became a single integrated system. . . . Mass individualism grounded in the democratic rhetoric of choice."[40] He also links such staunchly democratic media deployment to the advent of countercultural movements and moments, from John Cage's performances to the human be-ins that popped up in and around San Francisco in the late 1960s. Key to Turner's thesis is the contention that the technologies and ideologies of surrounds, "first came into being as part of the same urge to defeat the forces of totalitarianism that animated the most aggressive cold warriors," claiming that "for them, and for their backers in the federal government during and after WWII it was the job of the state to defend that diversity, at home and overseas. And it was the job of intellectuals and artists to develop modes of media and mediated interaction that could transform the integration of diversity into an experience that could be enjoyed by everyday citizens."[41]

While Turner's work is richly suggestive, it imagines the democratic world in and through an American guise. Turner's interpretation of the Soviet response to ANEM discounts the skepticism with which many Soviets met the exhibition. In fact, the archive of reception indicates a very uneven response.[42] Similarly, the "surround" schematic mutes the racialized and gendered assumptions that undergird the notion of choice and diversity as paradigmatically democratic. As I have indicated above, the syncretization of political choices and consumer choices occluded the manifest ways in which those choices were not really options at all, but rather constrained moments in which coercion and consent commingled while hiding the social histories of their availability. The suppression of the actual ideals of democracy for the *idea* of those ideals suffuses the entire environment of the exhibition. Admittedly, Turner is primarily interested in modes of interaction and attention, rather than representations (or what he might call texts) themselves.[43] But the images and sounds on display at ANEM shaped affects and moods at least as much as the technologies through which they were broadcast. In the development of perceptual skills, aesthetics matter not just in form but also in content.

The slippery terms of totalitarianism in the mid-twentieth century also deserve a closer look. While Turner casts his democratic surrounds within the struggle against totalitarianism, he does not fully explore the differences between Nazi Germany and Soviet Russia. But this distinction was being made by some intellectuals of the time, including W.E.B. Du Bois, Lorraine Hansberry, Paul Robeson, and Shirley Graham. As Vaughn Rasberry has argued, some African American intellectuals were rethinking the idea of totalitarianism in the late 1950s through the lens of racial terror in the United States. By reconsidering the political histories of colonialism, slavery, and Jim Crow, they juxtaposed the conflict between democracy and totalitarianism alongside the rise and fall of the color line.[44] Critical insights such as Rasberry's open up the dualism between East and West. In *The Racial Imaginary of the Cold War Kitchen*, I further explore this breach and the fantasy of historical progression that it troubles.

While some Soviets were impressed by the breadth and splendor of the American spectacle, many others proved resistant to the ideas of freedom and equality allegedly on display at the exhibition. Some proclaimed an aversion to the claims of superiority of a system that placed personal gratification over communal good. In rejecting the idea of a universal norm of femininity—and a correlative universal register of empathy—some revealed an awareness of the connections between the captivity of women and minorities in the Cold War kitchen and beyond. The point of attending to these responses is not merely to offer the other side of the story, but to reveal a key aspect of Cold War history that has previously remained murky: the unstable embeddedness of the United States in the Soviet Union and vice versa.

The kitchen debate serves as a through-line for each chapter, threaded from the segregation of the U.S. kitchen to its material mechanics and the emotional landscapes in between. Each chapter highlights a different aspect of the debate to reveal the layered ways in which the event was produced by—and productive of—key ideas about U.S. domesticity in the later 1950s. At the same time, I explore the ways in which the kitchen was importantly employed not only in changing the way Americans and Soviet imagined private life, but also in attempting to persuade Soviets to democracy.

Chapter 1 discusses how the Eameses' film, *Glimpses of the USA,* epitomizes the ways in which visual technologies intended as affective sources of ideological agitation were used to condition Soviet subjectivity. Chapter 2 reframes American claims of democratic diversity through the radical imaginary of Plath's *The Bell Jar.* Chapter 3 addresses the historical segregation of the American kitchen through the lens of Childress's *Like One of the Family* and Baranskaya's *A Week Like Any Other.* Chapter 4 looks at affective labors of the kitchen in the work of Hansberry.

Chapter 5 examines the film *Silk Stockings*, the Soviet counterculture youth group known as *stilyagi*, and the fashion of Christian Dior in Moscow, to show how the logic of the kitchen permeated popular culture. An epilogue examines the paradoxical plights of Marguerite and Marina Oswald, the mother and wife, respectively, of Lee Harvey Oswald, caught in the kitchen on the morning of November 23, 1963.

The places and spaces brought together here represent just two geographic locales among many possibilities. One might just as productively investigate the uses and meanings of the kitchen in India, China, Mexico or other sites—exploring how the interplay of domesticity and captivity might play out in ancillary or contested spaces in the global Cold War. Rather than reinstantiating a binary, however, I hope to trouble it from within by looking at the unequal and marginalized positions of women across the Iron Curtain and along the color line. *The Racial Imaginary of the Cold War Kitchen* takes up their texts and repositions them in the discontents of the global imaginary from which they came.

ENVY AND OTHER WARM GUNS: RAY AND
CHARLES EAMES AT THE AMERICAN NATIONAL
EXHIBITION IN MOSCOW

Every design is in some sense a social communication, and what matters is not so
much the importance of the object . . . as the emotional intensity with which the
essentials have been explored and expressed.

—George Nelson, *Problems of Design*

Our presentation gives as varied a cross-section of American life as can be found
today . . . we hope that among the visitors will be those who see the point underlying this effort—that capitalism does not exploit the common man at all, but bends
its most ingenious efforts toward raising his standard of living by offering him a
staggering diversity of goods.   —*Saturday Evening Post* editorial, August 1, 1959

WHEN CHARLES AND RAY Eames emerged from their plane in Moscow,
two days before the opening of the American National Exhibition, they
had in hand the seven reels of film that would debut as the central exhibition feature, *Glimpses of the USA*. Although the United States Information Agency (USIA) was in charge of the exhibition, no one in the State
Department had laid eyes on the film. Likewise, the American guides who
had been planted in the dome to aid Soviet viewers began their tours of
duty without a glimpse.[1] As Charles Eames noted, "Theoretically, it was a
statement made by our State Department, and yet we did it entirely here
and it was never seen by anyone from our government until they saw it
in Moscow."[2] Such secrecy was in keeping with the Eameses' habits; they
kept a tight grip on their plans for both the film and the dome in which
it would be screened. The couple was quite bold in their insistence on artistic and aesthetic autonomy. Nonetheless, the connections between the
designers' innovations and government aims were multiple.

Both the designers and U.S. officials were aware that ANEM offered
access to Russia on a scale unavailable since World War II; all were eager
to capitalize on this opportunity and turn it to their advantage.[3] Overall,

Nelson and the Eameses hoped to promote the message that better goods equaled better lives, that Americans had beat the Soviets in a race for better standards of living.[4] As Fred Turner has shown, however, these ideas of superiority had been influenced by the lessons of the psychologists, social scientists, and mathematicians who witnessed the destructiveness of fascism in World War II and, as a result, sought to devise new methods for combating totalitarianism. Equipped with the notion of a democratic personality, the Eameses meant to shape the minds of Soviet fairgoers. As Turner notes, the designers "took the fusion of Bauhaus aesthetics, Gestalt psychology, and pro-America psychological training born during World War II and turned it to a new purpose: integrating the psyches of our potential enemies, the citizens of the Soviet Union."[5]

U.S. postwar thinking about fascism rarely delineated the slippery terms of totalitarianism, however, and Sovietism was often collapsed into Nazism.[6] Meanwhile, having suffered devastating losses at the hands of Hitler's troops, the Soviets were preoccupied with defining themselves *against* fascism. U.S. approaches to the Eastern Bloc revealed little appreciation of this difference, and ANEM's designers appeared to understand Soviet culture as a product of top-down conformity that mirrored the dynamics of totalitarian power.

The fusing of the experiences of individuation and collective participation became the designers' stated aim. To this end, Nelson admitted that "the experiment is more one of communication than of design technique." This required what Nelson described as "a designer-government team."[7] As Nelson's terminology indicates, the ideals of market democracy and the exhibition's aesthetic principles and communication techniques were very closely allied. The architecture of the exhibition was designed to move Soviet visitors through space in ways that would activate their senses and turn them toward corporate America and democracy—and away from Soviet domination (see fig. 1.1).

The Eameses' idea of a democratic state of mind was based on the psychological theories of Claude Shannon, author of *The Mathematical Theory of Communication*, and Norbert Wiener. Shannon's theory of information understood communication as the individual transmission of messages—amplified, reduced, and repeated so as to be as clear as possible. And Wiener's concept of individuals as encoders and decoders linked the role of individuals to that of machines; both were at root "communicative organisms," comprised of information exchange. Though linked by processes of communication, individuals had the potential to be different from one another, and the channels of their "internal communication

AMERICAN NATIONAL EXHIBITION IN MOSCOW

FIGURE 1.1. Map of ANEM site plan, from "Designer's Comments and Extracts from a 'Log' on the American National Exhibition," *Industrial Design* 6.4 (April 1959): 50. Courtesy of Vitra Design Museum archive

[were] essential to the welfare of society."[8] The Eameses reworked Shannon's and Wiener's theories to link new modes of relaying information to the possibilities for a comprehensively inclusive democratic world. Their focus on the interactions between people highlighted the importance of *feedback* to the sustenance of this system. It is here—within the ANEM communications web generally, and at the site of the feedback loop more particularly—that this chapter pauses. The ways in which Soviet visitors were positioned at ANEM, how they responded to this positioning, and the opinions they expressed all destabilize the smooth operation of an instantaneous relay. Although the sampling of that reception is far from comprehensive, American guides on the ground in Moscow were perplexed about their Soviet audiences, and the USIA report indicates some fumbling incomprehension. At the time the fair closed, bureaucrats remained at a loss to explain why the exhibition was popular, or even if it had been popular at all. One limit of the theory of communication applied in Moscow is that it cannot imagine nor accommodate a message that goes astray, that does not produce a predictable response, thus rendering the feedback loop discontinuous. This short-circuiting of the system reveals the limits of the Eameses' idea of empathy in Moscow,

and likewise the limits of a democratic state of mind conceived within an exceptionalist paradigm. In this chapter, I link Nixon's quip about a "universal attitude" towards women to the active orchestration of public response to the exhibition, and ask how Soviet reception of the American exhibition troubled the attempt to appeal to the Soviets through sentiment.

First, I discuss the background and planning of the exhibition, in order to establish just how closely aligned were the efforts of designers and government officials to produce, on the one hand, an emotional convergence between Americans and Soviets and, on the other hand, a feeling of envy in the Soviet audience. An insistence on sameness depends upon a narrative of shared values and investments, while an insistence on difference requires a dis-identification with that very same narrative—the Soviet Union as the envious "other." Production of this double motion relied heavily upon an affective attunement of the audience with the exhibition's emotional circuitry, which was set up to display diversity as exemplary of U.S. ideals and principles at the same time that it curtailed those very principles through the tightly orchestrated management of the visitor experience. Next, I will take a close look at *Glimpses of the USA*, the film created for and screened at the exhibition by Ray and Charles Eames, arguing that *Glimpses* reveals the affective logic of the exhibit. Finally, I discuss Soviet reaction to the film and to the exhibition more broadly, to make the case that the Soviet audience had been misapprehended by the exhibition's designers. Some Soviet viewers not only resisted the universalizing tendencies of *Glimpses*, but also refused the presuppositions of envy that placed them as the inferior other.

Sent to survey Sokol'niki months before the first brick was laid, landscape architect Robert Zion noted, "the design criteria for an exhibition of this sort are very similar to those of a shopping center. We were, after all, a nation attempting to 'sell ourselves.'"[9] Although Nixon's team selected the stage for the debate, the entire exhibition was conceived as an experience that would convey the notion that better goods created better beings. With objects everywhere, possession and the pleasures of ownership were communicated not only as a prerogative of choice but also as the universally appealing mode of existence.[10] The Eames team designed the exhibition to communicate the appeal of surface consumption as the most fulfilling kind of selfhood. It was a romance of humanness based on a presupposition of shared values—not the least of which were acquisitiveness and greed—that articulated certain forms of subjectivity predicated on those values. This spectacle of stages, objects, and images portrayed the American way of life as a way of being *and* feeling; a mandate of happiness through conspicuous consumption so staunch as to be almost aggressive. The exhibit spoke clearly: we have stuff and it makes us happy.

The ideas developed in Los Angeles and advocated in Moscow thus advertised a specific kind of American experience, while eclipsing broader U.S. social relations. This elision did not seem to give the designers pause; they were concerned about whether or not the Russians would accept their presentation as accurate. Nelson noted that their "objective was to tell the truth as best we could about America and its institutions. The problem, only partly a designer's problem, was how to make the Russians believe it."[11] Finding a solution to this issue of credibility inspired Charles Eames to come up with this operating principle, borrowed from Shannon's theory of information systems: "First we reduce information to primer, then we simplify as antidote to anticipated Russian disbelief."[12]

Compression became the basis of the Eameses' missionary design principles. The use of the term "primer" to describe the process of information dissemination suggests not only a pedagogical mandate with Eames as instructor, but also the application of a neutral layer—in order to prime the audience for reception. Once reduced to primer, information would be simplified even further, creating a harmonious admixture of uniformity and noise-canceling belief. But what was communicated, how was it communicated, and to whom?

The designers' dogged attention to Russian disbelief echoed old assumptions about the Russian people as a huddled mass of backwardness, mired in a bygone era, and thus anxiously awaiting Western enlightenment. In this stock approach, the retrograde Russian people had only to be shown the light of consumer abundance and the ipso facto well-being and happiness of Americans to be convinced of Western superiority. For the designers, however, the potential for Russian disbelief lodged in the inflated version of the U.S. standard of living on display. Justified disbelief (about, say, the universal applicability of that standard) was to be ignored. Days before the exhibition opened, the *New York Times* reported that, according to *Pravda*, "The much vaunted bourgeois democracy has always been a paradise for the capitalists and slavery for the working people." The report proceeded to note that "The people of the Communist countries are the freest people on earth, *Pravda* contended, and it told Congress that 'elephants will roost in trees before your delirious ravings come true.'"[13] This Russian skepticism about U.S. claims of national superiority were denounced left and right in the U.S. media as delusions. In the United States, Russians were portrayed as not only ill-informed and uneducated, but so "deliriously" askew as to rely on outlandish comparisons to elephants roosting in trees. Who better than this poor misguided lot to prime for the Truth?

When *Glimpses* was screened at ANEM, however, it immediately became a different film than the designers imagined or saw back in Los Angeles. Within the Eamesian information relay, only the American voice was persuasive. But the conditions of intelligibility shifted as *Glimpses* gained access to a new community of meaning-makers. This chapter is an effort to trace the movements, both temporal and geopolitical, of that shift.

The Reel Bombshell

> The multiple projection of images . . . was not simply a trick; it was a method to employ all the viewer's senses. The reinforcement by multiple images made the American Story seem credible.   —Charles Eames

The pièce de résistance at the exhibition was the Eameses' film, *Glimpses of the USA*, described by the *Wall Street Journal* as the exhibit's "real bomb shell."[14] Over 3 million people saw the twelve-minute film, nearly five thousand viewers every hour. Projected on seven 20-by-30-foot screens, *Glimpses* soared above its audience, covering a span nearly the size of a football field. Overall there were about 2200 images, some moving, taken from sources as varied as Billy Wilder's *Some Like It Hot*; *Time, Life, The Saturday Evening Post, Fortune,* and *Sports Illustrated* magazines; advertisements and photographs by Ezra Stotter, Eliot Noyes, Eero Saarinen, and George Nelson; and theatrical stills from Broadway shows, including *A Raisin in the Sun.* Nelson called them "bits of visual data" and wrote that 80,000 square feet "was not enough to communicate more than a small fraction of what we wanted to say [which] resulted in a decision to use films as a way of compressing into a small volume the tremendous quantity of information we wanted to present."[15] To answer the question of scale—how to use small bits of data to convey massive amounts of information—the designers relied on compression. The dilemma implied by scale, this reduction of the vastness of American life to representative visual splices, was sidestepped by a focus on form: Masey noted that presenting information was not the only goal, and that the tactics of presentation were essential to the desired outcome. The designers used "carefully planned bombardment" to produce "envy" in their Soviet audience.[16]

Many descriptions of the film by Americans who saw it in Moscow confirm that *Glimpses* extended Nixon's proclamations in the kitchen and offered an image of American life as a universal way of being. "It has music by Leonard Bernstein and stresses human qualities with pictures of families and lovers and children," wrote a *New York Times* reporter.[17] But there was no mistaking that these human qualities were distinctly American. In government literature prepared for the seventy-five American guides working at the exhibit, the film was described in the following manner: "Reflected throughout will be how America lives, works, learns, produces, consumes, and plays; what kind of people Americans are and what they stand for; and America's cultural values."[18] Describing the project in advance to the *New York Herald*, George Nelson explained, "Primarily, we want to make a simple sincere statement about American life. . . . We feel in this case how good our design is isn't important."[19]

What is so interesting about the designers' repeated emphasis on simplicity is that it occludes the complexity of the film's design and mechanics. The logic of the Cold War kitchen—its evasions, oversights, and forced silences—dominated ANEM. *Glimpses* both resisted the impulses of that logic and repeated it. Presenting a workday in nine minutes and a weekend in three, the film strayed from the dominant version of the logic through its multiple screens and multiple media as well as its open-endedness, creating a form that moved viewers through modes of perception that were novel in the 1950s. At the same time, the film was constrained by an affective logic of universalism that kept it closer to the kitchen than its creators may have realized. Departing from linear visual patterns, *Glimpses* offered its viewers a collage of images and potential meanings forged by multiple connections. This was a great innovation by the Eameses, their contribution to the idea of information flow as a key to communication. In other words, the Eameses wanted to show more than a multiplicity of images; they wanted to reproduce the experience of multiplicity—through the consumption of images. A few years before Marshall McLuhan came up with "the medium is the message," the Eameses were fashioning ways to embed messages in the form with which they were presented.[20] In principle, the simultaneous, multiple, and fast-moving images attempted to create a kaleidoscope of possibility for open and diverse attention spans, refusing a lone perspective and a single take-away experience. The multiple available modes of perception showcased by *Glimpses* were likewise meant to condition subjectivity in its intended audience, aligning the Soviets with the principles of diversity and freedom of choice, and thus convincing them of the superiority of U.S. modes of being.[21] In *Glimpses*, incoherence itself could be considered one of the powers of democracy. In this sense the film reiterated one characteristic of the exhibition as a whole; audiences walked around in a loosely scripted fashion, without a singular point governing the seven-acre experience. They were not told how to move through the exhibition, but encouraged to follow their own pattern of encounter. Irma Weinig, a guide at ANEM, recalled that for Russians "the exhibition was a carnival: the brightest and most colorful spot in Moscow. Usually deadly serious and law-abiding, living in a world of clearly-marked 'don'ts' and 'don't touch's,' they were free to follow their own bent at the exhibit."[22]

At the same time, however, the flow of information in *Glimpses* was highly orchestrated and managed by the Eameses and their aesthetic principles. In appealing to an emotional circuitry based on notions of universalism, the film elided certain images that might have challenged such universalism. Notably eclipsing poverty, urban ghettoes, or dissent of any kind, the film used visual technologies to relay simple pleasures and streamlined environments stripped of any grittiness or depictions of hardship. Moreover the reception of *Glimpses* by Soviet viewers troubled the Eameses' attempt to make the film exemplary of universal emotions. Most Russians felt that the film "moved much too fast to comprehend" and also took issue with its premise, with how the American designers expected them to see it and react.[23] Although the film may have showcased a new logic of mass media, one in which a space is defined by its users, it also had a message. The filmmakers misgauged both how Soviet viewers would respond to this space and how they would experience that message.[24]

Although it may not have been their primary focus, Nelson and the Eameses were not unaware of the impact of affect on their design theories. In his 1957 book *Problems of Design*, Nelson begins with a chapter called "Design as Communication," in which he outlines the importance of emotion. "Every design is in some sense a social communication, and what matters is not so much the importance of the object . . . as the emotional intensity with which the essentials have been explored and expressed."[25] Without using the term "aesthetics," Nelson refers to some of the key ideas within aesthetic theory going back to Plato: the summoning of an emotional reaction in an audience. By moving beyond the aesthetic object, however, Nelson gestures towards a related register of experience, that of affect. Without naming "affect" per se, Nelson is talk-

ing about it—an experience of intensity prior to or outside of consciousness that is located in the body as a response to stimuli.[26] Addressing
what he calls "emotional intensity" in affective terms helps us to open
up the correspondence between thinking and action. It also requires us
to attend to the Soviet response to *Glimpses*, as that reaction shifts the
meaning of the film and of the space of the exhibition as a whole. This
exhibition was explicitly created for Soviet viewers (and only indirectly
for American audiences, who would be instructed by U.S. media accounts
of the Soviet reaction). How might we open up our memory of *Glimpses*
to take the Soviet response into account? One possibility is to examine
more closely the Eameses' use of visual bombardment to invoke envy in
their Soviet viewers.

Early in 1953 George Nelson and Charles Eames devised their "Sample
Lesson for a Hypothetical Course" in communication that Nelson eventually nicknamed "Art X." Devised for students at the University of Georgia, the aim of this course was to increase communication between people
and things by creating a presentation that activated all the senses. Using
"high-speed techniques for exposing the relationships between seemingly
unrelated phenomena," the approach included film, music, graphics, and
slides—as well as synthetic smells—all backed by commentary from Nelson and Eames.[27] This sample lesson was later developed and expanded
into Charles Eames's film *A Communication Primer* (1953) and its lessons were the basis for Ray and Charles's *Glimpses*. The multiscreen approach was a way to invite the viewer to make her own connections, and
thus her own meaning, from the montage of images before her. Again, a
promotion of diverse patterns of meanings at once promises democratic
differences of opinion—and even dissent—while belying an overarching
insistence on uniformity or consensus in experience and interpretation. In
Glimpses, this insistence was articulated through a romantic narrative of
life in the United States, a romance that covered over social and political
tensions and contradictions by using visual evidence of shared beliefs
about gender, sexual difference, and race—with which the Soviets were
asked to identify. These kinds of romantic narratives, which represented
the United States as a heroic figure, had been used throughout the Cold
War to bolster consensus at home; but how would such strategies work
in the Soviet Union, where the antagonist so crucial to U.S. romantic em-
plotments of heroism was also the target audience?

Although they were housed in separate facilities, the dome (which
became known as the "information machine") and the "jungle gym" of
goods were devised to be quite similar in function. Masey describes the

juxtaposition in the following way: "The plethora of images [in the film] would show to the Russian visitors the deluge of consumer goods in the Jungle Gym in authentic American settings. Nelson may have complained ruefully about being landed with the 'stuff' while the Eameses got to do the art, but in fact the overarching script was the same for both: create a visual proof of the abundance of American society. . . . each closely reinforced the message of the other."[28] According to Masey the film was a visual reassertion of the experience of the "deluge" of objects in the glass pavilion. Not only were the scripts for both the same, so too were their messages. The film simply provided an "authentic American setting" for the extraordinary range of consumer objects on display next door.

Although the USIA was initially reluctant to use a film to convey American life, Nelson and his team won over government skeptics by arguing that the display of consumer products and the components of the dome "all add up to the same thing: the presentation of believable information about America and its institutions and the way its people live and work."[29] Although Masey and Nelson evidently agreed that the two spaces "add up to the same thing," Nelson identifies different reasons for the convergence.

The presentation of "believable information about America" relied on the active creation of a visual argument that depicted a particular version of America. The "information machine" was, after all, a machine. And while heavy machinery may not have been in evidence in the dome, a message was evident. As one Nelson scholar puts it, "the dome had shown not the machine but its social implications."[30] Nelson's desire to create a streamlined environment in which visible mechanisms recede behind smooth surfaces and style is reiterated in the logic of the film.[31] *Glimpses* is a pretty picture, a thing of beauty, spellbinding; it also erases the social and historical machinery that made its production possible.[32]

Similarly, the film is not simply a setting for the objects it depicts, but in fact creates a setting for the viewers who behold it. The designers set the tone for the film's reception by focusing on mood. The Eames team designated that mood lights were to be constantly flickering inside the dome, dimming only when the screening of *Glimpses* was to commence. These multicolored mood lights greeted viewers as they entered the dome. The training book for the exhibition's guides was explicit: "As you proceed toward the center of the Dome, you will be struck by the spectrum of color. The aluminum roof reflects the various-colored lights within the Dome. The first thing which impresses the viewer is the full spectrum of colors—from warm yellows to reds and from blue-greens to violet."[33] The range of hues was meant to stimulate the audience for the screening of objects glimpsed in authentic American settings.

Such use of mood lighting returns us to the kitchen. In the futuramic kitchen of the pavilion, lights modulated from red to blue (depending on outside temperature to provide a "psychological benefit" to the house-wife.[34] The deployment of mood lights in the suburban kitchen suggests an awareness of domestic captivity and its depressing tendencies. Tech-nology is used to remedy these tendencies, to automate human response such that the mechanization of one's mood can compensate for bad weather. Picking up on this irony, the Soviet press pilloried Anne Sono-pol Anderson, the home-economist and guide in the RCA/Whirlpool miracle kitchen, who became emblematic of the captive woman-in-the-kitchen and the embodiment of an excess-driven, gadget-obsessed United States.[35] In a sense, Anderson embodied the very paradox of the Cold War kitchen—promoting both an excess of goods and the streamlining of clutter (read "absence of women") in a vision of the future. In the U.S. press, Anderson appeared in an article in *Look* magazine, produced by Gereon Zimmermann with photos by Bob Lerner. In the archive of these photos, we see RCA expert Bill Vitous—who traveled to Moscow with the kitchen—playfully posing with Anderson and Marcia Corley. In each of these photos Vitous is centered as the expert (see fig. 1.2), though he was absent from the display when it went live. Again the ANEM kitchen offers us an example of the ways in which human effort and emotion were managed and mechanized—technologized in the name of abundance, di-versity, and choice.

In the shaping of a narrative of distinct moods, experiences, and vi-sions, the dome and the pavilion reinforced one another. While the seem-ingly incoherent parade of artifacts and images seemed to reiterate all that was grand about American democracy—a belief system that cher-ishes and upholds diversity and difference—this very same pluralness sidelined alternative versions of life in the United States; in fact, it neces-sarily silenced these other modes of subjectivity. Consider the form of the multi-screened film: its use of discontinuity appeared to create a space of openness and possibility that was the site of its potentiality as com-munication. While opening the possibility for multiple interpretations, however, it rerouted this possibility through its constraint of sentiment, seeking to ensure social unity and invoke a universal response. In other words, it presented the experience of incoherence within a message of coherence—of unity. Inviting a mood of appeasement, reassurance, and unification, the film established a kind of affective attunement: as if to

FIGURE 1.2. Photo by Robert Lerner from *Look* magazine archive for "What the Russians Will See"; from left to right: Anne Sonopol Anderson, Bill Vitous, and Marcia Corley. Photograph Collection, Library of Congress, Prints & Photographs Division, reproduction number LC-L9-59-8225-B, frame 8.

say, "we are the same." At the same time, the film could only work as universal by suppressing its unseen others. The film's alleged plurality actually created the conditions for the curtailment of diversity and difference, and the necessity of stymieing dissent.[36] These strategies created a condition of reception that was much closer to the structures of totalitarianism than the filmmakers would have wanted to admit. But more importantly, these strategies also suggest that U.S. democracy and social injustice—racial terror, the sexual division of labor, and class divisions—were more intimately connected than not.

As is clear from the layout of the fair, the dome was the "first major structure greeting visitors."[37] It was the initial point of orientation for the entire exhibition. Thus, any readings of the objects in the pavilion next door would be shaped by the experience of the dome's film. Although the public did not require the film to make sense of the objects in the pavilion, those objects may have been better-articulated versions of themselves with the help of *Glimpses*.[38] The film gave narrative coherence to the deluge of objects; it reminded its audience why suppression of dissent can feel good. Recalling the impact of *Glimpses*, Masey wrote, "Everyone was mesmerized by the show. None of us had ever seen anything quite like it. Then the audience burst into wild applause."[39]

While the messages of the dome and the pavilion were fashioned from the same cloth, we cannot say that they were identical. Each allowed for misinterpretation in its own way. Following the impulse of a message gone astray, I want to return to the question of how the Soviet viewer was emplotted as an implicit antagonist in *Glimpses*, and how the audience did or did not respond to this, just as they did or did not respond to the film's racial ideology, one of normalized whiteness. In order to pursue these questions more precisely, we need to track what happened in the dome when the film was screened. What did the film evoke and promise? How did it engage its audience, not only in visual terms but also through emotional appeal, aural incitement, and textural sensitivity?[40] Films have a distinct texture, a feel, an affective resonance. All of these modes of apprehension and attunement were available to Soviet viewers when the colored lights dimmed, the crowds hushed, and the seven towering screens burst with motion.

Glimpses of Glimpses

> The seven-screen film presented in hectic, almost over-powering variety a great many external aspects of American life.   —"Report on American Exhibition in Moscow," usia Office of Research and Analysis

The film opens with a voiceover from Charles Eames, who introduces himself as the audience watches images of outer space. "We see the same clusters, the same nebula," he says. "They can be difficult to distinguish, the same stars, the same planets." Aerial views then reveal earth's changing landscapes as the narrator intones: "Our land is in some places cold, in others hot." As the point of view sweeps downward, the narrator states: "as in Russia, we have towns and cities where people are drawn together."[41] The film shows cityscapes and suburbs, pans across pools and apartment buildings, finally pausing at a home, where we see close-ups of milk bottles and the morning newspaper. The complex relationship between narrator and audience here is prominent. The disembodied voice is ungrounded, never attached to a body or a face. It positions the viewer as an authority, inviting the listener to participate in its vantage point, superior to the images, which are instructive, a sort of primer. The voice of the narrator knows these images and teaches us how to see what we see, bringing the audience into its cadences, to a shared place of being in the room together: "we," "we," "we," the intonations repeat, making it

FIGURE 1.3. A soviet audience watches the Eameses' film *Glimpses of the USA* in Fuller's dome at ANEM. Library of Congress, Eames File, Unit LC 13393 (H). © Eames Office, LLC (eamesoffice.com)

difficult to distinguish their referents, until a subtle shift acknowledges a slippery difference. "We" are all the same, but the movement to "our" followed by the implied "you" in "as in Russia" reinforces this difference. *Glimpses* borrows the form of a typical romance narrative, letting the audience identify with its protagonists through shared values and an implied conflict to be overcome or threat to be subdued.[42] But if these shared values are nothing less than our shared humanity, threatened by war, conflagration, and nuclear annihilation, then what outside force supplies that threat?

The threat is not only externalized. It is also, as the Soviets were sure to recognize, internal. The film deploys aerial views created by surveillance technology developed during World War II; in other words, these images of shared "humanity" are connected to and enabled by militarism. From an American perspective, the threat comes from the Soviets themselves. It is both external (bureaucratic warmongers) and internal (unless ordinary Soviets like you, the audience, join our side, you too threaten our implicitly superior way of life). As viewers, the Soviets were positioned to see themselves in the image the United States screened of itself. How could they not recognize that they were apprehended in a dialectical re-

FIGURE 1.4. Screens showing *Glimpses of the USA* at ANEM. Library of Congress, Eames File, Unit LC 13393 (H). © Eames Office, LLC (eamesoffice.com)

lationship between the United States and its Soviet other? A memo issued by Ralph White for the USIA picked up on this dynamic: "Indirectly and without any propaganda—in fact partly because of the complete absence of propaganda in the usual sense of the word—they [Soviets] were pulled out of their normal nationalistic Soviet frame of reference and given, at least momentarily, a feeling of kinship with the whole human race. At the same time they must have realized that it was America, their alleged enemy, that moved them this way."[43]

White's memo reveals the American conception of Soviets as nationalistic, differentiating them from the standard bearers of the human race—Americans. The pull toward a common humanity (imagined as Americanness) would happen through the visual and emotional incitement to sameness. However momentary or fleeting their sense of shared identification, the shift would occur as Soviets saw themselves as human in an American context. Moreover, White's statement suggests a lack internal to Soviet subjectivity—a lack that figured strongly in the idea of the Soviet as envious antagonist. Thus, if the film did not constitute "propaganda in the usual sense of the word," it did, as White underscores, present persuasive evidence of one version of U.S. life. As even the film's directors conceded, this evidence does represent a kind of visual propaganda, one that relied on presuppositions of identificatory sameness *and* difference.

Soviet viewers undoubtedly saw U.S. military escalation (along with the surveillance technologies deployed in the film) as a threat to their own peace. The images of families, lovers, and children paint a romantic narrative of U.S. domestic life, so reduced to essentials as to create a message of universality with the Soviets: the enemy humanized. At the same time, the film uses power, wonder, and awe—stock resources of the narrative of Cold War heroism—to overwhelm and disorient the viewer. While professing a shared humanity, the film also reminded viewers that Americans—in their insular, isolated, and gadget-oriented lives—owned more things. By 1959 the idea of Soviet subjectivity as implicit in the story of America was gaining traction in the United States. But the film screening in Moscow also suggests that Soviet citizens were coming to understand their subjectivity as henceforth transnational, which is to say, oriented in the eyes of another, towards an *other*. In asking the Soviet audience to see themselves in terms that had been set in advance by American designers, the film activated an understanding of Soviet and U.S. Cold War subjectivity as always already transnational. This kind of media-defined selfhood has become standard today, but in the Moscow of 1959, it was something out of science fiction. This is not, of course, a new point about the function of contemporary media and the shaping of subjectivity, but it does offer an alternative to the ways in which the American exhibition has been read in the past.

Housed next door to *Glimpses* was the widely discussed "Family of Man" exhibit, curated by Edward Steichen and with commentary by Carl Sandburg. (Both Steichen and Sandburg attended ANEM's opening.) Although *Glimpses* and "Family of Man" shared visual imperatives about the universality of human experience, "Family of Man" was not explicitly created for ANEM or for a Soviet audience. Containing more than five hundred photos from sixty-eight countries, "Family of Man" had been on tour since its debut at New York's Museum of Modern Art in 1955. It would eventually be seen in thirty-seven countries over an eight-year period.

In his accomplished study of the political and cultural contexts of the touring "Family of Man" exhibit, historian Eric Sandeen argues that "the power of sentiment was no match for the technological race with the Soviet Union and the space-age suspicions of the post-Sputnik era." Juxtaposing "Family of Man" with the kitchen debate and the general perception of ANEM as oriented on objects, not people, he reads the photography exhibit as "far removed from the drama of the newly instituted cultural exchange" in Moscow.[44] For Sandeen, "Family of Man" provides an example of how sentiment took a back seat to technology at the exhibition.

From another perspective, however, sentiment and technology were crucially intertwined—one was not exchanged for the other. With "Family of Man" on display next to the dome, sentiment combined with technology to take center stage. In fact, the function of affect in "Family of Man" was very similar to that in *Glimpses* and elsewhere in the dome. Even the USIA memo cited above suggests how essential emotion was to Soviet reception of the exhibition.

One of the key ways *Glimpses* aspired to create sentimental equanimity with the Soviets was through gendered forms of subjectivity. During the thaw of the mid-1950s, Soviet ideology claimed to have liberated women from the shackles of domestic drudgery even as Soviet practice maintained patriarchal attitudes. In spite of the fact that women were working outside the home, the domestic space remained unliberated—both the purview and the responsibility of women. In the late 1950s, the Soviet press brought back a previously minor term, *khoziajka*, the closest Russian equivalent of "housewife."[45] Unlike the middle-class housewives of the United States, however, this *khoziajka* was as comfortable wielding a power tool on the factory floor as she was engineering her family's meal plans.

In its depictions of the realm of the domestic, *Glimpses* assumes an international continuum of gendered forms of labor—the universal housewife. The film uses the sentimental authority of the feminine domestic space to create feelings of shared humanity—just as Nixon hoped to do when he stepped into the woman's place in that Moscow kitchen. The Eameses' own notes for the film highlight the quotidian, feminized space of the home: "people having breakfast at home, men leaving for work, kissing their wives, kissing the baby, being given lunchboxes, getting into cars, waving good-bye, children leaving for school, being given lunchboxes, saying good-bye to the dog, piling into station wagons and cars, getting into school buses, baby crying."[46] Absent in their grammar—but present as the agent—is the figure of the housewife whose ephemeral presence sets the emotional tone of these vignettes. In the film, as in these descriptions, we feel only traces of the American housewife. Although rarely pictured and never the subject of the action, she is the conduit: the indirect enabler of the scene, the disembodied hand extending a lunchbox or waving goodbye.

As the woman is reduced to domestic servant, we see how the housewife's labors are as much affective as they are physical. Her work has an

emotional texture, with maternal wealth romanticized as infinitely renewable, but also instrumental to the smooth functioning of the nuclear
family unit. These scenes of U.S. domestic life, accompanied by a musical
score by Elmer Bernstein, portray an existence where social and ideological uniformity creates peace; the domestic space of the single-family home
is presented as the launch pad of happiness.[47] The good life, American
style, depends upon the altruistic labors of women in the kitchen.

From here the film moves out of the private realm and into the public,
focusing on industry and urbanism: traffic, cars traversing bridges, tunnels, broad shots of cities which then become close-ups of skyscrapers,
the camera panning down to concerned urban faces. "Much to be done
and most of it in a hurry," the narrator opines. There is scant narration
as we move into the working and learning day. We see various images of
adults and children, then a scattering of schools where children are
"being prepared to meet the future years." The scale switches between
large and small, from close-ups to panoramas, as the film waxes pastoral, sailing past smokestacks to open fields and barns, flowers, plants,
and the hands of a farmer. It is here that we catch a fleeting glimpse of
migrant workers and African Americans, faces that are quickly passed
over as we move past factories called "the laboratories of private industry," where outside we see "the parked autos of the workers." Down
the road is "today's version of the old market-place": the shopping
mall. Supermarkets and Sears are featured within oversized parking lots,
where family cars wait as housewives gather supplies for the evening
meal.

Finally we are back in the realm of the domestic, where meal preparation closes the daylight hours. Women's hands work their way around a
kitchen. We are shown the dining table, families eating, the kitchen from
various angles, dishes being cleared, then cleaned by hand. And then it is
bedtime. So ends the workday in the USA.

Showcasing the kitchen as a space in which work is done by women,
the film now recalls its opening images. Although roughly proportionate
in screen time to other scenes, the kitchen scene compels greater attention.
We are in this space with greater intensity. The domestic images evoke the
efficiency of the miracle kitchen housed next door in the pavilion—but
through the figure of a woman's hands. The film's focus on the female
body (and not on appliances) seems to refute the mechanization of the
futuramic kitchen, as if to say this space is human, real, female—not technologized.[48] But the contradiction of the Cold War kitchen is exposed:

the woman's body is merely another gadget and her labors are revealed to be just as alienating as those of a factory hand. In short, she is cut off. If the Cold War kitchen sought to reduce modern excess through clean minimalist design, disposing of the emotional clutter accrued through long days of domestic toil, then it also threatened to eliminate women, just as it evacuated the emotion associated with women's quotidian chores. We witness this impulse in *Glimpses* by a singular focus on *hands*, as if the female body itself has become excess, a nuisance. Although the threads of women's labor are made visible through these hands, foregrounded and not forgotten, her labor is seemingly detached from her body. This focus on hands recalls the earlier image of the farmer's hands; in both scenes, the materiality of the bodies and minds of multitudes of workers have been removed.[49]

The emotionally cleansed workspace of the kitchen becomes the venue for a familial happiness that depends upon a woman's capable hands—no matter how disconnected. In this way the viewers are cut off from the reality of what it takes to get a meal on the table: anxiety, frustration, boredom, and even rage. The film's images are astoundingly calm, romanticized towards an ideal of efficiency and harmony in which the gendered and sexualized norms are clear.

The erasure of racial difference in *Glimpses* suggests that Soviet viewers also were meant to recognize themselves in this narrative.[50] The film's only suggestion of racial integration appears in an elementary schoolyard, with the image of a young African American girl in line with white school children (fig. 1.5). This could be interpreted as a nod to the U.S. Supreme Court's 1954 decision in Brown v. Board of Education and the federally mandated desegregation of U.S. schools. Or it might have been intended to allay common Soviet criticisms of U.S. white supremacy through the portrayal of peaceful integration. By placing the burden of racial difference on a child, however, this image suggests that racial inequities can be solved through a discourse of childlike innocence. To be sure, the Soviets were quick to denounce U.S. racial hypocrisy during the postwar period. Khrushchev opened the African Studies Institute just six months after hosting W.E.B. Du Bois in 1958. Du Bois went so far as to claim that Soviet pressure helped to speed some forms of restitution, including Brown v. Board.[51] This kind of amelioration did not stop Soviet visitors from peppering U.S. guides with questions about racism, lynchings, ghettoes, and interracialism.[52] Considering the furious response of South Carolina's U.S. senator, Strom Thurmond, to the proposed scenes of a ra-

FIGURE 1.5. Still photos for *Glimpses of the USA* taken at Westminster Avenue elementary school in Venice, California, across the street from the Eameses's studio. Library of Congress, Eames File, LOT 13186. © Eames Office, LLC (eamesoffice.com)

cially mixed barbeque and the staged marriage of an African American couple at ANEM's fashion show, this quiet image of integration belied the segregationist inclinations of U.S. officials in charge of the exhibition and its planning.[53]

Indeed, we need to reconsider this image in the context of other events at ANEM. *Look* magazine photographer Paul Fusco took several rolls of film at the integrated wedding scene as well as the fashion show. These photos (which I also discuss in the preface), show the staged marriage party of Norma and Gilbert Noble.[54] The scenes of revelry and celebration were intended to be part of the display for Soviet viewers, just like Anne Sonopol Anderson in her miracle kitchen. Fusco's photos offer portraits of inverted viewership, with the actors and the audience looking at one another within the larger frame of the lens (see figs. 1.6 and 1.7). Though certainly staged, some images appear at least partly spontaneous, with guests raising their glasses to the bride and groom, cavorting on the dance floor, drinking vodka from the bride's shoe, and beaming over the bridal gifts. Although *Look* put one photo from Fusco's slides on the cover of its June 21, 1960, issue, there was no discussion either of the controversial wedding scene or of ANEM within the magazine's pages. The stunning images of the Nobles in Red Square (see figs. 1.8 and 1.9) were passed over, their figures covered by a ribbon of text.

FIGURE 1.6. Norma and Gilbert Noble clink glasses at the interracial wedding party at ANEM. Photo by Paul Fusco. *Look* Magazine Photograph Collection, Library of Congress, Prints & Photographs Division, reproduction number LC-L9-59-8427-K, frame 14.

FIGURE 1.7. Norma and Gilbert Noble greet Soviet onlookers during the interracial wedding party at ANEM. Photo by Paul Fusco. *Look* Magazine Photograph Collection, Library of Congress, Prints & Photographs Division, reproduction number L9-59-8427-M, frame 37.

FIGURE 1.8. Photo of Norma and Gilbert Noble in Red Square, July 1959, by Paul Fusco. *Look* Magazine Photograph Collection, Library of Congress, Prints & Photographs Division, reproduction number LC-L9OIA-59-8427-1.

FIGURE 1.9. Photo of Norma and Gilbert Noble in Moscow, July 1959, by Paul Fusco. *Look* Magazine Photograph Collection, Library of Congress, Prints & Photographs Division, reproduction number LC-L9OIA-59-8427-2.

In the context of these erasures, the schoolyard scene feels even more flimsy, weak, and paradoxical. With the exceptions of this image and a lone head shot of an African American man in glasses and beret, *Glimpses* does not show pictures of Americans who are not racially coded as white until the three-minute weekend addendum. "On Saturdays and Sundays there is time to relax," says the narrator. "Time to catch up on small jobs around the house." Men mow the lawn while kids read the comics—emblems of the middle-class weekend as a site of leisure. Native Americans, Asians, Latina/os, African Americans, Jews, and Muslims are represented only in the context of religious worship or racially segregated community activities. But weekend activities for white (or "non ethnically identifiable") Americans include art shows—visiting an exhibit of Picasso, Kline, and Leger at MoMA—having picnics, flying kites, riding horses, skiing, sailing, flying, boating, playing football, hanging out at the beach, and watching baseball at Yankee Stadium. Louis Armstrong and Ella Fitzgerald make brief appearances after Althea Gibson, Jackie Robinson, and the Ringling Brothers circus. Their bursts of song taper into fireworks.[55] In the end, the film returns to a domestic scene, with handholding and warm embraces among family members, including shots of the Eameses' grandchildren. Images of forget-me-nots, the "international symbol of friendship," close the film.

I want to pause here to elucidate the racial complexities at work in these closing minutes of *Glimpses*. Although we have a more liberal use of racial inclusion (as opposed to the racial erasure offered by Nixon's discourse in the kitchen debate), the underlying principle remains similar. "Ethnicity" in the film is marginalized, presented as a playground or weekend activity, comparable to a pastime. Similarly, adult African Americans are reduced to stock characterizations as athletes and entertainers. Overall, the images of non-whites are tokens, moments of inclusion that limit the portrayal of racial mixing and integration. Ethnic groups are seen fraternizing among themselves, not in integrated urban neighborhoods, and certainly not in integrated suburbs. This kind of visual bombardment echoes both the militaristic aspects of what Buckminster described as "weaponry into livingry" and what a *Saturday Evening Post* editorial (cited in the epigraph to this chapter) called "staggering diversity." These descriptions of capitalism share aggression as a key defining principle; echoing this surface terminology, the exhibition featured an almost violent portrayal of what Cedric Robinson has termed "racial capitalism," a phrase he uses to describe the fact that capitalism feeds on racial differentiation.[56] Such dependence on the inequities of racialization is evidenced throughout *Glimpses*, as white Americans—in contrast with Americans of other ethnicities—are seen participating in what would undoubtedly have seemed to Soviet viewers as bourgeois activities: sailing, skiing, horseback riding, golfing, and mowing the lawn. At the same time, this implicit superiority of white pastimes (via a class mantle) could easily have appealed to the Soviets' own sense of racial entitlement. Racial inclusion was a principle—not an ethos—in Soviet Russia. Racialism and its systemic dependence did not end with Marx.[57]

Finally, what any viewer might make of U.S. racial heterogeneity is not only evacuated to the weekend (far from the domestic tranquility of the suburban workweek), it is closed over with the image of white domesticity. Nestled into the comforts of the isolated nuclear home, we are reassured of our universal "sameness" with forget-me-nots. In other words, the racial contours of the United States have been raised only so that they can be better erased, forgotten, eclipsed, smoothed over. The machine becomes invisible. A Soviet viewer can remain snug in a shared feeling where whiteness reigns—a color schematic reinforced by the pallor of the flowers that close the frame. The appeal is gestural, textural, scripted within a fastidiously planned and primed environment to win over hearts and minds.[58] According to Masey, "The Russians whispered 'nezabutki' [forget-me-nots] and there were tears all around."[59] Charles Eames noted, "We could tell they were getting it emotionally by the way they drew in their breaths at certain scenes, and oh'd and ah'd at others."[60]

Getting It: What the Soviets Saw When They Saw Glimpses

> Does Mr. Nixon really think that the Soviet people are so naïve as to believe that the American military bases, which are placed thousands of kilometers from the USA and very close to the Soviet Union's frontiers, are intended to defend America's frontiers—on whom no one has made or will make attacks? —Yakov Victorov for Moscow Radio[61]

> Poor little house! During twelve days of your existence more was said about you than any other exhibit here. —Unsigned guestbook comment

According to the reports sent back to the United States, *Glimpses* was one of the most popular attractions at the exhibition, second only to color TV and cars. What made *Glimpses* popular? Charles Eames' phrase, "they were getting it emotionally," packs a powerful punch. But what, exactly, were "they" getting? It is difficult to gauge the answer to this question with certainty, of course. But we can contrast the recorded comments of Soviet viewers with American expectations to show that, while Soviets may have been fascinated with American-made objects, they did not mistake goods for government. In other words, the message may have gone astray. Even if *Glimpses* was "not propaganda in the usual sense," it was an ambivalent success at best. To quote Norman Winston, a real estate developer who served as special advisor to the USIA during the planning of ANEM, this was hardly "the makings of a revolution."[62] Expecting the Soviets to be swept off their feet by universal emotions was a grandiose, if not foolhardy, assumption; thinking that this reaction would translate into a longing for the American ideals of life, liberty, and the pursuit of happiness was a tactical error.

To understand how Soviets responded to *Glimpses*, we must acknowledge that they were not naïve viewers of cinema but experienced filmgoers, with access to a range of Soviet and foreign films. Movies were cheap and plentiful. Fifteen kopecks—about the cost of a loaf of bread—was the standard ticket price. Moreover, Soviets were accustomed to seeing Cold War animosities depicted in stark terms on the screen. The film historian Jay Leyda notes that the Soviets produced many anti-American films in 1949 and 1950, including Alexandrov's *Meeting on the Elbe*, Kalatozov's *Conspiracy of the Doomed*, Romm's *Secret Mission*, and Room's *Court of Honour*. After the death of Stalin in 1953 and Khrushchev's 20th Congress revelations in 1956, film production shifted away from patent Stalinist propaganda and towards the adaptation of Russian classics.[63] A number of plays and novels were translated for the screen, including *Letyat zhuravli* (*The Cranes are Flying*), which took the Palme d'Or at Cannes in 1958. While Soviet audiences of the late 1950s were well schooled in the evils of capitalism, their viewing practices—along with their sense of public culture—had become, in the words of historian Jeffrey Brooks, "more secular and rational."[64] By 1959 a trickle of contrary opinion had appeared in media outlets, questioning (if not overturning) the three previous decades of Soviet norms.[65] Though Soviet viewers remained inclined to see the United States as the enemy, they also were likely to have some room for questions.

However fascinated they were with American goods, Soviets were probably not convinced that Americans had greater life satisfaction. Soviet films from the late 1950s expressed strong opinions about happiness and what constituted it. Films from this era were marked by a repetition of the idea that happiness comes from a passion for work well done. As one film historian put it, Soviet thaw films seem to follow a "formula that commitment to hard work and the good of others will be rewarded by personal happiness."[66] Far from the object-dependent logic of contentment as lodged in consumer abundance, this same critic argues that, "From film to film material well-being is represented as being an obstacle to happiness."

While the argument has been made that the architecture of information flow at ANEM is in many ways more instructive that the content of the exhibition's materials, we should remember that Soviet viewers were accustomed to sophisticated film techniques. Eisenstein's experiments with montage and the Russian formalists' notion of defamiliarization informed Soviet cinema. The top-down logic that typifies the idea of a single image-driven frame was not the only kind of cinematic semiotic available to Soviet viewers. Perhaps too easily paralleled by undifferentiated totalitarian power structures, this technique overlooks other aspects of the Soviet film lexicon, including variable camera angles, close-ups, short shots, and juxtapositions. In other words, montage was already part of a logic of choice, variety, and multiplicity wherein Shklovskian estrangement might approach the allegedly superior mode of Eamesian free association within a given system of aesthetic control.

Seeking to reclaim some of the Soviet historiography often overlooked in U.S. accounts, Susan E. Reid has done the most substantial and distinguished work on the Soviet response to ANEM. Two of her essays, "Who Will Beat Whom?" and "Our Kitchen Is Just as Good," together lay out the methodological problems of trying to characterize or capture how Soviets responded to the exhibit.[67] Sources on the U.S. side include dispatches from Moscow and reflections made by Americans involved with the exhibition after they returned home. All of these include reported speech and observations by journalists (most of whom did not speak Russian), thus such evidence can hardly be considered the final word. On the Soviet side, there are guest books or comment books in which visitors recorded their thoughts about the exhibits. Reid rightly concludes that "these comments cannot be considered to be authentic, unmediated reflections," as they were produced in a context of multiple and simultaneous constraints. The USIA report on ANEM supports Reid's insight, noting that "every Soviet citizen who wrote in these books knew that what he wrote might be seen and disapproved by a Party member or MVD agent."[68]

Nonetheless, these comment books do offer some patterns of response and what they have to say about the exhibition, especially as it speaks to the misperception of the Soviet audience by ANEM's designers, is instructive. Although they provide problematic data, these comments cannot be fully discounted. In their variety and discordance, they refute the largely held assumption that ANEM was a resounding success. More importantly, they provide evidence of an audience that was in some ways prepared for an onslaught of consumer envy. (As I discuss below, Khrushchev anticipated both the contours and contents of ANEM, and state media outlets were ready to denounce the exhibition's excesses.)

The guest books held in the USIA archives reveal diverse opinions. The array of responses reflects the ways in which *Glimpses*, in its efforts to represent diversity and multiplicity of meaning as the crown jewels of U.S. democracy, framed the Soviet experience in its own limited terms. Many Soviets not only rejected the claims of diversity, they also rejected the very terms of the viewing experience. As I emphasized earlier, Soviet self-understanding at ANEM was not static, but produced in response to the image that the United States projected of itself. To suggest otherwise (as is often the case in American Cold War studies) is to remain within the same U.S.-centric framework as the exhibition's planners. The recorded comments—both positive and negative—suggest that many Soviet viewers felt misunderstood. In other words, the audience perceived itself to be inaccurately addressed and, understanding itself to be misrepresented, refused to take up the subject position intended for it: as self-interested and materialistic, easy prey for the enticements of market capitalism. "Excuse us," one commenter writes, "but frankly speaking, your American way of life, which you demonstrated at the exhibition, does not appeal to us. Your exhibition shows that its organizers do not know our people." Another notes, "The exhibition shows how little the American organizers know about Soviet people. They wanted to astound us with trinkets rather than with technical innovations."[69] This awareness reveals a refusal to take up the expected site of addressee, troubling the agency's claims of a feat of "international communication."

To read through the comment books is to find these sentiments repeated again and again. Despite the books' shortcomings as unbiased evidence, they provide a powerful portrait of the Soviet response to the American message. (These quotes can be found in a variety of sources, including the USIA memos and the NARA archives; they have been helpfully retranslated into a more idiomatic language by Reid.)

> The Exhibition does not give anything to the mind, nor to the soul. It looks like a haberdashery store. There are more sofa cushions than things which might please us and let us understand what kind of people Americans are.
>
> You must understand our psychology. Russians come to an exhibi-

tion to learn, to extract from somebody else's experience what
    might be useful for their own.

The exhibition does not impress me. It resembles an advertisement
    more than an exhibition of a country that is a leader in the area
    of technology. The impression is created that America is more con-
    cerned with comforts and amusements than with education and
    spiritual enrichment.

Leaving the exhibition, I carry with me an impression of glittering
    saucepans.

If this is the American way of life, then it is the American way of life
    we should overtake.

We expected the American Exhibition would show something grand,
    something similar to Soviet sputniks, and you Americans want to
    surprise us with the glitter of your kitchen pans and the fashion,
    which do not appeal to us at all.

I am not with you, but I congratulate you!

Is it possible that you think our mental outlook is restricted to every-
    day living only?

It is calculated to stun the Soviet people. However, you cannot sur-
    prise us with kitchens and TV sets.

Having seen the typical house of an American family, I decided to
    write my impressions. Yes, it is a typical little house of an Amer-
    ican family of Browns. Poor little house! During 12 days of your
    existence more was said about you than any other exhibit here.
    People began talking about you before you were brought to our
    country. There you were criticized because you were too expensive
    and because you were not typical of American conditions where
    thousands of families were cooped up in slums and it was laugh-
    able for them to hear you were typical. . . We Russians say "All
    this unquestionably is very nice. Thank you, Americans, for trying
    to show us Russians what houses should be built and how to
    furnish them. Many thanks, but such light-weight buildings do
    not please us and do not foist on us your manner of living."

Many of the comments were signed, although some remained anonymous. Yet even the more positively inclined comments do not reveal a
desire to throw over their government for U.S. ideals:

Okay, Yankees! Some day we will catch up with you in all areas
    where we lag behind. But in general we wish you well and would
    like to hear the same from you addressed to us.

I am sixty-four years old and I am very glad I lived until I could per-
sonally visit the American National Exhibition for which I thank
its initiators from the bottom of my heart. I am a small man and I
particularly liked the spirit of the following exhibits: circarama, geodesic dome, and Family of Man. I am also grateful for the pepsi-cola.
A very good impression from the Exhibition and its organization—
everything can be touched and examined. Americans are a very
likeable people. We want to be friends with you.
Best of all I liked a conversation with the American lads.[70]

If diversity was presented as the promise of U.S. democracy, and this
promise gave the designer-government team leave to curtail the portrayal
of actual diversity, then the showcase of abundance on site enabled the
evacuation of income differences from the exhibition. Whether their comments were positive or negative, one thing is clear: the Soviet respond-
ents were unconvinced of the superiority of U.S. ideals vouchsafed by
goods. This response confounded the exhibition planners. Why wouldn't
the Soviet audience be stunned by the superior standard of living, and
thus connect superior standards to superior politics?[71] Perhaps the USIA's
bureaucrats did not recognize that many Soviets took their ideology quite
seriously, or perhaps they could not fathom this fact. But the notion that
collective well-being was more valuable than individual possessiveness
had been vitally upheld during the 1950s. After carefully considering the
American exhibition, many Soviets rejected its premise.

This perspective is especially evident in a newspaper article by the Soviet novelist, Marietta Shaginian. Writing about Soviet disappointment in
the show, Shaginian punctures the cheery image of the "happy housewife"
and underscores the isolation and insularity she perceives in an ideology
beholden to the pursuit of happiness based on individual needs and desires.

The countless domestic conveniences of the Americans are interesting . . .
but they anchor a woman in perpetuity to her mission as "housewife," wife,
and cook. They make this role easier for her, but the very process of allevi-
ating individual housework, as it were, eternalizes this way of life, turning
it into a profession for the women. We love innovations that actually could
emancipate women; new kinds of houses with public kitchens with their
canteens for everyone living in the house; with laundries where big machines wash clothes not just for a family alone.[72]

Shaginian's article dismisses American ingenuity as superfluous to gen-
uine female liberation, contending that a professional class of American

housewives cocooned within their suburban homes does nothing to advance women's rights. In her opinion, the kinds of objects on display at ANEM are poorly pitched for a Soviet audience, and she sees no happiness in the gluttony of an appliance-laden subjectivity: "The organizers of the exhibition naively think that our Soviet viewer will be consumed by a thirst to posses 'things.' The electric kitchen, for example, which the Americans promise in the future, appears to us a very cumbersome thing in private life but a very convenient one for public cafeterias and big restaurants."[73] In her review of the American kitchen in Moscow, Shaginian gets to the heart of Soviet disdain. The exhibition's planners assumed that the American desires for self-sufficiency, convenience, and luxury were common denominators and that, like most Americans, the Soviets would be seduced by the splendors of consumption. But as Shaginian points out, "The tastes of Soviet viewers are different from those of the ANEM organizers."[74] To at least a few Soviets, the U.S. kitchen looked like a path to private captivity, not liberation.

For her part, Susan Reid makes sense of the Soviet response by showing that while the feedback was generally critical, it was hardly unanimous, and some commenters did express appreciation for American innovation.[75] The production of consumer goods in the Soviet Union increased after the exhibition, and Soviet repudiation of America's trivial concerns coincided with a more general appropriation of American models. While indebted to the research done by Reid, my interpretive approach is different.[76] I want to put pressure on the idea of envy used by the Nelson team as their primary ploy. Instead of rejecting envy as a flimsy emotional tactic fraught with obvious ideological holes, I want to delve into it more deeply. In the next section I will argue that the Soviets did not confuse envy of material objects with admiration of U.S. policies.[77]

ANEM's projection of happiness as something to be acquired through possessive abundance and the positioning of the Soviet audience as envious went hand in hand. In *The Promise of Happiness*, theorist Sara Ahmed gracefully traces the relationships between narratives of happiness (happy family, happy worker, happy citizen) and the marginalization of people who are not, for various reasons, happy. She uses the phrase "affect alien" to outline a "gap between the promise of happiness and how [we] are affected by objects that promise happiness."[78] The affect alien feels the wrong thing at the right time, or the right thing at the wrong time, "feeling at odds with the world or feeling that the world is odd."[79] Bringing Ahmed's ideas to ANEM, we see that the Soviet audience responded antagonistically, as what we also might call "affect aliens."

The exhibition and its deluge of objects did not make Soviets happy. Instead, it made them characters of envy.[80]

Orchestrating Envy

> We know the life we have is good. By the end of the summer, the millions of Russians who have seen our exhibit will know it too. . . . Unless I am a completely inept judge of human action, that experience is going to stir not only hearts but also desires. Let it. Let the Russians want what we have. Let them clamor for it.   —Norman K. Winston[81]

> I do not want to conceal the fact that during my inspection of your exhibits I not only experienced a feeling of satisfaction, but also, to a certain degree, a feeling of envy. But this is a good envy, in the sense that we should like to have all this in our country as soon as possible.   —Nikita Khrushchev[82]

The cover of *Life* magazine on August 10, 1959, shows the wifely quartet of Pat Nixon, Nina Khrushcheva, Ashken Mikoyan, and Tatiana Kozlova. In contrast to the clothing worn by the stocky and unfashionably dowdy Soviet women, Mrs. Nixon's outfit looks sharp and slim. Commenting on this photo, Beatriz Colomina argues that the gaze of Mrs. Kozlov—away from the camera and towards Mrs. Nixon—indicates that "she can't keep her eyes off Pat Nixon's dress."[83] This could have been envy—precisely what the American exhibition seems to have been designed to produce. And yet, if we pause over this negative affect, we might wonder about its transparency. Tatiana Kozlova's glance could also have signaled sisterly pride—or sisterly disdain.[84] In any case, the supposition of envy is easy to make. At the time, headlines such as "Six Things Mikoyan Envied Most in America" circulated widely in the U.S. press, much of the reporting about the exhibition was couched in terms of envy, and many contemporary critics have followed suit.[85] But even if we embrace envy as the principal Soviet reaction, might we not pursue the contours of this reaction, especially as it seems to set the emotional tone for U.S. coverage of the exhibition's reception?

In her compelling work on negative affects, Sianne Ngai argues that "the fact that we tend to perceive envy as designating a passive condition of the subject rather than the means by which the subject recognizes and responds to an objective relation suggests that the dominant cultural attitude toward this affect converts its fundamentally other-regarding orientation into an egocentric one, stripping it of its polemicism and rendering it merely a reflection of deficient and possibly histrionic selfhood."[86] Indeed, couching the entire display of American luxury as an effort to incite envy thrusts the Soviet visitor into a tired position of feminized viewer, locating a lack internal to the Soviet subject. The words "wonder," "pleasure," and "disbelief" abound in U.S. descriptions of the Soviet response, male and female.[87] And yet envy both feminizes and devalues its subject, suggesting a larger American anxiety over responses to difference. Positioning its object as superior, envy subsumes difference within an acceptance of inferior status. Contemplating, as Ngai does, envy as an antagonistic response provides a broader way of understanding the ways threats of cultural difference might have been in part neutralized by translating the foreign into the domestic: a little America in the heart of Moscow. Women and, by extension, all Soviet citizens become the characters of envy, victims of dour self-assertion and a negative relationship to goods that Ngai calls "unhappy possessiveness."[88] As *US News and World Report* claimed, "some displays are so tempting that Russian visitors 'liberate' items not securely fastened."[89]

When Khrushchev announced his "good envy," he made use of it in an antagonistic sense, asserting that Soviets were in fact poised to leapfrog over the United States in technological progress.[90] Khrushchev's invocation of envy as aggression resonates with the notion of envy in Melanie Klein's "A Study of Envy and Gratitude," in which she theorizes envy as the "angry feeling that another person possesses and enjoys something desirable—the envious impulse being to take it away or to spoil it."[91] In Klein's formulation, envy intervenes with the object in such a way as to change it, and likewise change the envious subject's relationship to it. Such an antagonistic response to the object creates friction, even aggression, sensing from the object a kind of persecution.[92] While Khrushchev's claims of imminent Soviet advancement were obviously overstated, they nonetheless offer us the opportunity to examine the U.S. media's obsession with Soviet envy as evidence of Soviet backwardness and inferiority. And they encourage us to see U.S. insistence on the Soviet envy of American possessions as in its own way a kind of needling harassment.[93]

With the broad initiatives of the Third Party Program underway, it is clear that Khrushchev was not fooled by ANEM negotiators into authorizing an assault of U.S. propaganda on Soviet territory. He and other party leaders were well aware of the kind of blitz the United States planned to launch at Sokol'niki. Anticipating that the fair would showcase consumer goods, they had prepared accordingly. As one of the guestbook comments noted, "people began talking about you before you were brought to our country." This sort of expectation not only changes the nature of the response (and in so doing makes the guest books all the more intriguing), but also suggests that there may have been a Soviet strategy afoot. Perhaps, as Gregory Castillo has argued, Khrushchev welcomed the modern conveniences showcased at ANEM as a means of "intended culture shock" to jolt Soviet designers and manufacturers into action.[94] The evidence of such preparedness was not lost on the U.S. press. In the days leading up to the exhibition, the *New York Times* reported that "Soviet propaganda has taken extraordinary pains to assure people here that the glistening display they will see—the model home and apartment, the working kitchen and automobiles and the like are by no means universally available to the average American worker."[95] And as Charles Eames noted, U.S. awareness of Soviet anticipation altered the designers' conception of the imagined addressee. But when the exhibition arrived, that imagined public shifted yet again, rendering discontinuous the feedback loop so key to the designers' formulation. The Soviet response went beyond identifying the misleading aspects in the displays of so-called "average" American dwellings and possessions. Some even denounced what seemed to them the morbid irrationality of the logic of abundance, of consumer excess. "What is this," the Russian newspaper *Izvestia* asked, "a national exhibit of a great country or a branch department store?"[96] Focusing on the split-level ranch nicknamed "splitnik," one humor magazine reduced the typical American house from its advertised splendor to a more realistic version of what the average American family could afford—a few objects splayed on the front lawn (see figs. 1.10 and 1.11).

At the time the Nixons arrived in Moscow, the Soviet Union was shedding its earlier notions of domesticity, favored under Stalin in the 1930s and 1940s and characterized by comfort and coziness. The new Soviet modern, not unlike the international modern movement, cultivated asceticism over plushness. According to Reid, the new Soviet aesthetic "was an austere, simple, 'contemporary style' that bore a close affinity to (and was directly informed by) international Modernism, both in its visual characteristics and in such imperatives as 'form follows function' and 'less is more.'"[97] As an article in the *New York Times* put it, the fringed lampshades of the nineteenth century that were popular under Stalin became emblematic of dated style.[98]

In this new era, women were to become the domestic tastemakers while the home became a domain of scientific management, corresponding with the mandates of Khrushchev's Third Party Program, which called for self-regulation rather than coercive oversight by the govern-

FIGURES 1.10 AND 1.11. "Puteshestviia v Ameriku za rubl"
(A trip to America for rubles). *Krokodil* 22, August 10, 1959.

ment. The transformation of women into domestic engineers required training, however, such that efficient housekeeping merited its own revised encyclopedia. (As I will discuss in my analysis of Natalya Baranskaya's *A Week Like Any Other* in chapter 3, managing the competing roles of "good Soviet woman and good Soviet worker" became more and more difficult.)

The standard reference for housekeeping was the *Kratkaia entsiklopedia domashnego khoziaistva*, which underwent a major overhaul between 1959 and 1966.[99] The 1959 edition pictured a rudimentary kitchen typical of the early postwar era (fig. 1.12). By 1966, the kitchen had become a point of reference for modern living (fig. 1.13). These updated kitchens featured increased cabinet space, variety in design and décor, and sophisticated color palettes. Such kitchen updating set the tone for the revised encyclopedia as a whole. Whereas the 1959 edition had been printed in black and white, the 1966 edition contained multiple sections with color images. These sections included instructions on how to choose complementary interior colors for paint and upholstery; how to

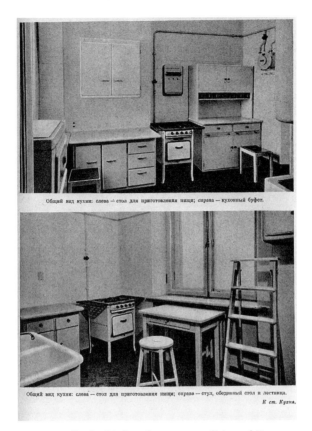

Общий вид кухни: слева — стол для приготовления пищи; справа — кухонный буфет.

Общий вид кухни: слева — стол для приготовления пищи; справа — стул, обеденный стол и лестница.

К ст. *Кухня.*

FIGURE 1.12. Soviet kitchen from 1959 edition of *Krat-kaia entsiklopediia domashnego khoziaistva.*

decorate the house fashionably with coordinating textures and designs; and instructions for how to operate new appliances, including TVs and hi-fis. Marking the advancement of everyday life in the Soviet Union, the kitchen had become a beacon of the future—not in an effort to be more like the United States, but in order to be more fully Soviet.

How did the Soviet world of consumer goods distinguish itself from the Western version? Unlike the extravagant displays at ANEM, the final word in Soviet homemaking was rational utility.[100] The movement towards a Soviet modern renders the Soviet reception of ANEM even more complex. It is no surprise that wonder, disbelief, ambivalence, disgust, and desire intermingle in the comments, making them impossible to pigeonhole. Modernization, rationalization, and standardization—the prescribed

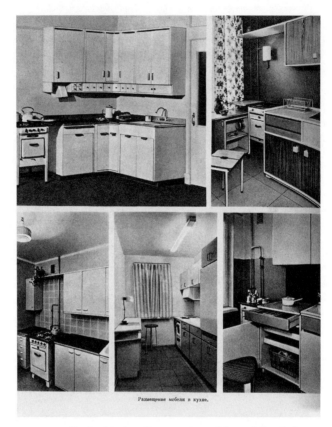

FIGURE 1.13. Soviet kitchen from 1966 revision of *Kratkaia entsiklopediia domashnego khoziaistva.*

"feeling states" of domesticity during the Soviet period—were entirely caught up by the difference between image and affect, between an American modern and a Soviet modern. Under Khrushchev's regime, women were to be the chief protectors of the state against consumerist gluttony and blind consumption. How then could the Soviet viewer make sense of the seeming paradox between modernity's asceticism and abundance? If the adage "less is more" held true, then what was the proper response to the "excess of images"—the visual bombardment—that sought to convey a message of democratic choice and technological convenience? Should a dishwasher provide a prosthetic emotionality or simply get the job done? Was the cut of Pat Nixon's dress purely functional or a pleasure to look at? Suddenly it could be both. How then could the Soviet viewer not be caught up in the gaps and inconsistencies triggered by envy? At ANEM, the American version of mid-century modern presented both abundance and efficiency, a celebration of excess and modern technology.

Some of this emotional inconsistency existed before Nixon's visit, of course, and can be seen in the contrast between the messy sociality of the communal kitchen and the state-subsidized private kitchen. Certainly the Soviets did not need the American kitchen to show them the simultaneous moods of contentment and streamlined efficiency—both were already in circulation by state decree. Would envy tempt Soviet citizens away from an imposed communality? Or would the Eamesian images of an American lifestyle seem like yet another administered mode of captivity, constraint posing as diversity?[101]

The American exhibition and the Eameses' instrumental contribution to it cannot be understood without considering this larger context. Debates about technological liberation, female happiness, and the individual's obligation to her community were already present in Soviet life before the exhibition opened its doors. The designers' reliance on a sort of visual bombardment to convey the superiority of a possession-oriented subjectivity may have created envy, but this was an envy that evidenced frustration, even anger, and irritation inspired by the foregone conclusion of Soviet subjectivity as inadequately evolved. In Khrushchev's model of consumerism, goods could benefit society, not simply the insular and isolated households of individual families. Most importantly, a plethora of household goods could also be incorporated into the lexicon as supremely Soviet. Even before the screening of *Glimpses* in Moscow, the domestic stage, changing modes of perception, and technologies of seeing and feeling were situated as international. At the time the exhibition opened, the Soviets already understood themselves as other to the American machine, both visible and invisible, present and absent. What we witness in Moscow, then, is both admiration and antagonism, a refusal to respond within the binary logic of the Cold War kitchen.

[2]

REFRAMING THE COLD WAR KITCHEN: SYLVIA
PLATH, *BYT*, AND THE RADICAL IMAGINARY OF
THE BELL JAR

A competent critic can do a good deal even for the most prominent writer. An in-
telligent critical article is like a bunch of birch twigs for anyone who enjoys a steam
bath—he lashes himself with the twigs as he takes the bath, or if he doesn't want to
do it himself, someone else does it for him.   —Nikita Khrushchev[1]

ALTHOUGH THE AMERICAN National Exhibition in Moscow seemed to
set the terms for reading the kitchen in the late 1950s, a reimagination
of the kitchen also was taking place in vibrant locales outside Moscow.
Percolating throughout literature, film, advertising, fashion, and other
cultural venues, the kitchen became an orienting concept for mid-century
U.S. women's subjectivity. Many of these texts demonstrate the centrality of the kitchen as both material object and symbolic concept to the
Cold War cultural front. If we pause over the proliferation of the kitchen
in women's literature from this era, we get a particularly rich reading
of the ways both canonical and lesser-known feminist fiction used the
kitchen to restructure the false dichotomies of this front. From Natalya
Baranskaya and Sylvia Plath to Alice Childress and Lorraine Hansberry,
women writers rewrote some of the key global polarities held in balance by
Nixon's rhetoric in the kitchen. Disrupting these polarities by invoking the
mutual embeddedness of the United States and the Soviet Union, the sexual
division of labor, and the instability of the racial discourses hidden in
plain sight in Moscow, their works offer a rebuttal to Nixon's postur-
ing in the splitnik kitchen. In so doing, this literature—from Childress's
Like One of the Family to Plath's *The Bell Jar*—radically reconfigures
the terms of the mid-century kitchen, offering a rejoinder to the two men
who debated in Moscow.

　　The Bell Jar is usually remembered as a tale of young female oppression within the patriarchal confines of early Cold War culture. Set on

the East Coast, the novel incorporates three characters that invoke Moscow: a Russian translator, a Russian suitor, and an African American kitchen worker. These marginal figures challenge the rhetoric of Nixon and Khrushchev's performance in Moscow, and force us to re-read the kitchen through the bind of heteronormativity. In this way *The Bell Jar* demonstrates how U.S. Cold War femininity was always already caught up in a summoning of the Soviet "other." Underscoring the awkward performance of masculinity in the Cold War kitchen, and the slippery and discontinuous production of meaning through translation, Plath's novel offers a counternarrative to standard accounts of Cold War femininity. With an alternative logic routed through the kitchen, *The Bell Jar* shows us how the fiction of an integrated American female selfhood (and its inadequate achievement) was correlated with those of designated Cold War others, such as Russians and African Americans.

Potboilers

In a 1962 letter to her mother, Sylvia Plath described the novel she was working on as an inferior piece of writing: "Forget about the novel and tell no one of it. It's a potboiler and just practice."[2] While Plath disparaged her novel as second-rate, her decision to dub it a "potboiler" turned out to be visionary. Published in 1963 as *The Bell Jar*, the novel has created even more of a stir in the years since Plath (perhaps disingenuously) disparaged it as kitchen fare. In fact, the kitchen context implied by the term "potboiler," coined for throwaway fiction written to pay the bills, may be one of the reasons its fuller associations have been overlooked.

For many readers, *The Bell Jar* summons something between rabid fascination and mute recognition. The book invites a feeling of empathy for the failure of its protagonist (and perhaps its author) to find solace in the postwar environment in which she is ensnared. The enticement of this readerly affect accounts at least in part for the book's stunning popularity more than fifty years after its initial publication. Sylvia Plath has become a sort of twenty-first century cottage industry, inspiring a major motion picture called *Sylvia*, an off-Broadway production based on *The Bell Jar*, the publication of the *Sylvia* screenplay, and a biography of Plath's estranged husband, Ted Hughes, called *Her Husband*.[3] Focus Feature's public-relations quip about the movie *Sylvia*—"life was too small to contain her"—seemed to inspire consumers. Although life may have been too small for Sylvia, she was large enough for everyone to have a piece of her.[4] Savvy marketing strategies and the cultivation of a kind of mass literary taste for the classics aside, the terms of female containment continue to plague Plath, decades after her death. The novel's enduring popularity not only indicates a cultural fascination with mid-century morbidity, it also exposes a fantasy of historical progress regarding U.S. women's emancipation. From the TV series *Mad Men* and *The Americans* to trends in architecture and design, the Cold War returns symptomatically, disclosing issues that have yet to be analyzed thoroughly. In the case of the *The Bell Jar*, the principal issue is a modern female selfhood defined by choice. In spite of the novel's continued status as a best seller, it has yet to be read in ways that fully appreciate its radical reconfiguration of this selfhood.

Due perhaps to an uncanny sense of perpetual female entrapment, the novel's protagonist, Esther Greenwood, and its author are compounded with millions of readers in a circuit of feeling: we are encouraged to feel with or through *The Bell Jar*. This circuit of emotion situates *The Bell Jar* alongside other fictions of sentiment—the novel participates in a process of substitution and repetition; the feelings that these processes instantiate then multiply through the novel's mass production. While much Plath criticism has attended to the various implications of such identifications for an Anglo-American, English-speaking, largely female audience, little attention has been paid to the moments in which such affection breaks down; that is, to the places in the book which, rather than inciting desire and identification, inspire distance and perhaps even dislike. Put another way, my line of inquiry in this chapter will not ask us to read against the circuit of sentiment, but to resituate radically the sentiments raised. While the discussion in chapter I sought a reevaluation of the success of the American National Exhibition in Moscow through the prism of Soviet reception, this chapter seeks a redirecting of *The Bell Jar* through the kitchen, through Russia, and through Plath's occluded racial thinking in order to discover what such redirection does to the sentiments that readers feel.

Before rerouting the way in which the novel is typically read, it is important to outline the book's complex publishing history—and the way this history has contributed to *The Bell Jar*'s conventional interpretation. The novel was published in England in 1963 under the pseudonym Victoria Lucas, then was reissued in 1967, this time with Plath's name attached to it. In 1971, against Plath's mother's wishes, the book was published in the United States. Plath's death a month or so after *The Bell Jar*'s first British publication has provided fertile territory for the author/protagonist conflation and made it very difficult to read the book using the other terms that it provides us. Plath's comment that the book was a "potboiler" hints at the degree to which artifice and unreliability might be some of its key ingredients; nevertheless, our attention is always tweaked in the direction of the autobiographical.[5] Even criticism that seeks to avoid such analysis ends up invoking Plath in order to stake a truer claim about the text. For example, one study is determined to track down every political journal that Plath read in an attempt to ascertain her opinions on issues as diverse as nuclear bombs and breast feeding and to connect her underlying beliefs to her literary output. As a *New York Times* reviewer remarked in 1971, "it's impossible to read *The Bell Jar* [without] the knowledge of Sylvia Plath's doom color[ing] its pages."[6] But if we insist on prioritizing the morbid Plathian prism as *the* primary means of investigating the novel, then we are likely to miss what I call its radical imaginary.

Like all novels *The Bell Jar* emerges from a specific context. It was written by an American living in London and its outskirts, during a period of heated political debate in the United States about national identity. Set in the 1950s, *The Bell Jar* provides us with the terms to think through this transatlantic intersection of impulses, offering key encounters that have remained overlooked in favor of more savory or sensational elements. This chapter turns to three characters that have not inspired much previous interest, perhaps because they have been obliterated by the seductiveness of the protagonist.[7] The otherwise marginal Russian and African American characters figure quite prominently at two key junctures in Esther Greenwood's tale.[8] The Russians appear during her first failed attempt to dispense with her virginity, while the "Negro" appears following her first failed attempt to dispense with her life.

The Bell Jar takes the form of a pseudo-memoir as nineteen-year-old Esther Greenwood, raised in Boston, recalls that "summer of 1953." On break after her junior year at college, she starts the summer with a plum internship at a women's magazine in New York City, then ends it by being hospitalized for severe depression. The summer turns out to be both more and less than Esther bargained for: more, in that she gains access to the Manhattan publishing elite and undergoes electro-convulsive therapy (ECT), and less in that both experiences are deeply disappointing to her. What begins as a promising adventure among the cream of college women devolves into a summer of catatonic misery, failed suicide attempts, and hospitalization. Along the way, the ferociously insightful and self-scrutinizing Esther meets a series of characters, female and male, who embody various types: Doreen the wild girl, Betsy the goody-good,

Dodo Conway the breeder, Jay Cee the mousy career woman, Buddy Willard the college boyfriend, Marco the Latin Lover. Esther criticizes all of them mercilessly, but she reserves the harshest criticism for herself. As readers we are privy to the incessant internal monologue with which Esther is preoccupied. We move with Esther's thoughts through her first suicide attempt, her ensuing attempts to recover, and her emergence from the asylum, Belsize, where she undergoes intensive psycho- and electric-shock therapies. Through it all, Esther's mother—a stenographer who has raised Esther alone (and who channels her own disappointments with life into Esther's ambitions)—plays the role of antagonist. Recited in the first person as a retrospective narrative set in the close past, *The Bell Jar* promotes identification with Esther. She is a type of her own: one that breaks molds in seeking to have it all—good looks, wealth, fame, marriage, a baby.

In this classic text, a denunciation of suburban, white, middle-class female constraint might seem an appropriate frame. In that context, a Russian and a Negro might appear to be curious interlopers, inviting readers to wonder about their presence in the novel.[9] In order to better understand the dynamics of the postwar kitchen as both a material and symbolic site, however, we should attend to these marginal figures in a tale in which the American kitchen and its narratives play a starring role. Interestingly, Betty Friedan's *The Feminine Mystique* was published in the same year as *The Bell Jar*. Identifying work outside the home as the balm for female malaise, *The Feminine Mystique* encouraged women to "go out and get a job!" Although women were certainly hampered or constrained by patriarchal attitudes and institutions that systematically removed them from the means of production in the 1950s, *The Bell Jar* connects the ideas of female discontent with the Russian and the Negro as important players in U.S. Cold War cosmography. Plath's novel thus allows for a rethinking of an overused notion of female containment. It elaborates on the alternative intelligences present in a narrative that also announces a kind of female domestic incarceration.[10] While Plath's novel demands to be interpreted in the context of U.S. domestic containment, its narrative has as much to say about American women's relationships to national narratives that place, displace, and replace women in an international, geopolitical world order as it does about the relationship between U.S. domestic incarceration and the asylum. Of course, these two discourses are not mutually exclusive; on the contrary, they are importantly related.[11]

Typically interpreted as a female *bildungsroman*, a "rite of passage from adolescence into womanhood, from psychic distress into mental stability,"[12] the book invites us to share Esther's descent into madness and her emergence from it through a potent solipsism. But the first-person narration that ensnares the reader—based on tangents, nearly a stream of consciousness—also presents a warning. If, as Esther constantly reminds us, she is a master of deception, might it not be important to read her against her word? The more Esther becomes self-absorbed, the more egregiously does she embody apathy towards the world around her. *The Bell Jar* offers impulses both towards mental health—an integrated selfhood—and towards the unfeasibility of such a selfhood. This is not, as is commonly thought, staged as an impossible choice between "motherhood" and "career." The conflict arises instead from the sexual, racial, and global terms of Esther's contradictory location. *The Bell Jar*'s ostensible emphasis on the cohesion of identity alongside the text's performance of this as an impossibility offer us an opportunity to query the ways in which isolated attention to selfhood and its inadequate fulfillment are a distraction from the embeddedness of that self in different matrices of power and interconnected networks of knowledge production. I do not mean to imply that the "personal" is not "political" or that *The Bell Jar* refuses a reading of U.S. sexual politics during the Cold War, interpretations that certainly have offered rich analyses. By reexamining the text, however, we can resituate what it suggests by these terms, by its links between the sexual and the political, as well as other Cold War framing devices.

In broad strokes, the political setting of the novel is crucial to its interpretation. Usually understood as a struggle based on two different types of ideological power—American capitalism versus Soviet communism—the Cold War is associated with entrenched polarities. This vision of hostile rivalry is based in a binary framework that squares American against Soviet, a framework that during the period enabled some U.S. citizens to determine a sense of self based in opposition to this Soviet other. Cold War critics have elaborated the means by which national narratives helped determine the key connotations and responsibilities of civic membership and participation.[13] These arguments about the role of narrative in building a sense of national community, naturalizing the relationship between people and territory, have created ways of analyzing and better understanding the relationships between subjectivity and citizenship during the Cold War period. Understanding the ways in which narrative can help to create social bonds among citizens has been key to a rethinking of the Cold War and the reach of its logic through various cultural and social strata.[14] To be sure, *The Bell Jar* participates with an almost gleeful abandon in the normalizing rituals of national narrativizing. Esther's search for selfhood through the dramatically opposed lives of poetry and motherhood offers us a character who throws herself against the limited options available to her like a furious pinball, aiming for and then bouncing away from discrete targets of female identity. But in spite of this dramatic pull towards the winning ticket of achieved selfhood, the text also resists an easy repetition of the ordinary sense of American Cold War sociality.

Herein lie the sexual politics of the book. The text strains to reassure us that Esther has emerged from *The Bell Jar* and written the document that remains as the material fact of her recovery. Esther's rebirth by electric shock therapy is undercut, however, by the multiple gaps the text summons: we are left with an uncanny sense of suspension.[15] What of the space between the novel's end and the writing of the narrative from a location of health and recovery? Ambivalence towards the narratives that would have assured us of the protagonist's success in a U.S. Cold War idiom—marriage and motherhood—is made evident in the book's opening pages. Esther mentions "the baby" (presumably hers) once in an aside, as if a baby could be brought in like a potted plant then left unattended.[16] The gap between the reputed remission at the book's close and the dubious maternal fulfillment at the narrative's beginning opens into a chasm. This space is punctuated by moments that suggest a negotiation of historically specific states of emergency.

The text's first sentence mentions the 1953 electrocution of Julius and Ethel Rosenberg, who had been tried and convicted in 1951 of conspiracy to commit espionage by passing information regarding atomic weapons to the Soviets. It has been suggested that Ethel Rosenberg can be interpreted as a ghost of Esther Greenwood and, moreover, that Esther's ECT, which serves as the source of her proverbial rebirth, can be juxtaposed with Ethel Rosenberg's death by electrocution.[17] After being interrogated about her wifely duties by the court ("Did you do all the chores of a housewife . . . cooking, washing, cleaning, darning, scrubbing?"), Ethel Rosenberg became suspected of bad mothering. Judge Irving Kaufman's sentencing statement accentuated her maternal failures:

> The evidence indicated quite clearly that Julius Rosenberg was the prime mover in this conspiracy. However, let no mistake be made about the role which his wife, Ethel Rosenberg, played in this conspiracy. Instead of deterring him from pursuing his ignoble cause, she encouraged and assisted the cause. . . . Indeed the defendants Julius and Ethel Rosenberg placed their

devotion to their cause above their own personal safety and were conscious that they were sacrificing their own children, should their misdeeds
be detected—all of which did not deter them from pursuing their course.
Love for their cause dominated their lives—it was even greater than their
love for their children.[18]

Ethel Rosenberg's status as a bad mother—an image the press went
to great pains to confirm—stays with Esther as a reminder that she must
conform to the era's dictates or risk excoriation.[19] In the 1950s, the consequences of bad motherhood apparently included a vulnerability to outside coercion and a susceptibility to Soviet influence, even perhaps the
risk of becoming a Soviet oneself. (The denigrations of motherhood in
general were forcefully articulated in Philip Wylie's popular *Generation
of Vipers*, published in 1942 and reprinted many times, which bemoans
the unhealthy cult of "Momism.") As Andrew Ross has pointed out, fear
of the Rosenbergs was based on a perception of their ordinariness, "not
because they harbored subversive, or violently revolutionary views (as
Popular Fronters, they did not), but because they were so much like an
ordinary, patriotic American couple."[20] At the same time, their liminality as Jews was never far from the surface. The cultural logics of anti-
communism, racism, and Momism come together through a belief in the
enemy within. The novel plays with this tentative logic, inserting Ethel
Rosenberg as a kind of *doppelganger* for Esther, and also introducing a
Russian translator as a shadow reflection, a woman who Esther tempo-
rarily but lustfully desires to be: "I wished with all my heart that I could
crawl into her."[21] By the binary logic of the era that the book both depicts
and undercuts, the Russian woman must be announced because she is
that which U.S. women must not be. Even more so than Ethel Rosenberg,
she is an enemy within, the sustaining other of U.S. Cold War femininity.

Who's Cooking?

> I strolled into the kitchen, dropped a raw egg into a teacup of raw hamburger,
> mixed it up and ate it. —*The Bell Jar* (119)

> Mikoyan really went overboard for electric mixers, openers, fryers, and other
> devices that make the American kitchen a complete contrast to its crude
> Russian counterpart. "No wonder your American women seem so pretty
> and dressed up," Mikoyan said. "They have all these gadgets to free their
> time." Then, as though taken by the prospect of being No. 1 Man with Soviet
> women, the No. 2 Russian said, with gallantry, "we have to free our house-

wives like you Americans! The Russian housewife needs help!" There's the
making of a revolution here!   —Norman K. Winston[22]

Plath's flirtation with the female translator both buttresses and undercuts the idea that the Soviet woman was the other to the white American housewife. Let us return briefly to the scene of the kitchen debate
with which I opened this book, a move made not—as Khrushchev might
have put it—so that the critic can lash herself with the twigs. Indeed, the
kitchen provides an uncanny undercurrent throughout *The Bell Jar*. In
the following passage, Esther offers an image that skillfully describes the
analogous relationship between woman and housewife during the 1950s:

> Often when I visited Buddy I found Mrs. Willard braiding a rug out of
> strips of wool from Mr. Willard's old suits. She'd spent weeks on that rug,
> and I had admired the tweedy browns and greens and blues patterning the
> braid, but after Mrs. Willard was through, instead of hanging the rug on
> the wall the way I would have done, she put it down in place of her kitchen
> mat, and in a few days it was soiled and dull and indistinguishable from any
> mat you could buy for under a dollar in the five and ten. And I knew that
> in spite of the roses and kisses and restaurant dinners a man showered on a
> woman before he married her, what he secretly wanted when the wedding
> service ended was for her to flatten out underneath his feet like Mrs. Wil-
> lard's kitchen mat. (84–85)

The kitchen functions as more than just setting here. In fact, the logic of
Nixon's rhetoric in Moscow remains front and center throughout *The
Bell Jar*—from Esther's sickness after a *Ladies' Day* banquet to the scene
when she throws gown after gown from the rooftop of her dormitory
(called the Amazon), in a rejection of consumer abundance. In the banquet incident, Esther gleefully stuffs herself on caviar and crabmeat, then
discovers that the food was "chock-full of ptomaine." In yet another invocation of the hypocrisies of the Cold War kitchen, Esther notes, "I had
a vision of the celestially white kitchens of *Ladies Day* stretching into in-
finity. I saw avocado pear after avocado pear being stuffed with crabmeat
and mayonnaise and photographed under brilliant lights. I saw the del-
icate, pink-mottled claw meat poking seductively through its blanket of
mayonnaise and the bland yellow pear cup with its rim of alligator-green
cradling the whole mess. Poison" (48). In the gown-tossing scene, Esther
dispenses with the contents of her closet after being attacked by her date,
Marco: "Piece by piece, I fed my wardrobe to the night wind, and flut-
teringly, like a loved one's ashes, the gray scraps were ferried off, to settle

here, there, exactly where I would never know, in the dark heart of New York" (111). In every way the novel is concerned with debunking what in other venues was called the "good life"—the house in the suburbs, the new car, the husband with a white-collar job, the cleanly scrubbed children raised by a full-time wife and mother—a life that required not only leisure time and consumer plenty, but also whiteness.

In that Moscow kitchen, Nixon declared that U.S. superiority was lodged in freedom of consumer choice, explicitly linking diversity to the right to choose. In this context, Plath's novel must be read as a direct engagement with the limitations of Nixon's proclamations. The vice president's collapsing of woman and housewife provides the ammunition for his pride in U.S. superiority, showcasing the supremacy of American ideas in the privacy of the home rather than on the battlefield.[23] Privacy, of course, was an operative term and, as Deborah Nelson has explained, ambivalences surrounding the private lie at the heart of containment rhetoric. Nelson writes, "The constitutional right to privacy represents a paradox: it both refused the logic of containment, which justified the intrusion into private life to protect the same privacy; and extended its logic by resting the right to privacy on the exceptional idealization of the home."[24]

But in Moscow, as in *The Bell Jar*, the idea of privacy hints at more than its own violation. Nixon and Khrushchev's debate marked the Moscow kitchen as far from a private space, of course, just as Esther's addressing of her private yearnings to a reader marks them as no longer private. In Moscow, American privacy encounters its own absence and, as in *The Bell Jar*, that absence occurs through imperfect translation: the reliance on poetic idiom. Because there is no word for "privacy" in Russian, Nixon's translator was hard pressed to render Nixon's terms: *lichnoe* (personal) or *chastnoe* (separate) are the closest the Russian lexicon comes to "private." In the Soviet context, the kitchen in the *communalka*, or communal apartment, connotes a place of separation, where running water may blur conversation so it cannot be overheard; it is also a falsely private place, a space that reinforces who's cooking as a matter of ideology. Even outside the communal kitchen, domestic space is always already marked as not private: housing is state-owned, and furniture and other domestic objects—including pots, pans, and the TV—are all government issue.

For Khrushchev, therefore, the kitchen is always a political site, and yet Nixon considers his movement to the domestic realm exemplary of democratic liberty, where ideas equal goods in the interest of female autonomy and an exceptional idealization of the home as sacred. As I argued in chapter 1, however, the U.S. suburban kitchen was in fact defined by a sense of captivity and surveillance. Thus the Russian translator could only partially convey the specificity of Nixon's claims, which based their victory in seemingly paradoxical claims of public *and* private triumph. Recalling the dissonance between U.S. media representations and Soviet reception of the American National Exhibition in Moscow, *The Bell Jar*'s portrayal of a Russian translator prompts us to trouble Nixon's reputed success in the kitchen debate. Plath helps us to see that the battle could not have signified for Soviets in the same way that it did for U.S. citizens.

Perhaps aware of Nixon's evasion of tensions concerning diversity and captivity in the United States, the Soviet press had a field day with the American portrait of the debate. One humor magazine, *Krokodil*, chided U.S. officials by reconstructing the exhibition's deleted interracial wedding scene.[25] If the United States was ready to admit, indeed to hail, the gendering of Cold War terms and terrain, fighting the war on an openly feminine front in which diversity equaled consumer choice (to square against forced captivity), then the Soviet insistence on putting racial diversity front and center at the exhibition underscored the *purported* exclusion of race from gender, the disconnection between ideas and goods. Indeed, as this pastiche displays, the Soviets would never tire of reminding the United States how race and gender are always a part of the ideological construction of U.S. citizenship, or about the ways in which a racial articulation always underlies the construction of the universality of the abstract individual as representatively male. Nixon's claim about a "universal" attitude towards women outlined in chapter 1 belies the fact that this attitude can be universal only so long as the abstract individual is universally male.

The Bell Jar's invocation of Russian characters helps us to further query this axiom. Universalism was not standard issue in the Soviet Union, where a uniform relationship to an Enlightenment intellectual heritage had been challenged by nineteenth-century Russian thinkers. These thinkers considered Russia different and superior to Europe, a formation reconfigured by the 1920s Leninist framework of a new society free of gender and racial inequity. In Khrushchev's day, this Leninist posture still resounded through socialist iconography and intent, if not in actuality. *The Bell Jar* helps us to see that perhaps it was patriarchy that marked the common ground of the debate, a transnational point of convergence. When troubled over shared terms, Nixon and Khrushchev finally agreed: "We can all drink to the ladies."[26] Their clink of classes elided the distance between "we" and "all," with the elite "we" and the populist "all" purportedly linked by the unifying principle of being "for the ladies." This elision reveals the link between their positions within a masculinist lexicon of Enlightenment philosophies, and thus outside the lexicon of racial and sexual heterogeneity. *The Bell Jar* instructs us that Cold War fictions depend upon race, and that a woman—defined by and privy to the universal compulsion of consumer choice—was always a racialized subject. In his convergence with Nixon, Khrushchev thus positions himself as at once popular and elite—occupying both places at once, his acts of unification and consolidation carried forth by the principle of being "for" the ladies. The organizing structure of the two leaders' (c)link relies on a kind of heterosexual contract, with Nixon's claims to universalism containing a directive in which this view of gender is the "good," the recruiting agent that no Soviet can resist. In a sense, diversity itself now becomes a captive term.

While the binding agent of heteronormativity was acknowledged through this raising of glasses, it was also built on a forced connection. Even the U.S. media highlighted the awkwardness of this display of male unity. *Time* magazine noted that "Nixon put his arm around Khrushchev, [and said] 'I'm afraid I haven't been a good host.' Khrushchev smiled and, underscoring the *weird aspect of the whole performance* turned toward the [male] American guide who had been standing in the model kitchen and said: 'Thank the housewife for letting us use her kitchen for our argument.'"[27] Khrushchev's indirect address of the absent housewife, via the translator, troubles Nixon's attempt to host this exchange as one between men, breaking the bond between himself and Nixon before it can solidify. Membership in a men's club, Khrushchev reminds Nixon, cannot be universal. The triangulated battle between men over women is a common mode of commerce, and Khrushchev highlights its artifice as a means of reducing women to goods through his refusal to hug Nixon back. His performance accentuates the uncanniness (*unheimlich*) of this scene and also calls attention to the absence of racial inclusion that Soviet dogma allegedly supported.

The portrayal of Russian meets American in *The Bell Jar* takes up the terms of the Nixon-Khrushchev encounter and shifts them. We are introduced to the unnamed Russian woman through Esther's much anticipated date with Constantin, a translator at the United Nations: "And while Constantin and I sat in one of those hushed plush auditoriums in the UN, next to a stern muscular Russian girl with no makeup who was a simultaneous translator like Constantin, I thought how strange it had never occurred to me before that I was only purely happy until I was nine years old" (75). Given all the issues that were debated in the summer of 1953—the Korean truce, fears of communism in the Middle East, U.S. trade embargos, the lingering instability following Stalin's death—it is telling that Esther's mind runs from her surroundings to her own troubled sense of self. She stares not at but "through the Russian girl in her double-breasted gray suit, rattling off idiom after idiom in her own unknowable tongue. . . . and I wished with all my heart that I could crawl into her and spend the rest of my life barking out one idiom after another" (75). The picture of the Russian girl that Esther draws for us conforms to stereotype: "muscular" and "stern," she defies American femininity, rebuking makeup and wearing dull clothing.[28] Although *Life* magazine may have announced a year earlier that "The Iron Curtain Look Is Here!," they were careful to delineate the difference between that "look" and the American one. (You can tell the American girl by her "slender gams").[29] As frumpy as this female appears, Esther is still drawn to her and, more importantly, to her "unknowable" language. The desire to become the Russian girl is not simply about a "negative identity politics,"[30] but rather about the alarming lure of a particular kind of speech: speech as empty speech. The language of idioms, after all, is one in which meaning is non-coincident with the literal. The text thus simultaneously suggests the enticement of national narratives which seem to offer identity as a solution and the foundation of that lure in rhetoric that is overblown, idiomatic, and empty. As Esther comments, to embody the Russian by "crawling inside her" would instantiate a particular kind of removed selfhood. Rather than a revelation of the "enemy within," she craves a return to the womb of empty speech: the little America in the heart of Moscow. Moreover, Esther's desire to expound idiom after idiom could be seen as an apotheosis of Plath's poetic technique, her investment in metaphor as a scene of transformation, of experience into language. As Alan Nadel has observed, Plath was "a radically metaphorical thinker, locating the meaning of things, of experience, in the transformation rather than what has been traditionally designated the metaphor's 'tenor.'"[31]

As the kitchen debate demonstrates—and *The Bell Jar* underscores—Cold War speech is empty; it requires articulation and then translation into imprecise idioms. Plath's summoning of a failed cross-cultural exchange does not invoke translation as failure per se; on the contrary, it reflects a desire to feel that emptiness or nothing as *something*, to make non-coincidence a mode of being. Although the scene criticizes "simultaneous translation" as inadequate to instantiate complete knowledge, the desire to be the medium of that exchange, to command that power, remains. We could see this as restaging the Nixon-Khrushchev encounter by emphasizing its weird performativity, its slippery discontinuous production of meaning. As Gayatri Spivak has argued, translation requires a certain intimacy, and in Plath's scene infidelity is exposed as key to the exchange of knowledge about the other.[32] What Esther voices is equal parts enforced misrecognition and desire. Here we should not forget that Esther's wish to sleep with a Russian, let alone *be* a Russian, is alarmingly un-American (taking the parallel to Ethel Rosenberg much further). *The Bell Jar* offers us the opportunity to see U.S. Cold War femininity as caught up in the weird performance—as perpetuated by the U.S. media— of the Soviet other. Indeed, Esther's whole encounter with the Russian woman talks back to a nostalgia for substance and sexual presence in which Esther, as a product of nation-building narratives, seems trapped.

Showing us how her desires are constructed through a narrative in which failure presents itself as the most promising alternative,[33] Esther next removes herself even farther from acting on them: "Then Constantin and the Russian girl interpreter and the whole bunch of black and white and yellow men arguing down there behind their labeled microphones seemed to move off at a distance. I saw their mouths go up and down without a sound, as if they were sitting on the deck of a departing ship, stranding me in the middle of a huge silence" (75). This self-imposed cocoon of isolation is not unlike the "white cocoon" of isolation Esther experiences at Belsize, the asylum where she inaugurates a recovery of sorts. In this scene, however, Esther is of the world but cut off from it: the international world of "black and white and yellow men" is a departing ship of political engagement.[34]

Elsewhere in the novel, Esther repeatedly demonstrates a full-throttle engagement in a political world in which her voice is quite audible. Given *The Bell Jar*'s multiple scenes of engagement with Cold War others, it would be remiss not to mention the figure of the Jew in this context. Jewishness is summoned not only by the notion of Ethel Rosenberg as Esther's alter-ego, but also in the novel's oft-cited story-within-a-story about a fig tree. Esther reads this story on the morning of her first conversation with Constantin, in a book called *Thirty Best Short Stories* given to her by a *Ladies' Day* editor as a consolation gift for the putrefied luncheon food (54–55). In the story, a Jewish man and a Catholic nun repeatedly reconnoiter behind a tree of ripe figs; there they witness the birth of a chick. Because their relationship is doomed (an angry nun shows up one day in place of the usual sister), Esther sees a parallel to her relationship to Buddy Willard, but the novel suggests other parallels pertinent to its radical imaginary, including Esther's inability to make choices about her own future.

The appearance of a Jewish character in the context of choice and the multiracial United Nations recalls the larger antagonism between U.S. and Soviet ideologies, between liberal democracy and socialist internationalism. In this antagonism the treatment of ethnic others, whether by U.S. Jim Crow laws or Soviet anti-Semitism, became a key basis for the cultural Cold War. Although I will return to the failed promises of liberal democracy and its false rhetoric of choice later in this chapter, the figure of the Jew suggests other failures. By 1953 many Jewish Americans who had forged early, substantial links to communism had taken their political affiliations elsewhere.[35] Soviet anti-Semitism had been widely reported in Europe and the United States, and 1952 had witnessed the execution of thirteen Yiddish writers and members of the Jewish Anti-Fascist Committee in the Soviet Union. (This event, which became known as "The Night of the Murdered Poets," was publicly denounced in 1955, after Stalin's death.) The presence of the inter-faith couple highlights a number of discontinuous links, including those between the Russian and the Negro; indeed, their presence makes impossible any kind of nostalgic championing either of liberal pluralism (the failed union of Jews and Catholics) or of Soviet internationalism, forcing us to confront head-on the promise and the disappointments of both.

Since the American idiom of *The Bell Jar* has been relatively well-rehearsed, let us follow the text's lead and turn to the Soviet idiom. Esther's reference to the Russian woman's "double-breasted suit" hints at more than bad taste in fashion. For Russians, after all, the double is an enduring model of national consciousness.[36] Geographically situated between East and West, yet falling under the sway of European thought (sometimes captured by nationalist *ressentiment*), Russian intellectuals felt that Russia had been wrongly dubbed as inferior to the West. In response to this slight, nineteenth-century theorists of Russian national identity angled for a place on the scale of world-historical progress established by their Western counterparts. Having been more or less dismissed by German idealist philosophy, Russian intellectuals believed that they had a key role to play in the future of world history. Russian formulations of doubleness provided a means of articulating alienation from Western philosophies of identity, and the belief persisted that an ability to embody both a Europeanness and a non-Europeanness, simultaneously, made Russians unique.[37] This providential duality is equally apparent in the intellectual genealogy of both Fyodor Dostoevsky and Vladimir Lenin, for whom the notion of nation presupposed that of gender.[38]

Khrushchev's democratic turn in the mid-1950s, in what has been called a period of political thaw, included a new interest in women's issues and the establishment of *zhensovety*, women-only councils devoted to developing ties between the Communist Party and women. In his 1956 speech to the 20th Party Congress, Khrushchev inquired about activity in party politics and pointed out that only ten members of the Central Committee were women; thereafter, he made women's issues more prominent, perhaps realizing that the inequalities of Soviet-style socialism had yet to be addressed.[39] In spite of Khrushchev's stated interest in these issues (which, as I discuss in the next chapter, included a bald concern for the declining birthrate), the "woman question" remained bound by the available masculine-oriented terms, in which diversity was part of a totalitarian ideology, and local knowledges were collapsed into the supersignified of doubleness.[40]

Some scholars of Soviet studies identify this masculine bias, understanding Soviet women to be oppressively housed under the "double burden" of domestic and workplace demands.[41] And in the postwar context, Soviet women were undoubtedly challenged by the dual demands of work and domesticity. But as we will see in the discussion of Natalya Baranskaya in chapter 3, women's articulation of resistance to state-sponsored demands has been largely subsumed by narratives of Soviet national identity that deploy a representatively male paradigm. Following Stalin's death in 1953, World War II—"The Great Patriotic War" against fascism— became the key symbol of a national identity whose international view was more retrospectively defensive than forwardly aggressive. Whereas male heroism was valorized by militaristic images of patriotism, robust images of maternity, encapsulated in the figure of Mother Russia, were used to suggest female endurance and maternal sufferance—normalizing the feminine into a romantic figure for a nation controlled by males. A resurgence of the traditional distinctions between the sexes signaled a turn to conservative "family values" and conventional gender roles. And the corporealization of the nation as mother rendered compulsory this relationship between the Soviet Union and its female citizens.[42]

Some Soviet women authors offered compelling revoicings of the notion of Russian cultural doubleness, taking as a point of departure the contradiction between Russian cultural messianism and the ostracism of the everyday, known as *byt*. *Literatura byta*—or literature of the everyday—grew out of a resistance to socialist realism, and became known as "socialist realism with a human face."[43] Developed during the postwar period, this literary movement addresses the life of ordinary people, typically in the first person, without editorial comment. Iurii Trifonov, Irina Grekova, Natalya Baranskaya, Maia Ganina, and Nadezhda Kozhevnikova are all identified with this movement, and their work is marked by a turn away from collective themes and towards personal ones, foregrounding the dissonance between party dogma and individual experience. Some of this *literatura byta* facilitated a reconception of the relationship between women and Soviet national identity, and explored the burden of articulating, differently, the cultural nationalism of the Russian double.[44] What, then, might it mean to read *The Bell Jar* within the framework of the everyday, or *byt*? Esther's relationship to the quotidian, in which the everyday is both the despised location of the feminine and the esteemed location of national superiority, would propose another identificatory detour through the *kommunalka* to suggest a longing for a selfhood not dependent upon a mystique of the Cold War other, the suppression of racial diversity, or the usurping of local knowledges into a supersignified.

Plotboilers

> The most effective kind of propaganda was defined as the kind where the subject moves in the direction you desire for reasons which he believes to be his own.   —U.S. National Security Council Directive, 1950[45]

Esther's encounter with a black kitchen worker at Belsize recalls the previously mentioned scene involving the Russian woman. The presence of the kitchen here again underscores the purported absence of race from the kitchen debate and likewise highlights the dilemma of U.S. female captivity during the Cold War. The black worker is introduced as follows: "Usually it was a shrunken old white man that brought our food, but today it was a Negro" (180). The logic of equivalences presented here suggests that the black man is not simply a substitute for a white man, but rather a substitute for a "shrunken old white man." (In other words, the worker's masculinity is equivalent to that of a decrepit white geriatric.) If this were not insult enough, he is accompanied by a woman "in blue stiletto heels" who is "telling him what to do," an image in which stiletto heels correlate to the insinuated sexuality of white femininity. Lodged in her unavailability to the Negro, the woman's sexuality articulates itself as superiority and bossiness: she instructs him and he obeys, while "grinning and chuckling in a silly way" (180). This black male is not only explicitly emasculated and nameless, thus establishing the sexual taboo that is ingrained in white supremacy, but he also performs his duties with token compliance.

In spite of his namelessness, however, the Negro is the one character in the novel who reads Esther accurately. Esther, as no one else has yet dared to announce, is a little shit. After listening to her impertinent order "we're not done . . . you can just wait," he responds by calling her "Miss Mucky-Muck." Later she complains when he serves two kinds of beans at the meal: "beans and carrots, or beans and peas, maybe; but never beans and beans" she growls. In retaliation, Esther kicks him and declares, "That's what *you* get" (181–82).[46] Esther's sense of entitlement propels her "you," hurling difference in its wake. What the text tells us is that Esther's character is grounded in her relationship to choice. This is her problem in a nutshell: she wants it all, but cannot have it. She is the American girl spoiled by choice, luminously portrayed in Plath's previous depiction of the rotting figs that surround Esther after her inability to make a decision about her future. That scene occurs when Esther is sitting between Constantin and the female Russian translator, after Esther has begun to chide herself for her inadequacies:

> I saw my life branching out before me like the green fig tree in the story. From the tip of every branch, like a fat purple fig, a wonderful future beckoned and winked. One fig was a husband and a happy home and children, and another fig was a famous poet and another fig was a brilliant professor, and another fig was Ee Gee, the amazing editor, and another fig was Europe and Africa and South America, and another fig was Constantin and Socrates and Attila and a pack of other lovers with queer names and offbeat professions, and another fig was an Olympic lady crew champion, and beyond and above these figs were many more figs I couldn't quite make out. I saw myself sitting in the crotch of this fig tree, starving to death, just because I couldn't make up my mind which of the figs I would choose. I wanted each and every one of them, but choosing one meant losing all the rest, and, as I sat there, unable to decide, the figs began to wrinkle and go black, and, one by one, they plopped to the ground at my feet. (77)

In rendering Esther as a spoiled ingénue in the later scene at the hospital, the text makes explicit the parameters of Esther's earlier choices, and who is implicated within them. Esther's negative reaction to the kitchen worker comes from his faulty presentation of her choices: it could be beans and corn, or beans and rice, but never beans and beans. The choice of beans and beans, of course, is no choice at all. Faced with this "no choice," Esther behaves badly, a "Miss Mucky Muck" whose conduct is as putrefied as rotten figs.

The book thus elaborates upon the differential possibilities of choice as they make themselves available to white women and African Americans during this era. Sandwiched between her exchanges with the kitchen worker is a brief scene in which Esther overturns a tray of thermometers so that the mercury balls glisten with potential dispersal, as she says "into a million little replicas" that, if pushed together, "would fuse, without a crack, into one whole again" (183). The book is clear about Esther's choice in the Cold War asylum: either you chose a million selves or one whole self. But the book also articulates the ways in which this dichotomy between the fractured and the whole is a false one. The government's stance on the relationship between woman and nation can be extrapolated from a 1950 U.S. National Security Directive that sought to move the subject "in the direction [the state desires] for reasons which [s] he believes to be [her] own." This anticipation of Althusserian interpellation, in which society conditions the self to be an ideal participant, was part of the "psychological warfare" necessary to systematically defeat the Soviets. As Frances Stonor Saunders has noted, such warfare was defined by the government as propaganda, a technique of the Soviet other, and it sounded a lot like brainwashing: "the planned use by a nation of propaganda and activities other than combat which communicate ideas and information intended to influence the opinions, attitudes, emotions and behavior. . . . in ways that will support the achievement of national aims."[47] Within this context, then, *The Bell Jar*'s ostensible emphasis on the cohesion of identity alongside the text's performance of this as an impossibility offers us an opportunity to query the ways isolated attention to selfhood and its inadequate fulfillment are correlated through Cold War others so as to produce "emotions and behavior" that will "support the achievement of national aims."

The fiction of integrated selfhood that the asylum offers Esther is one in which such integration relies on the Negro's marginalization, the repeated replication of Negro selfhood as always already broken. This brings us back to Nixon's proclamation of diversity as equal to the abundance of choices. What *The Bell Jar* teaches us is that, for Esther, the choice of being a million of herself or one integrated whole is not after all a choice—like the beans and beans, or the multiple plump figs, no choice is possible. This is *The Bell Jar*'s response to Nixon's claims, to the binary logic of an era in which to be a better or more integrated society is just another version of being plural—a million self-replicating pieces. This is not actual diversity, since that would require opening selfhood to difference. In a startling image, *The Bell Jar* does just that. Esther notes that, "Soon after they had locked the door, I could see the Negro's face, a molasses colored moon, risen at the window grating, but I pretended not to notice" (183). This image presents us with the black worker peering into Esther's prison, while suggesting that he could as easily be peering out from his. What we learn from this passage is that her imprisonment relies in part on his, and vice versa. This is, of course, the point that Esther pretends not to notice.

Although she and he are trapped, and his lack of choice is hers, these are not analogous locations. After all, Esther has the fiction of integrated selfhood at her fingertips, whereas he possesses a more limited access to that fiction. In a sense, Esther is more at leisure to be herself precisely because she is *not* one of the "others" identified in the novel.[48] Her kick tells us that this is no simple parallel, but one that relies on her misrecognition, a misrecognition which is so startling as to produce a kick. But we must recall that as readers, we also are targets of that proverbial kick: the "you" is us. That's what we get for buying the logic of *The Bell Jar*, the asylum, and the false premise of choice.

So, we might ask, is it only Esther's life that the book holds in balance? If, as Ruth Feldstein has argued, the liberal state emerged during the Cold War as a provenance of racial tolerance that went hand in hand with gender conservatism, *The Bell Jar* parts from such coupling, documenting how gender conservatism not only manacles white women but also correspondingly genders black men. If Friedan's "feminine mystique" derives in part from a lack of sufficient language to describe the constraints of patriarchy, then *The Bell Jar* responds by documenting how that language is indeed present (although perhaps not in the way Friedan's book imagined).[49] Plath's novel links the suffrage of white middle-class women to racial emancipation *and* the demystification of the Soviet other. Summoning these two key myths, the text thus offers a rebuttal not only to Cold War master narratives, but also to liberal feminist attempts to counter those narratives. Linked by their status as unnamed but crucial links to the maintenance of Cold War ideology, the Russian woman and the Negro are not coincidental extras—they represent the very forces that threaten to disrupt Cold War sociality, as well as the circuits of sentiment that continue to plague *The Bell Jar*.

The question remains: if the currents represented by the Russian and the Negro, respectively, are poised to capsize conventional readings of

The Bell Jar, why do these readings continue? Why does the book continue to enjoy such stunning popularity? One answer lies in the possibility that, although the Cold War has arguably ended, the terms and conditions of its master narratives continue to govern the way we read U.S. women's literature and Plath in particular. It could even be argued that the book promotes such misreading, encouraging us to bracket the seemingly extraneous markers of a global political consciousness and drawing us into a force field where author and text merge to the point of irreconcilability. Yet, as I have argued, this is a space dominated by the terms of female containment for which U.S. Cold War women's narratives are famous. Why should we retreat to or take comfort in these captivating terms? I am convinced that we should not.

The Bell Jar may offer a searing indictment of 1950s patriarchal U.S. culture, but it also provides a different or less obvious glimpse of this representation. Invoking ideas derived from Chandra Mohanty, the scholars Norma Alcaron, Caren Kaplan, and Minoo Moallem have argued that "[c]ritically reading the spaces between woman and nation as not only structured by patriarchy, we can begin to grasp the supra and transnational aspects of cultures of identity, . . . 'imagined communities of women with divergent histories and social locations,' woven together by the political threads of opposition to forms of domination that are not only pervasive but systemic."[50] In order to register these divergent histories and social locations, we must follow the clues *The Bell Jar* provides to signal an engagement beyond a longing for selfhood dependent on a suppression of difference, and the false premise of choice as key to female emancipation. The novel offers the enticement of national narratives that proffer integrated selfhood as a warning, one that we may, like Esther, "pretend not to notice" (183). The price we pay for this pretense is a perpetual entrapment in the terms of female containment. Indeed, in an era defined by a historical progression in which the Cold War is officially over, it may be more difficult to summon such alternatives amid a nostalgia for substance and sexual presence dependent upon the suppression of racial diversity and alternative intelligences. But if we trace the historical currents of *The Bell Jar*, we see the multiple ways in which the paradigms of the Cold War kitchen continue to haunt us, and the ways in which they continue to be disavowed. *The Bell Jar* offers us an eerie preview of the slippery slope premised by "choice" as equivalent to "diversity," of an equation between multiculturalism and the market. While a focus on the Negro and the Russian may not lead us to neat and tidy summations of the novel's many strands of consciousness, it does speak back to the picture of domestic female captivity in which Plath's work, and likewise her popularity, seem stymied. Moreover, if we follow what I am calling the novel's alternative logic—its radical imaginary—we find discontinuity, provisionality, and even misunderstanding are part of its transnational gesture.

[3]

ALICE CHILDRESS, NATALYA BARANSKAYA, AND THE CONDITIONS OF COLD WAR WOMANHOOD

Mrs. Richard M. Nixon described today how she and four other women sat and "didn't say a word" for close to six hours while her husband and Premier Nikita S. Khrushchev held their dinner table conference yesterday.

—*New York Times*, July 28, 1959[1]

BY BRINGING TOGETHER TWO overlooked facets of the U.S. Cold War kitchen—the locations of African American and Soviet women—this chapter builds on what I called the radical imaginary of *The Bell Jar*. Here I want to open up discussions of the kitchen to include some of its most vital inhabitants: the black domestic housed within the postwar kitchen, and the Soviet woman housed between kitchen and workplace. While chapter 1 examined the mechanisms through which the kitchen was staged and deployed as a space of exception at the American National Exhibition, and chapter 2 showed how that exception might be rebutted via Plath's literary re-narration, this chapter goes yet further in exploding the logics of the Cold War kitchen. In what follows I examine how traces and voices of antipathy to the kitchen were articulated from within its confines. Juxtaposing two versions of the Cold War kitchen in which the master's voice does not answer back with any kind of uniformity—or indeed in which such an American voice barely resonates—this chapter interrogates American exceptionalism by threading the terms of diversity and captivity through contrapuntal stagings of the marginalized women in the kitchen.

The African American writer Alice Childress and the Soviet writer Natalya Baranskaya worked at a great distance from one another. Childress wrote *Like One of The Family: Conversations from a Domestic's Life* in Harlem; Baranskaya wrote *A Week Like Any Other* in Moscow. And yet my somewhat jarring juxtapositions of geography and literary location are intentional. Bringing these novels into conversation enables us to see a deep correspondence between the two. Baranskaya's and Childress's texts register Richard Nixon's misplacement of the housewife in his debate with Nikita Khrushchev and redress that misplacement by constructing visions of diversity that belie an easy association between choice and the market. The ideological uses to which Nixon put the kitchen occluded its place as a site of women's domestic labor and racial segregation. Conversely, both texts present a heterogeneity not reliant upon the captivity of women and minorities (or the erasure of their histories of inequity). Both put women back, as it were, into the kitchen. Rather than occupying a transparent position of captivity, however, the housewife in each text announces herself and her kitchen labor as material, not ephemeral. Together theirs is a dissident feminist poetics of the kitchen. Unlike the absent housewife showcased at ANEM, whose emotional life is rerouted and mechanized with the advent of technological progress, the women in these novels proclaim a physical and emotional presence, thereby challenging the Cold War kitchen's sphere of sentiment, meant to ensure social unity and universal emotions. Far from an internal essence, however, these versions of presence speak to a feminist transnationalism in terms of material infrastructure, showcasing media and its dissemination as one way of thinking through the stumbling blocks of interracial coalition.

The distance between the two novels also could be measured in time. While Baranskaya's novel was published in the late 1960s, Childress wrote the pieces that would become *Like One of the Family* throughout the 1950s. Although it is tempting to read *A Week Like Any Other* as the product of a different historical moment, it is also important to see Baranskaya's novel as the product of a Soviet consumer culture that was seeking to catch up to its American counterpart. Given this condition, we must read through a lens of critical belatedness when considering the circulation of U.S. culture in the Soviet Union. Baranskaya accentuates this kind of temporal delay through the actions of her main character, Olga Voronkova, who is always running, always late, and thus never able to be coincident with her historical "present." Eric Hayot makes a helpful point about periodization, claiming that despite challenges to chronology and linear time in theorizations of history, conventional periods remain intransigently fixed in our intellectual, pedagogical, and institutional practices.[2] While the publication moments of these two novels do not overlap, both books are deeply connected to the crises of a woman's relationship to labor, in both capitalism and communism. These crises—and the responses to them—create a coherence along the lines of what Hayot proposes, organizing new periods in which "telescopic models lead from the small to the large, rather than the reverse."[3]

Looming large in the background of both novels is the figure of the American housewife, who figures broadly in the emotive realm of the African American domestic worker and the Russian working woman as an image around which their emotional lives are constellated. At once attached to the idea of a conversation among women and defiant of the conversation relegated to them, both writers demand a revision of the terms of recognition accorded to them, and both texts articulate alternative intelligences about the relationships between diversity and captivity in the early Cold War moment. In this sense, we can see these novels making a case for the contingency of internationalism; it does not offer a straightforward path out of domestic suppression, nor does it unfold along the same terms of domination contained within a nation state.

The correspondence between these novels is not only thematic, however, it is also formal. Both use an unconventional form to inscribe their meditations; similarly, both demonstrate how form shapes content. Childress deploys gossip—that so-called feminine genre—and casual conversation between women, whereas Baranskaya uses a falsified diary, another traditionally feminine form. Within these breaks from the typical, both Baranskaya and Childress endeavor to theorize correspondence—similarity, difference, overlap, partiality, coalition, and diversity—without resorting to captivity, the very terms collapsed together by the discourse of the American Cold War kitchen.

In Childress's case, the shape of the text existed before the novel was published; at least thirty of the novel's chapters were written originally as columns for *Freedom* magazine. *Like One of the Family* relies on a vernacular intellectualism indebted both to its periodical origins as a column titled "Conversations from Life," and to its community of *Freedom* interlocutors. Edited by avowed communist Louis Burnham and staffed by W.E.B Du Bois, Alphaeus Hunton, and Paul Robeson, *Freedom* was dedicated to promoting links between African America and decolonization movements in Africa and Asia. Its masthead carried the slogan, "Where one is enslaved, all are in chains." Alongside articles by Eslanda Robeson, Lorraine Hansberry, Beaulah Richardson, Thelma Dale, Shirley Graham, Victoria Garvin, and Claudia Jones, Childress's columns helped to shape *Freedom* as an experimental magazine. During its tenure from 1950 to 1955, *Freedom* realigned terms of the familial, the racial, and the national through a dynamic mix of social democracy, anti-racism, and anti-colonialism. As fictional pieces, Childress's contributions offset the news-oriented shape of the magazine, shifting attention to the powerful imaginary of a black female domestic worker. Her pieces, among the magazine's most popular, also undercut the predominance of news about men that the publication showcased, and thus moderated in key ways the focused attention on a representative black masculinity as the face of radical blackness.[4]

Moreover, Childress's novel is ever conscious of its own form. Plotless, it is a novel under erasure, its chapters best described as non-narrative installments. The formal strategies of *Like One of the Family* speak to the location of the domestic worker as both central to and marginalized by Cold War narratives of the kitchen, thus appropriating its own contributions to *Freedom*.[5] Written as conversations between women, the chapters are elocutionary missives. Each begins with a salutation in which Mildred Johnson, a black domestic, greets her good friend and neighbor Marge in the space of an urban kitchen and then goes on to discuss her day and/or a topic from popular print headlines. To read Mildred's addresses to Marge is to engage in their conversation. At the same time, this kind of engagement indicates a wider horizon of exchange. Recollecting their initial form as newspaper columns, the chapters perform a similar kind of summoning of their public.[6] Within this summoning, new modes of sociality are imagined in conversations in which the kitchen is the central conceit. These communicative modes reconfigure the relationship between diversity and captivity as announced at ANEM by placing a black feminist internationalist at their core, thereby challenging the mechanized affect of female domesticity and racial homogeneity in the U.S. kitchen that was advertised in Moscow.

Originally published in the prized literary journal *Novyi Mir* in 1969, Natalya Baranskaya's *A Week Like Any Other* made a sensation when it hit the streets, quickly selling out its first printing and becoming one of the most sought-after publications for months following its appearance.[7] The story describes the everyday life of twenty-six-year-old Olga Voronkova, who works as a research assistant in a science lab. Using a first-person narrative, Baranskaya chronicles the pressures of Soviet life on this young worker, wife, and mother. Structured like a diary, the form of *A Week Like Any Other* plays on a state mandate that Olga keep a personal record. (In the story, all of the women who work at Olga's institute are asked to provide a detailed account of how they spend their time.) *A Week Like Any Other* thus immediately summons the image of Nikolai Gogol's civil servant in "Diary of a Madman," whose account of his descent into madness is also a thinly veiled record of petty bureaucracy in nineteenth-century St. Petersburg. Moving between the personal and the official, Baranskaya's novel records one week, but covers much more than seven days: the diary is neither spatially nor temporally accurate. In this sense, it both attends to the assignment of journal-keeping and moves beyond it. Divided into seven installments, *A Week Like Any Other* rehearses Olga's movement between the unstable poles of attention and distraction through which we witness the shadow of Moscow's kitchen protocols. But Olga's ensuing madness, as her husband Dima calls it, reveals an affective layer of Soviet female consciousness that chafes against the confines of the American kitchen; this is a consciousness that cannot be recuperated in American terms.

"Hi Marge!"

> It's a rare thing for anybody to find a colored family in this land that can't trace a domestic worker somewhere in their history. . . . How 'bout that, girl! —Alice Childress, *Like One of the Family*[8]

Alice Childress is best known today for her 1955 play *Trouble in Mind*, which was revived in 2011 at Washington's Arena Stage to much critical acclaim. This production coincided with the publication of Childress's *Selected Plays*, edited with care and precision by her collaborator and friend Kathy A. Perkins.[9] Prior to this flurry of critical interest, Childress was relatively marginalized, forgotten by most dramatic anthologies and rarely included in course syllabi. Yet Perkins calls Childress an "American theater pioneer," whose plays were characterized by interracial casts and strong black female leads.[10] Although Childress was the first black woman to have a play produced by Equity actors (a revue of *Gold Through the Trees* in 1952), this credit was often given to her *Freedom* colleague, Lorraine Hansberry (whose work I discuss in the next chapter). Childress also is reputed to be the first woman to win an Obie award, for *Trouble in Mind*. Other plays include *Wedding Band*, *Wine in the Wilderness*, and *The African Garden*. Childress also wrote the novels *A Short Walk* (1979), *Rainbow Jordan* (1981), and *Those Other People* (1989), the young adult novel *A Hero Ain't Nothin' but a Sandwich* (1973), the children's story *When the Rattlesnake Sounds* (1975), and a play for young audiences, *Let's Hear it for the Queen* (1976).

Originally drawn to New York from her native South Carolina to be an actress, Childress joined the American Negro Theater (ANT) in 1941. Three years later, she was nominated for a Tony for best supporting actress for her role in *Anna Lucasta*, the play that launched the career of a young Ruby Dee. After nearly a decade of acting, Childress became fed up with the paucity of decent roles for black women and decided to try her hand at writing. Her first play, the one-act "Florence," published in *Masses and Mainstream* in 1950, tells the story of a young woman who has fled the South and abandoned her young son to pursue her acting dream in New York.[11] While waiting for a train to fetch her daughter back from the big city, Florence's mother meets a white woman who proposes to help Florence by recommending her for a maid's job. In response, Florence's mother sends Florence the money she was planning to use to bring her home. These themes of domestic labor, the racialization of gender, and the lure of an urban elsewhere recur in many of her works.[12]

In a series of autobiographical essays and interviews from the 1980s, Childress characterized herself as someone who did not like to look backwards. Indeed, later in her life she all but expunged her earlier affiliations with the Left and the black Popular Front.[13] With this in mind, it is difficult to establish a full picture of her commitments and affiliations during the early 1950s, the period during which she worked in close proximity with her *Freedom* collaborators and created the character of Mildred Johnson. Thanks to the research of scholars such as Trudier Harris and Elizabeth Brown-Guillory, along with the more recent literary history by Mary Helen Washington, we know that Childress belonged to a number of leftist and communist theater groups and collectives, not only the ANT, but also the Committee for the Negro in the Arts. Along with Claudia Jones, Shirley Graham, and Hansberry, Childress also was a member of the Sojourners for Truth and Justice, the internationalist women's organization formed in 1951 to support black victims of McCarthyism and protest injustices against black women.[14] As Washington points out, much of the information about Childress's background comes not from her own accounts but from those of the FBI, who kept a surveillance record on her for at least a decade. Whether or not this hounding by the government was enough to cause her faltering associations with leftist politics, Childress made a concerted effort in her later life to distance herself from her earlier communist associations, citing a version of presentism, part of a desire to never look back. Perkins sees Childress's reinvention of herself as commercially motivated. But Washington astutely (and, I believe, correctly) identifies this recalcitrance as of a piece with what she terms Childress's "idiosyncratic radicalism."[15] As a writer and playwright who continued to compose black-centered pieces that focused on the underclass and relatively powerless, Childress created racially radical works to her own tune. *Like One of the Family* was the product of an important moment—when black radicalism, cultural progressivism, Soviet communism, aesthetic modernism, and an anti-colonial internationalist vision all collided. The novel and its presentation of that errant cosmopolitan text—the kitchen—must be considered in that framework.[16] For it is here, within the kitchen, that the gaps and continuities between these discourses become most audible.

As the title of *Like One of the Family* implies, the protagonist Mildred Johnson is precariously positioned as both insider and outsider to two key constructs of women's everyday life in U.S. Cold War cosmography: "the family" and "the domestic."[17] She is "like" a member of the family, but not "one" of them. Just as Mildred torques a certain presumed groundedness of Cold War family, so too does she reorient the domestic and its usual associations. As an adjective conjoined with "sphere" or "front," the domestic is the stereotypical location of white suburban femininity. That notion of the domestic is queried by a turning of its adjectival links into the noun that describes Mildred's already unruly personhood. Mildred is thus from the outset a complexly conceived character, one who embodies a certain doubleness that hinges on a grammatical alterity—a shift between adjective and noun. As a domestic, Mildred is the person upon which the family relies to keep it together. The "like" in the title simultaneously implies similarity—this one is like that one—and desire—this one likes that one. But the idea of *like* also introduces the limits that these two meanings suggest: to be in a state of likeness is also to be different from. Mildred's selfhood is thus structured through a model of apartness, a model that retains the multiple significations of a layered term. Apartness describes both that which is included and that which is not; that which is required to maintain a sense of unity, and that which marks the unit as different from itself.[18]

All of the novel's sixty-two conversations take place inside the kitchen of a black domestic worker. It is within this space that the novel's heroine, Mildred, recounts for her good friend Marge the daily battles she has with her white employers. As Brown-Guillory notes, these employers either "treat her like she is invisible or . . . try to overwork and underpay her for her services as a maid. Unlike the docile, self-effacing, one-dimensional domestics often found in American literature, Mildred is assertive, intellectually superior, quick-witted and dignified. She questions authority, attacks stereotypes, and challenges white bias."[19] In other words, Mildred generates friction.

The friction caused by placing the black domestic at the center of the narrative recalls the energies of Childress's collaborator and ally at *Free-*

dom, Claudia Jones, who was the secretary of the Communist Party's National Women's Commission and, at age thirty-five, the youngest black woman to be a party member. In 1949 Jones published her seminal "An End to the Neglect of the Problems of the Negro Woman" in the leftist journal *Political Affairs*.[20] This essay was prophetic in its insights about the links between black feminism and Marxism, and the omission of women of color in Marxist theorizing of the 1940s and 1950s.

In her monograph on Jones, Carol Boyce Davies identifies these critical links as class struggle, anti-imperialism, and the structural position of black women, as articulated in "An End to the Neglect" and in Jones's lesser known "We Seek Full Equality for Women," also published in 1949. Together these essays offer the framework of "superexploitation" to explain the absence of black women from theorizations on the Left. Jones's main purpose is identifying black women as forerunners of political change, the incipient vanguard of a revolutionary labor movement. She writes, "The triply-oppressed status of the Negro woman is a barometer of the status of all women—and that the fight for the full, economic, political and social equality of the Negro woman is in the vital self-interest of white workers, in the vital interest of the fight to realize equality for all women."[21] Placing the Negro woman at the forefront of revolutionary change is a move that echoes formulations from the 1930s by Langston Hughes, whose interest in Soviet Central Asia correlated women's advancement with a revolutionary vanguard from which the U.S. Left had much to learn.[22] Key to Jones's reformulation of Marxism-Leninism is her citation of Department of Labor statistics that identified black women workers not only as primary income earners but also as primarily laboring in service industries, including a majority as domestic workers in private families. Jones used the phrase "catch-all, fall-back" to describe the domestic profession for black women, who were hard pressed to find work outside the home in the postwar period because of racism, job scarcity, and societal expectations. At the same time, these women were often subject to media stereotypes characterized by *The Beulah Show*, as mammies stuck in the kitchen.[23] Arguing that this stereotype may have a proleptic force of its own, Trudier Harris notes that "the integral place of the domestic in black American experience suggests that the black woman as maid is the basic historical conception from which other images and stereotypes have grown."[24] In *Like One of the Family*, however, Childress turns the implicitly negative association between domestic work and image into a source for commendation. Mildred observes that, "domestic workers have done a awful lot of good things in this country. They have taken care of our brothers and fathers when the factory gates and office desks and pretty near everything else was closed to them (36–37). Using the black woman domestic as her mouthpiece for black communalism, Childress announces the deeply sedimented structures of inequity that shape black women's lives inside and outside the domestic framework, and advocates for collective protest and unionization for all workers in service professions.[25]

Childress's connection to Langston Hughes in subject matter and choice of emblematic character is not arbitrary. The creation of Mildred is indebted to Hughes's Jesse B. Semple, whose "simple" stories of living in Harlem appeared in a serialized column for the *Chicago Defender*. Like Mildred, Simple has a friend with whom he shares his quiet philosophies and to whom his questions and stories are addressed—in his case the demure Boyd. While Mildred is certainly more strident and uncompromising than Simple, both Mildred and Simple are unpretentious raconteurs who expose white hypocrisies while standing up for justice for the black masses. That Childress had Simple in mind when creating Mildred is almost certain; as Mary Helen Washington has pointed out, in 1950 Childress adapted *Simple Speaks his Mind* for a stage show called *Just a Little Simple*.[26]

The similarities between Mildred and Simple end at Mildred's advocacy of black women's rights. Each chapter opens with an invitation to Marge (and the reader) to "come on in." The coffee is usually on, and Mildred is ready to get down to serious elocutionary business. Making use of her captive audience, Mildred rehearses a quotidian indignity or a popular news item, and her voice appeals to the elliptical Marge with a desire for recognition, understanding, empathy, and appeasement. In the course of her elocutions, Mildred confronts racism, advocates for civil rights, and champions collective resistance. Her language draws from the criticism of racial liberalism in the 1950s forwarded by the Left, and thus shapes this portrait of black radicalism as one that forwards feminist consciousness as key to societal change. In advocating for the centrality of domestic laborers to the sustenance of the black community, Mildred notes, "After freedom came, it was domestics that kept us from perishin' by the wayside" (37). The titles of the chapters range from "On Sayin' No," "All About My Job," and "I Liked Workin' at That Place," to "Why Should I Get Upset?" "Ain't You Mad?" and "Discontent."

In the eponymously titled opening chapter, Mildred debunks the myth that black domestics are included in the familial circle. Mildred hears her employer, Mrs. C, say to a guest, "She's like one of the family. We don't

know what we'd do without her! We don't even think of her as a servant"
(1). After the guest leaves, Mildred confronts Mrs. C:

> I am not just like one of the family at all! The family eats in the dining room
> and I eat in the kitchen. . . .You think it is a compliment when you say,
> "We don't think of her as a servant," but after I have worked myself into a
> sweat cleaning the bathroom and the kitchen, making the beds, cooking the
> lunch, washing the dishes and ironing, I do not feel like no weekend house
> guest. I feel like a servant. (3)

Proclaiming that the work she does is part of an economic exchange,
and not out of the "kindness of her heart," changes the nature of the
family into which her employer would interpolate her. Mildred not only
makes material the day labor she provides for the housewife, she blocks
the fantasy of the family as a space of sociability in which intimacy
and identification can bridge racial difference. Her work creates a feeling state of difference that exhibits the alterity of being alike and apart
simultaneously—like but not (one) of the family.

But insightful as it is about these structures, the work also cautions
against the gesture of humanizing the black domestic as a solution to
racism's inequities. In other words, Mildred has no desire to be "like" or
even "of" the family, per se. The idea that black people need to "prove"
their humanity to be accepted by a white court of judgment is rejected
tout court. On the contrary, a later chapter suggests that trying to unpack
the humanity of people repeats the same problem of differentiation over
and over again.[27] In rejecting identity politics, Mildred's accounts of her
days open up a more useful way of understanding difference: through a
prism of power displays, including those of consumption, the dissemination of information, and narratives of shared labor.

The Female Ghostess

This kind of alterity speaks to the larger and more pervasive iterations
of the American housewife in early Cold War culture. In these iterations,
well-rehearsed by the U.S. exhibition in Moscow, the housewife cleaves to
an image: June Cleaver, picket fence, pot roast, Jell-O molds—whatever
the association, there is an image of domestic incandescence attached to
it. Call it iconic—after all, icons are known for being known—for this
image participates in a logic of public persuasion. In *No Caption Needed*,
Robert Hariman and John Lucaites offer a helpful framework for understanding how iconic images work by combining elements of "mainstream

recognition, wide circulation, and textural impact"—all of which position the housewife as a site for ideological relay and as a site of ideological excess. In this sense, the iconic housewife follows the five vectors of influence that Hariman and Lucaites identify as important for an iconic image: it communicates social knowledge, reproduces attendant ideology, shapes collective memory, and provides figural resources for communicative action.[28] Though we might call this housewife image iconic, however, it is not an iconic image, per se. In fact, a range of images can be summoned by the ideas of female domesticity in the 1950s. There is no single image of the housewife commensurate with, say, Dorothea Lange's "Migrant Mother" of the 1930s, or as recognizable as Marilyn Monroe's billowing skirt in the *Seven Year Itch*. So while we can lay claim to a commonsense understanding of what this female looks like, we also might wonder why this is the case. What are the conditions of intelligibility for this iconic image that lacks both an icon and a singular image?

Perhaps what our communally summoned images have in common is less about the specific picture than about the sensibility or emotional register brought to the fore by the image: an affective component of female domesticity. In this sense the housewife image bears witness to something that exceeds words, at the same time that it presents a visual commonplace. Captured in or by the ordinary are relations of power that seem natural, articulated as they are through seemingly banal signs of housewifery. But why do we see what we see? How can we think about this ordinary image as a perception? Again, what are the conditions of intelligibility that make this so? And what are the alternative registers of intelligence put under erasure so that these conditions might emerge?

In order to underscore the rhetorical ambivalence in which the American housewife is enshrined, and against which Childress's and Baranskaya's texts agitate, I turn to an advertisement published in a 1956 issue of *Time* magazine (fig. 3.1). This advertisement for a Kitchen Aid dishwasher boasts that a new appliance will solve the disappearing hostess phenomenon. Its caption reads: "How to bring a Ghostess back to life." The ambivalence housed in the promise of consumer choice via the assertion of domesticity's liberating vectors is deeply embedded here. In effect this ad introduces the same housewife conjured above: absent and present at the same time. "You know what a 'ghostess' is," the advertisement reads, "that's a hostess who disappears right after the meal." The ghostess is the figure that haunts the hostess, the apparitional "G" that adheres to her figure, even when she is present. The duty of the dishwasher is to scrub away that "g," return her to her rightful place as autonomous host-

FIGURE 3.1. Advertisement for Kitchen Aid dishwasher.

ess. The acts of purification, cleansing, and mechanization rehearse the emotional affectlessness of a kitchen devoid of emotional engagement. And yet, as that pesky "ghostess" might remind us, the kitchen is also the space of overwrought frustration, rage, girl talk, female sociality, and appetite. Proper domesticity, in acquiescence to the manicuring tendencies of the modern appliance, exhibits itself as the device for the organization of the emotions.

This ad documents the ways norms of domesticity sought to strip women of the emotional equivalents of freedom, autonomy, and sociality and replace these emotional valences with appliances. In this sales pitch, and across the spectrum of middle-class, consumerist domesticity more broadly, appliances became prosthetic devices for the emotions. According to Kitchen Aid, the appliance brings her "back to life"; it becomes the site of her emotionality, which is paradoxically automatized like a dishwasher. This rerouting of affect through appliance is an eerie reminder of the housewife's *de rigeur* emotional absence, the dedication of her emotional life to the labors of home maintenance. In the Kitchen Aid version of life (and elsewhere), emotion itself becomes a domestic chore. Thus technological progress recreates the material practice of domesticity, but in so doing it also creates more work. Simultaneous to an erasure of white women's labor in the home is the advent of a new consumerist model—in which consumption itself becomes a middle class woman's labor. This is nowhere better illuminated than in the planned obsolescence of appliances. Their proverbial demise, in three to five years, promises to bring about the burden of more consumer choices, and the perpetual resurrection of the ghostess.[29]

As Jones and Childress and others involved in the Popular Front were well aware, however, the term "domestic" outlined a subjectivity, that of *the* domestic, frequently African American, who labored in the white, middle-class, hostess's kitchen. With this in mind, it would be remiss to not discuss how the changing shape of postwar labor was reflected in advertisements aimed at the American housewife. The rise of the labor movement—and with it the value and cost of labor—helped to transform the way racialized classes emerged. As the possibility for securing cheap labor declined, a portion of the working class merged with the bourgeoisie, resulting in a middle class that failed to correspond with traditional Marxist formulations. These were people who sold their labor but had some purchasing power, as well as upwardly mobile consumer sensibilities. While the traditional bourgeoisie relied on a cast of servants and clung to elite taste in consumer goods and services, a variant middle class found—with the help of government funding and support— that they had the resources to achieve bourgeois status, including home ownership, cars, TVs, and relatively expensive appliances like the dishwasher.[30] Although the aspiring postwar middle class could not afford a house full of servants, they could afford a day-laborer like Mildred now and again. Thus, as Alan Nadel observes, "appliances were the mediation between proletarian employment and middle class sensibilities."[31] Black women domestics like Mildred and Marge served as traces of the proletariat within middle-class homes. In this sense, black domestics were ghostesses in their own right, haunting the mutated middle-classness of their employers by consistently reminding them of their own, intimate relationship to the working class. The relationship between domestics and their employers as one that depends on this haunting trace of labor corresponds with that broader cultural inability to fix on the housewife's iconic image—and the conditions of intelligibility that at the same time render this image so familiar.

Mildred's intrusion into the white familial fantasy requires a vacillation between female subjectivities, between presence and absence. The novel opens with the words, "Hi Marge!" Commencing with the summoning into being of an imagined other, Childress's novel insists that we ask and re-ask, as Mildred does, "Where is the Speakin' Place?" The implied repetition of this question throughout the book gives shape to black women's location in the matrix of American selfhood and black radicalism, offering this complex site as a model for a dissident sensibility. Mildred takes up the space of the provisional subject with monologues that are, as evident from their first word, performative—they call into being "a public [that] exists by virtue of being addressed."[32] Rarely does she subsume her speeches into succinct narratives. Rather, her installments range over and around various topics from decolonization to polishing silver.

Although the novel's opening line brings the character Marge into being, we never learn much about her. Marge is Mildred's interlocutor, the subject with whom Mildred engages in conversation.[33] Indeed Mildred comments at one point that she would "lose her mind if she had to come home after a hard day of work, rasslin' around in other folks' kitchens" and not have Marge to confide in (34). Mildred notes, "you are not only a good friend but you are also a convenient friend and fill the bill in every other way. . . . Well, we are both thirty-two years old; both live in the same building; we each have a three room apartment for which we pay too devilish much. . . . We both come from the South and we also do the same kinda work: *housework*" (33). However instrumental Marge is to Mildred's soliloquies, Marge's agency is usurped by Mildred's recapitulation of Marge's words into her own.[34] All we ever know about Marge are the ellipses that represent what she would have said or what she probably said. In fact, the novel doesn't present a conversation at all—it presents erased conversation, setting up a female intimacy into which the reader is pulled into the position of the silent and yet necessary Marge. It is the positioning of the reader, here, within that conversational dyad, that helps us to think about the shape of the collectivity summoned. Recognizing that black women were not typically the ones addressed by public media, and especially by newspapers, the voice of Mildred addresses an *absence* in public address. This conversation not only calls into being an interlocutor but also asks for connection: "feel with me, feel with us,"

Mildred's words seem to say, modeling a kind of pedagogical imitation for her readers.[35] Making black working-class women not only the subject but also the audience, the interweaving of Marge and Mildred makes use of the notion of black American doubleness to shift that paradigm. Through the characterization of Marge, the novel calls attention to black women's marginalized location in a masculine rhetoric of doubleness. What we get is an improper repetition of double consciousness, a feminist theorization of black selfhood that uses intimacy between working-class black womanhood as its model. By posing a doubled black womanhood at its unstable center (what, after all, is the center of a conversation?), *Like One of the Family* intervenes in the absenting of black women from accounts of black radicalism during the Cold War, accounts in which white history largely signifies black absence, and black presence is largely represented by black men.[36] At the same time, *Like One of the Family* offers the movement from the conversational dyad to a larger, unknowable audience as a model for thinking about how connections are made, about how a radical collectivity might be fashioned from those who have yet to hear themselves addressed as subjects.

Because the novel is consumed with broaching the questions of enunciation and location, the multiple Mildred/Marge asks: from what position *can* a domestic speak? If there is an answer to this question, it seems intimately connected to this question of audience. Michael Warner's formulation of gossip as a unique instance of public discourse helps us to think through this particular formation. Gossip in *Like One of the Family* includes debates not only about recipes and lingerie, but also about history, politics, and workplace entitlements. Through a range of topics, Mildred's soliloquies demonstrate how sharing information—even and especially if it is information that has been overheard—can enable engagement that is not uniform, but open to dissensus, contest, and debate. Warner writes:

> Gossip might seem to be a perfect instance of public discourse. It circulates widely among a social network, beyond the control of private individuals. It sets norms of membership in a diffuse way that cannot be controlled by a central authority. For these reasons, a number of scholars have celebrated its potential for popular sociability and for the weak-group politics of women, peasants, and others. But gossip is never a relation among strangers. You gossip about a particular people and to particular people. What you can get away with saying depends very much on whom you are talking to and what your status is in that person's eyes. . . . Intensely

personal measurements of group membership, relative standing, and trust are the constant and unavoidable pragmatic work of gossip. An apparent exception is gossip about public figures who do not belong to the official social network made by gossiping, especially when official or unofficial censorship makes scandal unreportable by more legitimate means. About such people it is possible to gossip among strangers, and the gossip often has both reflexivity ("People are saying . . . ," "Everyone knows that . . . ") and timeliness (hot gossip versus stale news).

It is this latter version of gossip that interests me, for it provides a way of conceiving the "stranger relation" of Mildred's internationalism, her sense of the connection between U.S. civil rights and decolonization. Gossip is a rhetorical conceit for Mildred—she isn't concerned with what she can get away with, as veracity is not part of the equation. Likewise, her interlocutor is purely imagined, set up as a model for those who care to listen. Mildred's topics include female bosses, missionaries, the West Indies, links between apartheid in South Africa and Jim Crow, education, and step-ladder speakers; one chapter is titled "What Does Africa Want? . . . Free-dom!" (174). In bringing the world into the black urban kitchen, and vice versa, Mildred is catapulted from the heuristically domestic confines of the kitchen. Gossip, as a staged way of articulating overheard conversations or commenting on conversations around her, enables Childress to open this world to the audience she addresses and, in so doing, helps to create.

At this uneven intersection between the national and the international, Mildred pursues the question of black female location in a passage that opens with an ellipsis, signaling Marge's interlocution: ". . . Who do I mean by 'we'? I mean the two of us right here or rather I should say any-body that was listenin' to the program" (197). In a short speech, Mildred ironizes the benevolence of missionary work (the subject of the radio program) but also extends that irony to the question of location. "Who do I mean by 'we'?" she asks, repeating Marge's question. That collective begins as a dyad then extends to the unknown shape of "anyone listenin' to the program." The social imaginary of this "we" is comprised of an unpredictable alliance of co-listeners in which the speakin' place is also a place of potential overhearing and miscommunication. Mildred recalls this space as she addresses Cold War politics directly. Sneering at newspaper reports that violence against blacks must stop because it "plays into the hands of the *Russians* and makes bad *propaganda* which they can use," Mildred responds, "I suppose that if we was real chummy with all the countries in the world then it would be all right to kill our people" (202). Mildred's statement here moves from "I" to "we" to "our"—threading black female consciousness through official national consciousness and a more ambivalently nationalized "people." She speaks not only to the question of representing black voices, but also to the question of their location, the space of enunciation for a radical black collectivity. In so doing, she not only demonstrates the key role of Russia as a conceit in the fomenting of a U.S. Cold War consciousness that seeks to disentangle the domestic from the international, but also reveals how Mildred's feminist consciousness precedes or serves as an antecedent to her internationalism. Moreover, Mildred's elocutions voice a black vernacular discontent that is didactic, underscoring the power as well as the potential misunderstandings of media in fomenting a feminist black transnationalism. Her vocalizations speak to a problematic at the root of black transnationalism, its tenuousness as a political movement because of gendered asymmetries and lack of consensus along the color line.

This posing of a hypothetical subjective space recalls the Kitchen Aid ghostess, reminding us that while middle-class women's labor may have changed shape with the arrival of the dishwasher and the postwar boom in household appliances, the domestic's labor remained ineradicably working class. Mildred's staunch insistence on standing her ground in the kitchen and proclaiming her difference from the housewife undercuts the claims of the labor-saving Cold War kitchen. It is not Mildred's time that is saved by the advent of appliances. In the chapter titled "All About My Job," Mildred exposes the myth of bonds between women across class divisions. Mildred is asked by a white matron about her occupation, and replies that she does housework.

> "Oh," says the matron, "you are a housewife."
> "Oh no," says Mildred, "I do housework." (35)

Three years after the publication of *Like One of the Family*, Betty Friedan would claim that American housewives suffered from a problem that had no name. But Mildred was leagues ahead of Friedan and ready to name this problem. For Mildred, the material practice of domesticity is not only about home maintenance based on a consumerist model, but also about the hands-on labor that creates social difference and that would remain transparent if we believed in an undifferentiated continuum of female bonds created in the American kitchen.[37] As the dishwasher advertisement so pointedly reminds us, the American ghostess poses on the threshold of kitchen and proper dining room—a permeability of boundaries rarely afforded Mildred.[38]

Childress's text implicitly challenges what would later come to be the rhetoric of the Cold War kitchen exemplified in Moscow. The American kitchen's history of segregation—and the affective states associated with this history—create and compound the experience of blackness. Childress calls attention to a racial subjectivity that will later be overlooked in Moscow. Formally and thematically, the text provides an improper repetition of American housewifery, a black feminist theorization of racialized and racializing affect that opens up the differential space between women in the kitchen.[39]

"Plastics, My Boy, Plastics"

Perhaps no one was more surprised than Natalya Baranskaya when *Nedelia kak nedelia* became an instant literary sensation upon its release in 1969. At the age of sixty-one, Baranskaya had already completed a career at the Pushkin Museum in Moscow, and though she had written several short stories, none of them had been published to great success.[40] Eventually printed in twelve languages, Baranskaya's novel garnered her renown not only in the Soviet Union but also internationally, where she is arguably more widely read than in Russia. Part of this appeal can be attributed to the novel's deceptively straightforward prose and its engagement with what is known as *literatura byta*, or literature of the everyday. I argue, however, that the novel's international popularity is linked to the ways in which a trace of the West shapes Olga Voronkova's tale in surprising and unpredictable ways.

In *A Week Like Any Other*, we hear another version of Childress's reconfiguration of mid-century female domesticity, told through a different set of associations. The conceit behind Baranskaya's novel is a bureaucratic questionnaire, issued by state sociologists to address Russia's "insufficient population accretion," and given to all the women at the scientific institute where Olga works. This survey asks them to record "hour by hour, in the given period of time, a week," how much time they spend on housework, child care, and leisure (24). The ostensible object of the questionnaire is to provide the authorities with a statistical understanding of the declining Soviet birthrate.[41] But what the questionnaire actually provides is a template on which Olga can voice, in the first person, the various pressures upon her at work and at home, and the inability of Soviet ideology to mitigate these competing demands. Although Olga has much to be thankful for by Soviet standards—two children, a loving husband, a decent apartment, and a very good job—she is unhappy, relentlessly self-scrutinizing, and looking for relief from the stresses of her everyday life. Like Childress's novel, the story has no plot. Nothing momentous happens in the week: Olga's daughter gets sick, Olga is late to work, Olga and Dima fight, Olga is consoled by her coworkers. Events are characterized by their quotidianness—their lack of a narrative arc. As Benjamin Sutcliffe puts it, "the everyday is an unending travail of missed buses, hungry children, and omnipresent lines. . . . Women's *byt* is a series of recurring problems, whose ordinariness does not help . . . characters solve them."[42]

The intimate view we are given has some features in common with other contemporaneous *literatura byta*, in which the everyday life of ordinary people is addressed without editorializing or comment from an omniscient narrator. In Russian literary studies, Baranskaya's novel has been discussed both within this framework and its female literary corollary, known as *zhenskaia proza* or women's writing, and with good reason: by investigating the contingencies of everyday life rather than following an officially sanctioned script, the novel invites intimacy with the stresses of Soviet women's lives.

As Helen Goscilo has commented, the novel raised women's consciousness about gender inequities in the home and workplace, stirring controversy "chiefly because of its sociological, rather than literary value."[43] Discussed as realist verisimilitude, the novel both reflected and inspired public debate about women's "double burden" and the ways in which liberating women to the workplace did not challenge an underlying patriarchy or assumptions about the sexual division of labor within the home. While there were no literary reviews of the novel when it appeared in Russia, it has since been taken up in the West as emblematic of Soviet women's literature from the period.[44] Indeed, there is something quite prescient about Baranskaya's depiction of women's work/life balance—a harbinger of debates to come in the United States.[45]

Within Olga's consciousness of the thwarted embodiment of an idealized Soviet selfhood, there is a key engagement with the West. Like Childress's novel, this story renders a feminist consciousness that is itinerantly international, and women are at the center of a tale with an implicit internationalist impulse. What do we make of this impulse and the resulting story of an impossible female subjectivity?

A Week Like Any Other uses both formal and thematic tactics to render the texture of Soviet selfhood. Revealing the double bind of women who work both outside and inside the home, most of the survey's questions presuppose what Soviet women workers do when they are not at their jobs: they work. As Maria Mies points out in *Patriarchy and Accumulation on a World Scale*, "the high rate of employment of women in [the Soviet world], the limited availability of public services and communal facilities . . . and the refusal of men to share housework means that women have much less leisure time than men and are constantly overburdened."[46] Indeed, Baranskaya highlights the pathos evoked by the very term "leisure," letting Olga linger over the word like a lost friend: "Dosug . . . ekh, dosug, dosug . . . Slovo kakoe-to neukliuzhee 'do-sug'" [Leisure, ha, leisure. . . . The very word is somewhat awkward: lei-sure].[47] Resentment over what Mies calls "the persistent and reinforced patriarchal attitudes of men, who fill their leisure time with drinking and watching TV without bothering in the least how the housework is done," provokes both ire and guilt in Olga.[48] Throughout the Soviet era, motherhood was extolled as a patriotic duty. Olga feels this pressure deeply, both as a mother and as a Soviet. She is fully identified with the emotional labors of family life and also aspires to be a good citizen. But her involvement and concern are presented as always lacking—never enough on either front. Olga's story becomes one of feminine anxiety to achieve the unfeasible paragon of Soviet female glory: good Soviet and good Mother. Her failure is captured in the contrast between the stark and staccato beat of the sentences that open the story, and the interludes of lush prose in which Olga daydreams about her honeymoon with her husband. This shift between anxiety and distraction enables her to remain close to the ideal of romantic love and the promise of reciprocity she anticipated in that love.[49] In this manner Baranskaya renders the undoing of this promise of exchange, which then becomes the potential undoing of Olga's site of enunciation. As Edward Brown has noted about the tempo of Baranskaya's prose, "Everything is told in a frantic present tense dominated by verbs for hurrying, worrying, and scurrying . . . quick short sentences, incomplete snatches of dialogue, remarks thrown back over the shoulder as one rushes downstairs."[50]

Preoccupied as it is with the place of enunciation for Soviet women who are burdened with achieving the impossible integration of "good Soviet/good mother," Baranskaya's novel recalls a question I asked of Childress: from what position can a *like* but not an *of* articulate selfhood? The story opens with Monday: "begu, begu" [I'm running, I'm running]. Although Olga is in a hurry, it is clear that she will never catch up. Temporality is structured in the text so that Olga is always behind; she is never coincident with the present. Rather, Olga runs through the frantic pace of the story beneath a mandate that she "couldn't possibly forget":

"you won't be late with the testing," her boss asks her, "will you?"[51] As the reader knows, however, Olga has already forgotten, and she is already late. As the poet and literary scholar Thomas Lahusen notes, "Olga's time is made up of the absence of it."[52]

Temporality is not the only site of potential erasure for Olga: silence becomes another place of seeming absence. Instead of assuring her boss "no of course not," she "keeps silent," asking herself, "how can I be sure?" Olga negotiates these conflicting roles with an active, vernacular silence, not unlike Childress's character, Marge. Although her encounters with her male superiors at work lead her to repeatedly remain silent, for example, as readers we are privy to the workings of her active mind. In this way the novel shows how Olga maintains her sense of self despite an anxiety that charges through the text like a ticking time bomb. In her day-to-day activities, Olga keeps from losing her mind by shifting between hyper-vigilance and inattention. She is emotionally present for her husband and family, then loses track of time at work and misses her train home. Instead of proposing an integration of the selves put forth here, Baranskaya's text suggests that this kind of erraticism is actually an ordinary form of Soviet feminine consciousness. In the end Olga does not come apart, although one might argue (as her husband does) that she is unraveling. Rather, her undoing is part of her mode of competence. This puts the reader in the position of trying to make sense of Olga's world and her modes of perception.

Like Mildred's, Olga's consciousness is shaped by the overarching binarism between East and West. Olga is a valued scientist, working to develop a new fiberglass to help fulfill the Five Year Plan, one of a string of state plans intended to push Soviet industrialization ahead of the West. The mention of plastics—and Olga's involvement with them—is not incidental here. Plastics played a central role in the utopian visions of a modern Soviet society. As one East German scientist put it, plastics "represent a revolution in technology that contradicts in every way the conservative capitalistic relations of production" because they enable "a dialectical unity between utility and economy."[53] Thus, Olga's very occupation bespeaks her embeddedness in a cultural logic in which the West plays a starring role. But perhaps even more suggestive than plastics are the particular ways in which the United States is named, located, and signified in the text. The presence of Americanness speaks less to a globalizing momentum of the market than it does to an unexpected mobilization of that impulse.[54] When Olga and her husband Dima try to have a conversation, Olga moves from the kitchen to the common room, suggesting that they talk about Jim Garrison (a prominent conspiracy theorist in John F. Kennedy's assassination).[55] And when Dima, again poised on the threshold of the kitchen, suggests that Olga quit her job so that he can have a more relaxed life, she denounces him as a capitalist. To not talk about the family—to escape *byt*, the everyday occupations of the household—Olga exhibits her worldliness by choosing JFK's death as a topic. Aware of the competing claims on women that each nation makes, she sees a capitalist or Western attitude towards women and work as one that collapses women into housewives and makes presidential discussion superfluous, the association of women with the everyday (*byt*) inescapable. Olga staunchly refuses to disengage her emotions to accommodate her husband's appeal for a life of felt simplicity, a life that would render her timelessly feminine.[56]

Although she is a respected scientist at work, Olga is apparently a failure at the scientific management of her home. Khrushchev's Third Party Program encouraged self-regulation rather than outright coercion. Instead of focusing on the containment of "women's needs" within the home, the Soviet project increased mechanization in the collective world—building laundries, communal dining halls, and daycare facilities. As the saying went: *byt ne chastnoe delo* (the everyday is not a personal affair). It is Olga's failure to blend these two worlds—to make her home run like clockwork and her office more maternal—that sustains her anxiousness. Using the prescribed feeling states of Soviet domesticity— modernization, rationalization, and standardization—as their ammunition and armor, women were to be the bulwarks against the seductions of capitalism. However, these imperative states are at odds with the ways in which Olga experiences her domestic life.

Thus, negotiating female selfhood in *A Week Like Any Other* requires less focus on identity and more on the false emotional iconography of Soviet womanhood, as Olga's co-worker puts it, through the integration of "good mother/good worker."[57] As the conceptual artist Martha Rosler has pointed out, female emotionality in Russia "was expelled except in representations of leaders' public appearances, where woman could be permissibly depicted as overcome with justified emotion. . . . Women were shown in a state of emotional uncertainty only in those instances where they were waiting the return of husbands who were fighting for their country."[58] And while Baranskaya's women are ensnared in the uncertainty of opting to be both, they are also enmeshed in the racial coding of the Russian nationalist project. These women are constituted in part by a presumption of universal womanhood demanded by the doubling rhetoric of the state: one that produced multiracial iconography but operated within largely sedimented presumptions of (white) Russian superiority. Thus Soviet women's place is assigned a hierarchical function of superiority in which whiteness operates through its own privilege of not knowing and diversity is made to feel like a kind of Western exploitation. But Olga's story also opens to the impossibility of that kind of racial foreclosure. If diversity feels like Western exploitation, it is, as the story reveals to us, already part of the Soviet configuration. Diversity does not have to mean captivity. *A Week Like Any Other* seeks to move the horizon of exchange beyond the wavering terms of selfhood to a larger collective.

One such collective emerges in the middle of the story through the invocation of the words "hully gully." "Hully gully" is introduced as a wake-up call, announced once as Dima and Olga begin their day (51). Dismissing the compelling cultural routing of this reveille, the notes to one edition explain that "hully gully" are "nonsense words from a popular song."[59] In fact, "Hully Gully" was a 1960 dance song by the Olympics; it was covered by many other artists, including the Beach Boys in 1965. The song title refers to an unstructured line dance that consisted of a sequence of steps called out by alternating leaders and enacted by everyone in the audience at the same time.

While it may have been the Beach Boys who made the hully gully most popular, they were simply following a trend—fusing (some might say appropriating) an African American dance into their own idiom. Scholars have traced the hully gully in U.S. culture as far back as 1894, when "hully-gully" or "hull da gull" referred to a phrase in a children's game.[60] So while Baranskaya's femininity may be contained within the problematically "white" contours of Russian national identity—that which would dismiss the words "hully gully" as nonsense—her novel also breaks with the racializing confines of that model. In fact, Baranskaya's story makes use of silence to foreground how evasion may serve as both strategic dissension from and point of intervention with the cultural norm. Anticipating the articulation of an already present heterogeneity, silence becomes Olga's speakin' place.

Squeezed between the dual impossibilities of good worker and good mother, Olga finds herself waking up in the middle of the night. She says: "What is disturbing me? I don't know. I lie and listen to the silence." Silence, it turns out, isn't silence at all, but the steady pace of a clock ticking "like a drum roll" (54). We are left waiting for the "Hully Gully," the "wake up call." With its African American resonances, this signals more than simply the U.S. intrusion into Soviet daily lives; rather, it signifies women's negotiation of this intrusion, of the burdens of multiple demands, and of a female "as if" yet to be elaborated. In this way the hully gully represents another little America in the heart of Moscow. However, the distance between this version and that offered by the American National Exhibition is significant.[61]

Given the itinerant articulations of domesticity in Childress and Baranskaya, we might ask again about the conditions of intelligibility for the iconic image of the American housewife. And in order to answer this question we need to return to the photo op in which Nixon and Khrushchev are poised at the threshold of the splitnik kitchen—just as the ghostess is poised at the threshold of the Kitchen Aid kitchen, Mrs. Jones is hovering at Mildred's kitchen door, and Olga paces from room to room. These threshold spaces speak to the constitutive and yet unstable presence and absence of women who are implied in this kitchen context. Those who refuse to reiterate the housewife image, those whose engagement with the West takes them elsewhere, must be returned to visibility. Thinking comparatively about Russian and American work in this way enables us to attend to the silenced figures of otherness that undergird Cold War narratives such as those surrounding the kitchen debate. Through such unlikely juxtapositions we may better comprehend the lesser-known narratives, the silenced linguistic and affective registers, that continue to adhere to the figures, images, and emotions through which we commonly identify a period.

At the same time that the debate announced the highly politicized interior of the kitchen, it revealed the mutually constitutive relationship between Russianness and Americanness in the Cold War era. While Nixon's rhetoric turned the kitchen into a space that erased histories of gender and racial inequities, Childress and Baranskaya used it as a space to highlight their subjective experiences of these inequities, and likewise framed it as a place of resistance. These writers' refusal of an affective conditioning of erasure marks their works as extraordinary. Together their texts reveal that homogenous temporality itself is a fiction. *Like One of the Family* and *A Week Like Any Other* present a means of excavating that rupture, of working through the exclusive logic of the Cold War kitchen. The epigraph that opens this chapter marks the reticence of Pat Nixon and Nina Khrushcheva while their husbands debated the meaning of the Cold War kitchen, bearing witness to the constitutive silence of women in Moscow. We can therefore more fully appreciate the contrary voices offered by Childress and Baranskaya. Accentuating the removal of alternative feeling states of domesticity, their characters offer a means through which we might transform the kitchen into a speaking place of broader sociality. More than a half-century later, we should heed what their kitchens have to say.

[4]

LORRAINE HANSBERRY AND THE
SOCIAL LIFE OF EMOTIONS

The question is not whether one will make a social statement in one's work—but only what the statement will say, for if it says anything at all, it will be social.
                                                                    —Lorraine Hansberry[1]

To perceive texture is never only to ask or know What is it like? Nor even just How does it impinge on me? Textural perception always explores two other questions as well: How did it get that way? And What could I do with it?
                                                                    —Eve Kosofsky Sedgwick[2]

WHEN LORRAINE HANSBERRY BURST onto the theater scene in 1959 at age twenty-nine, winning accolades and attention for her play *A Raisin in the Sun*, she was already a well-established writer. Hansberry had been a key correspondent for Paul Robeson's *Freedom* magazine. She had traveled internationally, become engaged with decolonization movements in Africa, was particularly impassioned about the Mau Mau rebellion in Kenya, and was a critical proponent of black feminism. Over the previous ten years she had filed stories on many topics, including the representation of African Americans on TV, the gathering of the Sojourners for Truth and Justice in Washington, D.C., and the election of Kwame Nkrumah in Ghana. One notice in *Freedom* plugged Hansberry's grit and determination in the early 1950s: "Hansberry triples in brass in our office as subscription clerk, receptionist, typist and editorial assistant and correspondent . . . and takes a leading part in the progressive activities of young people in the world's largest Negro community."[3] As an activist deeply committed to global black enfranchisement, Hansberry followed the news of African independence movements just as closely as she threw her energies into civil rights demonstrations in the United States.[4] Although Hansberry's outspoken radicalism may have mellowed throughout the fifties, she continued to advocate for a socially conscious artistic practice, one that plumbed the depths of racial suffering and accentuated

the linked fates of "the African people and twenty million American Negroes [as] inextricably and magnificently bound up together forever."[5]
Hansberry's quieter criticisms at the end of the decade were prompted
by the political environment: redbaiting, surveillance, isolation, jail time,
deportation. By 1959, many of the people associated with Hansberry's
early years at *Freedom* (including Alice Childress) had rethought their
leftism or been hounded into the margins.

While the success of *Raisin in the Sun* was certainly not a fluke, its
somewhat daunting celebration left much of this prior life behind. Hansberry was known to complain about her play's reception. The white
press embraced *Raisin*'s tale of a black family confronting the racism of
postwar Chicago, celebrating its putative color-blind and integrationist
message—a triumph for the American narrative of patient, melting-pot
assimilation. But the play was seen as accommodationist by some in the
black press, a concession to bourgeois white standards and dreams.[6]
Hansberry lamented that neither side accurately engaged her play's politics, and that the Younger family was transformed into an "every family"
of the middle class.[7] In missing the major points of Hansberry's play,
these reviews reiterated exactly what *Raisin* decries—the exclusion of
mid-century black experience, in all its variety and multiplicity.[8] For political scientist Richard Iton, such misreadings suggest a transition from the
black Popular Front politics that characterized Robeson's *Freedom* to the
integration-oriented civil rights movement of the 1960s. Iton argues that
the popular reception of *Raisin* reveals this key shift, writing that "the
downplaying, and in some instances suppression, of themes related to anticolonialism, diasporic consciousness, and intraracial class distinctions,
along with the implicit engagement of gender relations, mark her creation
as a significant turning point in both black politics and popular culture."[9]

It is here, then, that we might pause to consider the ways *Raisin* reframes the binaristic struggle between the United States and the Soviet
Union to raise questions of U.S. citizenship in innovative and sustained
ways. For those who think of *Raisin* as the story of a family in Chicago,
this may not seem an obvious approach. And yet, Hansberry's radical
interest in the domestic turns out to reflect the U.S.-Soviet struggle, particularly in relation to black affective experience. In earlier chapters of
this book we have seen the ways in which U.S. officials deployed race as
part of a national narrative of inclusiveness in order to counteract Soviet
propaganda that alleged U.S. hypocrisy along racial lines. Beginning in
the late 1940s, U.S. notions and narratives of racial progress and interracial harmony began to feature African Americans. Rather than show-

FIGURE 4.1. Photo by Howard Sochurek of Norris Garnett, one of four African American guides at ANEM, with Tania Sochurek and others. Courtesy of Tania Sochurek

casing capitalism as an evil complicit with white supremacy, this kind of racial progressivism proclaimed the future as bright with cross-racial solidarity. *Raisin*'s appearance at this crossroads, when accounts of racial tolerance began to tour abroad (see fig. 4.1), offers a means of querying the idea of black Americanness that traveled overseas, and in so doing avoided the trajectories of Paul Robeson, W.E.B. Du Bois, Claudia Jones, Alice Childress, and other black internationalists with whom Hansberry was associated earlier in her career. *Raisin*, in Iton's words, created a "blueprint, a particular sentimental economy" for the understanding of black class relations and their connections to coloniality.[10] But how could this economy have been so underappreciated, so misunderstood?[11]

Rather than reading a certain internationalist politics back into *Raisin*, this chapter looks at Hansberry's best-known play through a different prism in order to better understand the registers and economies of its sentiment. Keeping in mind the international trajectories and circuits involved in *Raisin*'s complex narrative, I return the play to the seemingly banal idiom it offers us: that of the domestic. For all of its insightful commentary on decolonization, the legacies of slavery, civil rights, and black nationalism, the play is, at its roots, a play about home. The framing narrative is about a black family attempting to move from one home to another in the 1950s. How might we understand the commonplace of the domestic, then, to be connected with something like geopolitics? My argument is that better and more secure links to the transnational are hidden, as it were, in plain sight. With most of the action happening within the cramped confines of the Younger's makeshift kitchen, the play espouses the centrality of that space—as always already an international construct—to mid-century black working-class lives.

Using the affective emotional landscape associated with all things domestic—from the post–World War II home front, to the home threshold, to the notion of female servitude in the home—Hansberry's play makes a key intervention into the frameworks that ground much of the era's conception of American exceptionalism. In challenging then-existing frameworks of domesticity, the play displays the ways in which the American home (as ideal, as concept, as emotional template) was used and misused in the 1950s and early 1960s by politicians and policies that sought to disengage domestic politics from international ones—while still showcasing the American home as an international ideal. As we began to witness in the previous chapter, this double standard also relied on a range of emotional states—an economy of sentiment—that occluded black experience and placed black domesticity and its diasporic consciousness under erasure. This kind of misprision of the domestic on a larger, national scale likely enabled the many misreadings of the play to which Hansberry so vehemently objected. In fact, by highlighting emotions summoned by the Youngers' movement within and around domesticity, the play underscores the correlation between affect and a range of social resonances that move us far from the play's setting on Chicago's South Side.

In her understanding of emotions as social forms, Hansberry was no doubt in conversation with the impressive work of her *Freedom* collaborator and colleague, Alice Childress (whom I discussed in chapter 3). Both Hansberry and Childress had an uncanny ear for conversation, for black vernacularisms, and for the deep correspondences between women's rights and black enfranchisement. (Coincidentally, it was Hansberry who reviewed a production of "The Emperor's Clothes" in 1952, writing that Childress had proved she was "unquestionably one of the finest actresses in the theater on or off Broadway.")[12] Hansberry likely owes Childress a debt for her characterizations of black working-class women. *Raisin*'s Beneatha, in all her irreverent and active questioning of the confines of her life, certainly recalls the vibrantly insubordinate Mildred, the protagonist of Childress's *Like One of the Family*. Although Childress was the first black woman to have a play produced professionally on Broadway, her fame was eclipsed by Hansberry's success with *Raisin*.

Unlike Childress, who was born in the South and raised in New York City by her formally uneducated grandmother, Hansberry came from a solidly middle-class and urbane background. Her father was in real estate, and his lawsuit against Chicago's restrictive covenants (Hansberry v. Lee) went all the way to the U.S. Supreme Court. Growing up on Chicago's South Side, Hansberry was surrounded by black cultural luminaries. Her mother's living room was the stage for an informal salon at which figures such as Langston Hughes, Katherine Dunham, and Paul Robeson were frequent guests. Although their backgrounds could not have been more different, Hansberry and Childress came together in their political leanings, emboldened feminism, and embrace of drama as a privileged literary form. Like Childress, Hansberry chose the performative space of the theater to expose the upheavals in 1950s U.S. domesticity. Set almost entirely within what is identified as a "cramped little closet which ain't now or never was no kitchen" (49), *Raisin* uses the tension between the Younger's cramped confines and their expansive dreams to prime its characters and its audience for the surge of social emotions that it conjures. As Hansberry was well aware, the stage play is a form for which the summoning of an emotive realm is key to its reception. At the same time, however, this form creates risks—due to the unevenness of exchange, multiple levels of incommensurability, and the opportunities for both communication and miscommunication. Perhaps that is why the play became Hansberry's form of choice: it provided a means of emphasizing the range and importance of feelings that are too easily dismissed as individual or all "inside one's head." Theater is undeniably social, and a stage play with many narrative strands accentuates this sociability.

Raisin showcases this aspect of theater's sociability by foregrounding the emotion with which the Cold War era is most associated—fear—along with some of fear's fallout emotions, namely weariness and rage. In so doing the play demonstrates that these emotions are not privately held but in motion. *Raisin* takes old, prescriptive ideas about individual emotions—ideas that see emotions in a framework of temporal psychology—and reprograms them.[13] In *Raisin*'s logic, emotions are difficult to elaborate not because they are deeply lodged in the characters but because they are ephemeral and contingent, at once singular and collective.[14] Occupying threshold spaces of betweenness that recall my preoccupation with liminality in the previous chapters, fear, weariness, and rage help to reveal the ontological ambiguity of the Youngers as mid-century African Americans.

Providing us with an anatomy of affective frameworks in which the Youngers are situated, *Raisin* posits a theorization of the social life of emotions that strains against dominant Cold War tropes.[15] Instead of a simplistic, flattened-out subjectivity, these emotions reveal a connectivity —not just among the Youngers but beyond their family and into the world—from Walter to his money-scheming friends in the neighborhood, from Asagai to Nigeria, and from Beneatha to her college peers, to name a few. Moreover, domesticity in *Raisin* shifts from a typically female purview to focus on Walter and the importance of domestic emotions to his awkward masculine selfhood. *Raisin* mediates the terrain between psychic and social lives, showcasing the ways in which an emotional landscape associated with mid-century African Americans plays out in a very particular way to register collective reverberations.[16]

To understand just how interwoven these elements are in *Raisin*, we must recall that Hansberry wrote her play in correspondence with the major events and thinkers of her time. That period included major publications by Betty Friedan and Hannah Arendt, the space race and Sputnik, decolonization movements, and the U.S. assertion of global domination through consumer culture. In all of these contexts, domesticity played a starring role. Indeed, just a few months after *Raisin* opened on Broadway, Nixon and Khrushchev faced off in the splitnik kitchen at the American National Exhibition in Moscow. While that kitchen was used as a site for the broadcasting of white exception, *Raisin* rebutted the very premises of such a state.

Just five months before Nixon touched down at Sokol'niki Park, the American Society of African Culture (AMSAC) hosted the First Conference on Negro Writers in New York City. Modeled on the *Presence Africaine* conference in Paris in 1958, the New York conference sought to address the cultural and political links between the United States and Africa. With the prominent exceptions of Ralph Ellison, James Baldwin, Robert Hayden, and Paule Marshall, the meeting gathered some of the best-known black writers of the era, including Langston Hughes, Saunders Redding, Julian Mayfield, Lorraine Hansberry, Frank London Brown, Sarah E. Wright, Harold Cruse, and Alice Childress. Despairing the absence of a literary journal devoted to black globality, the conference attempted to negotiate the slippery terms of race, coloniality, black agency, the publishing industry, and aesthetics—issues sorely lacking a solid home in public discourse. AMSAC offers an unstable parallel pole from which to contemplate the American National Exhibition in Moscow. Although similar issues come to the fore when one considers both events, the conference foregrounded the complexities of addressing leftist black radicalism in 1959, while ANEM all but ignored them. While it was never on the radar of the designers of ANEM, AMSAC put forth what Nixon later occluded in Moscow: the ways in which slavery and coloniality shaped the alleged binaries of Cold War discourse.[17]

The efforts of black cultural producers to address the global polarity of the Cold War's cultural front were erased in the volume of conference proceedings, edited by AMSAC president John A. Davis and entitled *The American Negro Writer and His Roots*.[18] Most significantly, the book leaves out Hansberry's opening address, "The Negro Writer and His Roots." In her revisionary history of the conference, the literary historian Mary Helen Washington argues that this volume obscures the work of the more radical speakers of the conference, including Hansberry. She recovers the AMSAC archive, documenting it as a site of ideological struggle over representing race in the Cold War. Hansberry's contributions to AMSAC, just months before *Raisin* made its debut, necessitate a rethinking of this moment as shaping not only the confrontation of black radicalism with integrationists at home, but also the staging of ANEM as a global site for Western triumphalism. As we have seen, Nixon's rhetoric in Moscow presented a one-sided view of the mechanics of the American kitchen. The official account of the proceedings at AMSAC was similarly distorted. In Washington's account, *The American Negro Writer and His Roots* represents a "hidden, missing, manipulated, distorted view,"[19] which is reflected in its selection of both papers and photos. What interests me here, beyond the historical proximity of AMSAC and ANEM, is the warping of the relationships between Moscow and New York, as well as the intellectual vibrancies at work in the received accounts of both events. One of the aims of this chapter is to reactivate the conscious and unconscious hopes and longings—the deferred dreams, as Langston Hughes wrote in the poem that became the inspiration for *Raisin*'s title— displaced by the progressivist accounts of history for which *Raisin* has served as a pivotal marker.

For most theatergoers, *Raisin* did not immediately summon the global polarities on display in Moscow. The reasons for this are multiple, but among them may have been the prominence of other persuasive domestic fictions in circulation in the 1950s. *Raisin* immediately entered the sphere of popular literature that addressed the phenomenon of the contemporary suburbs. In its direct engagement with suburban narratives, *Raisin* tussled with works like Sloan Wilson's *The Man in the Gray Flannel Suit* (1955) and John Cheever's *The Wapshot Chronicle* (1957) and

The Housebreaker of Shady Hill (1958). In this context, the play takes on the moods of the white middle class typified by these books, as well as the affective range of its primary audience—many of whom may have come in from the suburbs to see the play (and likewise helped to make the play so popular). Someone thumbing through *The New Yorker* on the train into the city might have perused Cheever's "The Scarlet Moving Van" or "The Persistence of Desire," but it is unlikely that this reader confused the middle-classness of the suburbs with their racial exclusivity: these aspects were givens, understood markers of spatial and temporal uniformity, however pernicious and undemocratic. Such literary representations in which the suburbs are presented as less comforting and more alienating are, for Catherine Jurca, key to the affective dislocation of white middle-classness in the 1950s and beyond. In her study of the white suburban novel, Jurca describes this process as one of "sentimental dispossession," through which white suburbanites saw themselves as spiritually impoverished by their prosperity.[20] Jurca's scholarship prompts a question about the *correspondence* between cultural representations of white desire for home ownership and those of mid-century African Americans, such as the Youngers. What these narratives have in common is the figuration of home ownership as a source of emotional and material stability. Yet the play demonstrates how difficult it was, if not impossible, to achieve this national norm, much less feel alienated from it, and how hard it was not only for the black middle class with which the Youngers are symbolically fused in the play's misreadings, but also for the black working class that the play addresses.

Topically, the suburbs suggest a rationale for the deracinating and class-collapsing tendencies of the play's reception, its universal appeal to middle-class aspirations and expectations. Yet these tendencies completely contravene Hansberry's assertions about the links between civil rights and decolonization. In an interview with Studs Terkel, Hansberry declared: "before you can start talking about what is wrong with independence, get it."[21] Her declaration would seem to hold true for the play's approach to black equality, as it seeks to gauge the depths of injuries inflicted upon those denied the opportunities of suburban mobility. Striking out against the presumptions of the American middle class as its every-class, the play registers Hansberry's thoughts from her lecture, "The Negro Writer and His Roots," omitted from the published proceedings of AMSAC. She writes that, an "illusion which it seems must be dealt with is the idea that our country is made up of one huge sprawling middle class whose problems, valid though they are as subject matter, are considered to represent the problems of the entire nation, and whose values are thought to be not only the values of the nation but, significantly enough, of the whole world!" (5). Hansberry attributes such false consciousness to "our particular form of organization of industrial society," thus pinpointing capitalism as a racial project. Further, Hansberry implicitly allies herself with those who more boldly exposed the limitations of this project, including Paul Robeson and W.E.B. Du Bois, declaring that: "it is idle to argue the patriotism of those who call this question to our attention. It is more relevant to recognize its truth and to alert the people of this nation to that truth" (5). For Hansberry it is the "devious purposes of white supremacy" that have poured the foundation for the forced negation of the "most robust and important" fact of our time: the inextricable connections between African peoples and African Americans (6).

With these glaring racial and class disparities as background for the play, it would be hard to argue that the yearning for privacy with which the suburbs have long been associated could be understood as racially equitable terrain in *Raisin*. In his landmark study *Crabgrass Frontier*, Kenneth Jackson argues that "the single family house responded to the psychic value of privacy."[22] As *Raisin* documents, the Youngers desire for privacy is connected to psychic deprivation and a longing for self-possession that distinguishes it from white middle-class longing. Although longing may be the common affective register, it manifests itself through different routes. For a working-class family like the Youngers, the suburbs are not a wasteland (as critic Lewis Mumford would later announce); instead, the suburbs represent yet another site of racial privilege denied them.[23] The backlash against the suburbs came in part from the literature that they spawned, but before you could depict the anomie of suburban destitution, you had to "get it"—gain access to that emotional privilege and its psychic values. *Raisin* demands to be read in this context, especially as the dream it proffers (and defers) is one in which a yearning for home-ownership appears to cut across race, class, and, gender, while at the same time rendering each of these categories all the more affectively legible.

In U.S. reporting about the kitchen in Moscow, there were no white women, and no Lena or Ruth Youngers—black women typically hired to do a white woman's housework. As Childress's *Like One of the Family* makes evident, the black female servant may have been the presence less fully evacuated from the kitchen by the postwar boom in household appliances, and by the related focus on the kitchen as command-central not only for U.S. families, but for the discourse of U.S. superiority as well. A ghost of the proletariat, her day labor haunts the middle-class kitchen. As in *Like One of the Family*, the term "domestic" signifies more than private home or national home front: it also outlines a subjectivity, that of *the* domestic. In *Raisin*, Ruth asks Mama: "Don't you get up and go work in somebody's kitchen for the last three years to help put clothes on her back?"[24] Like Childress's novel, *Raisin* evokes the tripartite structure of the domestic at play in Nixon's rhetoric in Moscow. As housekeepers, Ruth and Lena Younger perform gendered forms of work that congregate around the affects—nurturing and caretaking—that become invisible, part of the forgotten forms of social production through which the invisible threads of capitalism weave their tacky web. As a chauffeur, Walter also performs work that is affective. He serves at the pleasure of his boss, doing chores that involve caretaking of varied interiors, human and automotive. The play offers the domestic neither as consumerist fantasy nor as a mechanism for celestial escape, but rather as an articulation of what would be left out of the conversation in Moscow. Given the inequities of the postwar housing market, the pointedly racist and sexist contours of the GI bill, and the common practices of redlining or applying restrictive covenants, Hansberry's play rebuts Nixon's claims about the splendors of freedom arrayed as consumer choice. Instead, *Raisin* boldly charges into uncharted territory: brimming with the emotional valences of the kitchen—frustration, weariness, and rage—and the messy sociality occluded in Moscow, the Youngers open up the discussion of the domestic.[25]

Home of the Brave

"Black brother, hell!"   —George to Walter in Hansberry's *A Raisin in the Sun*[26]

The play opens on a weekday morning at the Youngers, where Walter and his wife Ruth live with Walter's mother, Lena (also known as Mama); Walter's sister, Beneatha; and their son, Travis. While the family goes about their morning routine, we learn that Ruth and Mama work as housekeepers and Walter as a chauffeur. Beneatha attends college, where she has attracted two suitors—George, a business major from the black middle class, and Asagai, a Nigerian prince. Moved intellectually and emotionally by the connections between U.S. civil rights and decolonization, Beneatha has aspirations to be a doctor, while Travis looks up to his father as role model.

    The energy that fuels the plot comes from an exchange of life for money. The family is expecting a check of $10,000 from an insurance company, following the death of Walter Sr. ("THAT MONEY IS MADE OUT OF MY FATHER'S FLESH," Walter emphasizes,[27] concretizing the always proximate potential reduction of black masculine subjectivity to currency.) Mama wants to use some of this money to support Beneatha's ambitions, but plans to use part of this inheritance as a down payment on a house in the Chicago suburbs. Walter, on the other hand, imagines investing the money in a neighborhood liquor store with his friend Willy Harris. In anticipation of the check's arrival, Mama has been deliberating about what to do but remains uncertain. The play's action follows the family as they receive the money, lose the bulk of it to Walter's scheme, then come together over a decision to move into a white neighborhood in Clybourne Park—once Mama has secured a down payment. Over the course of these exchanges, Beneatha's engagement with African nationalism takes center stage, as does, in turn, Walter's derision of her intellectualism and of George's "capitalist" cartoonishness. Money (and its related ontological ambiguities) thus becomes a sustaining force throughout the play.

While *Raisin* was interpreted as endorsing integration as the key objective of mid-century African Americans, Hansberry understood the family's decision to move as about futurity.[28] In the interview with Studs Terkel, Hansberry explained that Asagai gave the statement of the play:

I don't know how many people caught it. Beneatha says to him you are always talking about independence and freedom in Africa, what about the time when that happens and you have crooks and petty thieves who come into power and they will do the same thing, but only now they will be black you know—what is the difference. And he says to her that this is virtually irrelevant in terms of history. When that time comes there will be Nigerians that step out of the shadows and kill the tyrants. Just as now they must do away with the British and that history always solves its own questions, but you get to first things first. In other words, this man has no illusions at all, he just believes in the order that things must take, he knows that first before you can start talking about what is wrong with independence, get it: and I am with him.[29]

In other words, the decision to move is a version of the emphatic imperative to "get it." First things first. In this framework, the sacrifice of Walter Sr. reflects a step towards emancipation, a process that sustains not only the play's trajectory, but also its willpower, its life force. In this way, Hansberry's *Raisin* offers crisis as a means of thinking about possibility. Without mapping out the exact coordinates of what this future looks like, the play offers opacity, attending instead to the micro-practices of the Youngers' everyday life, wherein the possibility for change takes shape. Sociality is premised on transformative moments that push beyond available models for thinking about the future. *Raisin* offers a refusal of closure, of a denouement beyond the script's pages; the future, at best, is uncertain. In the play's temporality, no one knows how this history will play out, although the recent bombing of a black family's Clybourne Park home gives us one sign. As Fanon Che Wilkins has commented, "*Raisin* does not end through a resolution of the central contradictions of American democracy but instead suggests that greater challenges await the Youngers and the larger world in which they live."[30] In fact the play's use of affect enables such contradictions to be highlighted precisely because the relationships between actions and passions, between reason and the emotions, remain in unresolved tension when the curtain closes. It is after all the affective impulse, charge, and uptake of the closing scene (when the neighborhood representative Lindner appears with his final offer to the Youngers) that produces Walter's change of heart, thereby showcasing the correspondence between the mind's power to think and the body's power to act, no matter the consequences.

Some of these consequences are meant to seem immediately palpable to the Youngers. Historians Becky Nicolaides and Andrew Wiese have commented that while the postwar suburban housing boom opened opportunities for housing ownership and upward mobility to millions of whites, "blacks and other racial minorities faced hostility at every level of the suburban housing market. Behind these defensive ramparts, an expansive sense of white identity and privilege took shape, supported by federal largesse, protected by local government and private enterprise and pampered by economic abundance to which whiteness was the key."[31] Even William Levitt, the developer of Levittown, commented: "I have come to know that if we sell one house to a Negro family, then ninety to ninety-five percent of our white customers will not buy into the community."[32] Echoing Levitt's assertion, historian Dianne Harris makes a strong case that the very idea of the nuclear suburban family is a mythical narrative built with the bricks and mortar of racial exclusion. She writes: "It was far easier and more acceptable to admonish suburban dwellers to cultivate distinction and privacy for the sake of democracy, than for the preservation of an economic ideology that was inherently linked to racial assignment and to the preservation of all-white suburbs."[33] Harris argues that following World War II, racist government policies undergirded the housing industry, such that these industries became complicit in the formation of what it meant to be American—white, middle-class, suburban. Making "white" Americans out of every new homeowner in the nation, these industries helped to shape a new subjectivity.

The Youngers' decision to move is likewise not about a free range of options but rather about the coercion of a market closed to black choice. In his 1986 reassessment of the play, Amiri Baraka claimed that, "there is no such thing as a 'white folks neighborhood' except to racists and to those submitting to racism."[34] In practicality, however, there were white neighborhoods, the various contours of which have been rehearsed for us by geographers, urban historians, and sociologists. In spite of the respective richness of these varied studies, the white neighborhood has been approached as largely limited to feminine associations with domesticity. As Jurca points out, "literary scholarship on the home has continued to be confined almost exclusively to nineteenth-century texts and contexts and to the experience of women."[35] While the home may be a general familial preoccupation, the kitchen—more than any other room—exemplifies the disenfranchisement of black women. As we saw in the previous chapter on Childress, African Americans are located as domestic workers in the kitchen of the home from which white middle-class suburbanites typically feel alienated. In *Raisin* this connection foregrounds the racialized mid-century domestic as well as Walter's masculinity and the range of emotions he must navigate in order to find himself outside the grasp of capitalist greed (his interest in owning a liquor store in the ghetto) and inside the dynamics of resistance. Fastidiously aware of the conflation of race, affluence, and suburbia—as in the images of happy white families laid out so carefully at ANEM—the play closes with an affectively pregnant unknown.

First Things First

What kinds of emotions does the play highlight as the nodal points of affective connectivity? Act 1, scene 1, offers stage directions that focus on weariness and fatigue: "A section of this (the living) room, for it is not really a room unto itself, . . . slopes backward to provide a small kitchen area. . . . The single window that has been provided for these 'two' rooms is located in this kitchen area. The sole natural light the family may enjoy in the course of a day is only that which fights its way through this little window" (23–24). The kitchen as the sole source of light is more than just an obvious metaphor for hope; it is staged as an affective rebuttal to the canned formula of 1950s domesticity, constellated as it was around the

American kitchen.[36] In contrast to the suburban kitchen, the Younger's kitchen is not even a room but an area, marked by dreariness and indirect light from a cramped window (about which I will say more in the following section).

Noting that the light must "fight" its way through this window, I'd like to pause on the embattled sentiments within which the entire Younger domestic scene is situated. Just prior to the introduction to the so-called kitchen, Hansberry's stage directions also disclosed that:

> The Younger living room would be a comfortable and well-ordered room if it were not for a number of indestructible contradictions to this *state of being*. Its furnishings are typical and indistinguished and the primary feature now is that they have clearly had to accommodate the living of too many people for too many years—and *they are tired*. (23; emphases added)

What we glean from these anthropomorphizing descriptions of the apartment's interior is that the affective "states of being" embedded within the domestic are important. Pitting comfort and orderliness against everyday life, these contradictory states of being comprise the emotional anatomy of this play. Showcasing what is not comfortable is also a means of showcasing who is not comfortable—and the characters fitting this description are multiple. Indeed, we might ask, who of the Youngers is comfortable? Certainly not Walter and his ill-fitting manhood, nor Ruth and her undisclosed pregnancy, Mama and her will to move beyond the kitchenette, Beneatha and her budding black feminism. By externalizing the emotional register of objects and their owners so forthrightly, the play suggests that these are not the affective states of private individuals cut off from the world. By imbuing objects with feelings, *Raisin* messes with the idea that feelings can become objects with lives of their own. As Sara Ahmed has argued, feelings become objects "only by the concealment of how they are shaped by histories, including histories of production (labor and labor time), as well as circulation or exchange."[37] But what if objects become feelings? Instead of concealing the histories of these feelings, *Raisin* showcases them as unstable material objects, offering their poor, tired, and weary presences as documentation of how they have been used.

The stage directions that open the play continue to offer object lessons on the Younger's emotional landscape.

> Now the once loved upholstery has to fight to show itself. . . . The carpet has *fought back by showing its weariness*, with depressing uniformity, elsewhere on its surface. Weariness has, in fact, won in this room. Everything

has been polished, washed, sat on, used, scrubbed too often. All pretenses but living itself have long since vanished from the very atmosphere of this room. (23; emphases added)

In penning such specific dramaturgy, Hansberry points to the uncomfortable proximity between personhood and things for mid-century African Americans. Indeed, there is something Marxian here, the spectral shape of objects mixing with people to imply the very thingness of the Youngers as working-class blacks struggling to survive. In his work on the historical ontology of objects, Bill Brown has argued that "even as we point to a certain moment in a certain place when and where it is no longer possible for a person to be a slave, we nonetheless find, in the post-history of that moment, residues of precisely that possibility—in other words, an ongoing record of the ontological effects of slavery."[38] The play sets up this worn-out terrain, spreading ontological ambiguity like a blanket for the Youngers to perform upon. This template suggests not only that the idea of "personhood" as such will be continually called into question by the play's very premise (and its dependence on the inheritance that represents Walter Sr.), but that a major tension will exist between the racial weariness of Cold War life and the possibility of challenging the "depressing uniformity" of its objects. Indeed, the play opens with the sound of an alarm clock: a wake-up call for the Youngers and the audience alike.

A few moments later, Walter erupts at Ruth: "Man say I got to change my life, I'm choking, baby! And his woman say—[in utter anguish as he brings his fists down on his thighs]—Your eggs is getting cold!" (33). At first glance, Walter's anguish may read as poignantly individual, and yet the play tells us that his pain reaches beyond him. It surges along a nodal circuitry, creating a dense transfer point for both Ruth's weariness and Beneatha's impatience. From Ruth's response to Travis's request for lunch money, to Beneatha's African tribal reverie, the play demonstrates over and over again that emotions are places of connectivity; that they are, as *Raisin* emphatically teaches us, deeply social forms. The play's emotions are produced by the ambiguous personhoods of the Youngers, hovering as they do between the unstable poles of subjecthood and objecthood, part of a long legacy in which black Americans were denied political enfranchisement and inclusion.

The scene that closes act 1 reveals the paralyzing proximity between these two frames of being for Walter, and the psychic toll of existing within this ambiguity on a day-to-day basis.

WALTER: Do you know what this money means to me? Do you know what this money can do for us? Mama, Mama, I want so many things. I want so many things that they are driving me crazy. Mama look at me . . .

MAMA: I'm looking at you. You a good-looking boy. You got a job, a nice wife, a fine boy and—

WALTER: A job. Mama, a job? I open and close car doors all day long. I drive a man around in his limousine and I say, 'yes, sir; no, sir; very good, sir; shall I take the Drive, sir,' Mama, that ain't no kind of job . . . that ain't nothing at all. (73)

In this part of the scene, Walter proclaims that the affective labor of chauffeur, much like that of the housekeeper, is deadening to him. The repetitive acts of tending to the rudimentary emotional needs of his boss place Walter in a position of feeling less human, more automaton. Like the work he performs, Walter has become practically invisible. For Walter this amounts, in his estimation, to a "big, looming blank space—full of nothing" (73). The great big nothing of his future looms in such a way that Walter feels desperate for action, some change in the pattern and texture of his day-to-day life so that he will feel more in control of his own destiny, not simply the "yes man" that he has of necessity (and perhaps desperation) become. The stakes for Walter become even clearer as the scene continues, when his words equating money and life recollect Hansberry's comments at the American Negro Writers Congress a few months earlier: "O, the things that we have learned in this unkind house that we have to tell the world about! Despair? Did someone say 'despair' was a question in the world?" (7).

MAMA: Son—how come you talk so much about money?

WALTER: Because it is life, Mama!

MAMA: Oh. So now it's life. Money is life. Once upon time freedom used to be life. Now it's money. (74)

Walter's emotions are those of someone who is stuck. The weariness he displays in his place of betweenness—where the lure of money does indeed feel like the only possible escape—is a threshold emotion, one on the border between selfhood and object. He is stuck in a logic that reduced the value of his father's life to $10,000. And as far as he can see, his own life is being crushed to nothingness by the same, repetitive, logic. No wonder he is going crazy! Is Walter a man or is he money? His father was transmuted into money, wasn't he? What is the value of black personhood?

This question shimmers in the air around the play, creating a prickly space of unease for the Youngers and the audience alike. In this scene Walter shows us how the sensory perception of belief is often an ill-fitting match with cognitive "beliefs"—a disjuncture that reveals what Eve Sedgwick has called "texture," irreducible to ideology.[39] This very "graininess"—the space between Walter's beliefs and his passions—is the affective space that sustains the play's recurring tensions between life and money.

Later, during the play's climax, when Walter rejects Lindner's offer to sell back their deposit on the house, Walter proves that his declaration about the easy equivalency between money and life is incorrect. Life is not money. But it is Asagai's words that reveal Walter's contorted logic. Asagai first asks: "Isn't there something wrong in a house—in a world—where all dreams good or bad must depend on the death of a man?" Asagai goes on to see his own situation as directly linked to this injustice. Where are we all going he asks, and then replies: "I live the answer" (135).

Just as Asagai lives the answer to this insuperable question, so too does Walter at the play's close. Following Hansberry's declaration that, "first you must get it," Asagai and Walter move forward into the unknown. Nigeria was on the verge of independence in 1959, after years of resistance against the British. In *Raisin*, Asagai and his country are shifting, transitioning, creating movement and momentum. Similarly the Younger family creates action that unsticks bodies from being perceived as things first, people last. All are in motion. Nigeria and the Younger family, Asagai and Walter, all are in the thick of what I earlier called graininess: the space where answers cannot be foreseen, where belief and its sensory perceptions collide. Together Asagai and Walter affectively reproduce connections between the domestic drama in Chicago and the decolonization movement in Nigeria. Where will the interconnected legacies of slavery and colonialism take us?

Threshold Emotions and the Picture Window

I want to return now to discuss more fully what I earlier referred to as the threshold emotions of stuckness. Like Mama's "feeble little plant growing doggedly in a small pot on the windowsill" (39), the Younger family is determined to escape their weariness. All over the play we see signs of objects and people refusing to stay in their places, battling against where they are supposed to be. The stage directions indicate that Mama's plant becomes a metaphor for her family, "growing doggedly in a small pot."

But the window, the single source of light for the entire apartment, has been relatively overlooked by critics, in spite of Mama's repeated references to it. As she places her plant on the windowsill, for example, Mama asks, "Lord ain't nothing as dreary as the view from this window on a dreary day is there?" (53).[40] *Raisin* uses the window as a feeble version of potentiality, creating a threshold space that gives us insight into the mechanisms that drive the Younger's family unit. For all its soiled emotions and despairing hope, Mama's dreary little window indicates both potential movement and the false transparency of social relations.

In choosing this window as a point of reference, Hansberry draws a brushstroke of domesticity that ranges far from the way in which home windows were showcased in the 1940s. As wartime industry turned to home building, picture windows became standard issue in the prototypical suburban house. These suburban neighborhoods were almost exclusively the domain of middle-class whites, and their built environments and concurrent shaping of race have been taken up by social historians and geographers.[41] For example, the historian Sandy Isenstadt has pointed out that, to the modern eye, the picture window functioned in ways material and psychological. He writes: "If indicators of lost autonomy and racial contagion were everywhere in an urbanizing world and psychic distress was the unhappy result, then a sweep of space over an unpopulated and untroubled landscape was good therapy while recuperating at home; an assortment of modern troubles could be offset by the good graces of extra large spaces."[42] In their very transparency, then, these windows were a key part of the vanishing of social relations and belief systems upon which suburban environments were built and through which corresponding social power was organized. In helping to sweep away the psychic distress of racial contagion and lost autonomy, picture windows did more than simply enable a particular view of the landscape. By establishing "ownership" of the view, such windows made architecture not only a way of seeing landscape but also of owning it. Moreover, the idea of owning the view, indeed the idea of ownership itself, implied a prerogative of subjectivity at a far reach from the Younger's position between subject and object, and outside of ownership as prescribed by the mid-century racial lexicon.

Windows offer two ways of seeing, of course, and so embodied some of the tensions within the idea of privacy that came to increasingly characterize the suburban racial landscape. While functioning as signs of status that suggested emulation, windows also could be curtained to insinuate distance: this seesaw of enticement and rejection can be linked to tensions within possessive individualism and the obsession with the private around which notions of postwar subjectivity and class identity came to be constellated.[43] Indeed, the picture window stood for the false notion that there could be a "visual corrective" to affronts felt in the racially mixed urban world that could be ameliorated at home, with individual psychology rather than political action. Isenstadt cites ad copy for *House Beautiful* that brags: "Picture windows blend the exterior and interior in a remarkably effective manner and create an air of spaciousness that defies description," noting that "the picture window was the threshold of an emotive realm that outstripped rational explanation."[44] In essence, if not in fact, the picture window did away with reality and its messy sociality.

For some theatergoers in 1959—even those for whom the cracks in the picture window may have been evident—the contrast between the threshold emotion posed by Mama's window and the threshold emotion offered by the suburban picture window could not have been greater.[45] The emotive realm proffered by Mama's window is hardly a picture of the deracinated sublime, a place where emotions "outstrip rational explanation." In stark contrast to the anomie-blocking picture window of suburban middle-class America, the Younger's kitchen window reveals the stifling air of a world all too immersed in troubled landscapes. Before it became a banal relic of mass consumption, cheapened in cost and character by its sheer ubiquity, the picture window was a way of seeing landscape by recasting interior architecture in the light of a destabilizing inside/outside binary.[46] In the 1940s, Thermopane even championed a "glass designed for happiness" promotion that tied middle-income consumer demand with factory supply. As larger windows became markers of class status, "small but spacious" became the common moniker for a window-enhanced home (see fig. 4.2).

The Youngers' window dismantles the snugness of this inside/outside binary in quite a different fashion. The smells, sights, and sounds of their urban life are hardly the sensations to produce a transformative sylvan scene. This is not "happiness" glass. Rather, the threshold emotions showcased in the play—and made vivid by Mama's window—are emotions that result from being stuck in a place between visibility and invisibility, between personhood and objecthood. The view from the Younger's window is far from transparent.

Although I have been calling it "Mama's window," in the larger context the window was in conversation with the vision of a resituated domesticity that featured the suburban husband's instrumentality to domestic life. Domesticity, the suburban home and, to a lesser extent, the kitchen have been taken up as key sites in the discussion of white middle-class

FIGURE 4.2. Libbey Owens Ford advertisement from an August 1959 issue of *The Saturday Evening Post*, featuring Thermopane glass, a technology patented in 1930 that featured two planes of glass with an insulating air seal between them.

FIGURE 4.3. *Life* magazine, January 5, 1953. Getty Images

subjectivity. Although typically the domain of women, men were no less important to these domestic ideals. That the house served as a framework for this iteration of selfhood is nowhere better illustrated than in the January 5, 1953, cover from *Life* magazine.[47]

In this photo, the window is open and the family is nestled inside (see fig. 4.3). The husband towers over his wife, who is eye level with two children as she looks glassily at the camera, while the baby is propped (precariously) on top of the window sash. What hangs in balance is no less than the future of the nuclear family, and Dad has his hands on this future. The unmistakable message is that men are in control; women may do the housekeeping and shuttle around the children but, as Lizabeth Cohen has convincingly demonstrated, the consumer's republic is the male's domain.[48] The window presents an inverted relationship to privacy: there are no curtains here; rather, the scene is pure spectacle, entreating us to gaze at the family on display, fish-bowl like, for our enjoyment.

This scene at the window is echoed in *Raisin*, act 1, scene 1, when Walter peers from his own window at the passers-by below: "Just look at 'em down there. . . . running and racing to work" (27). The Youngers must do their own racing that morning—not to work, but to the communal bathroom that they share with their neighbors. Walter's mounting rage comes from an awareness of his participation in this system of accumulation through speed—industrial capitalism—and his subjection to its deprivations—the slumlord housing and the shared toilet. Like *Life* magazine's featured family, the Youngers are on display. Unlike those white middle-class paragons, the Youngers are a family whose microcoordinates—in particular their relationship to privacy—shape them as working class and black. As Dianne Harris has explained, the linking terms "privacy," "individuality," "democracy," and "American" served as code words for "white" and "middle class" in the popular sociological literature of the 1950s, which sought to stem anxieties about overconformity in the suburbs by focusing on autonomy and leisure—neither of which are enjoyed by the Youngers.[49] In this context, designing inwardness became a means of preserving democracy. Turning one's back on the world was sold as the counter to conformity, which was associated with communism, the lower classes, and racial minorities.

In spite of these prominent differences, the family in *Raisin* does share some commonalities with the exemplary *Life* family. The play echoes the photo's male chauvinism, domesticating Walter while at the same time pronouncing his dominance as the hero of the house. (At the play's outset, Mama holds the check, but she gives up her matriarchal position of power by handing the money over to Walter.) Mama's deference to Walter refuses the stereotype of the black matriarch that was reified by Daniel Patrick Moynihan's 1965 report, "The Negro Family: The Case for National Action." Some critics have claimed that, by the end of the play, we are so fully caught up in the realization of Walter's dream that issues of sexism are subordinated to those of race; in other words, that the play champions the cause of racial freedom as representatively masculine, to the marginalization of black women's concerns.[50] However useful these critiques are (and I do believe they are useful), they also overlook the affective circuitry at work here, in which Walter's bold denunciation of white fear connects with the cause of the Younger women, making it—and them—visible, rather than subordinating either to his singular manhood.

It must be kept in mind that the very motivating forces behind the picture window and its affects—happiness glass!—were the forces that strove to negate the existence of families like the Youngers. The vision afforded by the picture window is what John Kenneth Galbraith described in his classic 1958 work, *The Affluent Society*: that of the "self-perpetuating margin of poverty at the very base of the income pyramid . . . largely unnoticed because it is the fate of a voiceless minority."[51] In contrast to the open window pictured above, meant to hide the belief systems upon which suburban environments were built, Mama's window gives voice to this minority.

Walter's declaration (in act 2) that he is like a volcano invokes the combustion not only of his own rage but of others too. This admixture of rage, bitterness, and spite creates a prickly space that bears closer attention, particularly in the exchange between Walter and Beneatha's would-be suitor George.

> WALTER: I see you all the time—with the books tucked under your arms—going to your [British A] "clahsses." And for what! What the hell you learning over there? Filling up your heads—[counting off on his fingers] —with the sociology and the psychology—but they teaching you how to be a man? How to take over and run the world? They teaching you how to run a rubber plantation or a steel mill? Naw—just to talk proper and read books and wear them faggoty-looking white shoes . . .
>
> GEORGE [looking at him with distaste, a little above it all]: You're all wacked up with bitterness, man.
>
> WALTER [intently, almost quietly, between the teeth, glaring at the boy]: And you—ain't you bitter, man? Ain't you just about had it yet? Don't you see no stars gleaming that you can't reach out and grab? You happy? —You contented son-of-a-bitch—you happy? You got it made? Bitter? Man, I'm a volcano. Bitter? Here I am a giant—surrounded by ants! Ants who can't even understand what it is the giant is talking about. (85)

In this famous scene, weariness morphs into bitterness then sizzles into rage. These feelings travel hissing and crackling as if along live wires; they are the result of years of black disenfranchisement. Hansberry once noted that: "The foremost enemy of the Negro intelligentsia of the past has been and in a large sense still remains—isolation."[52] But these are not isolated emotions; they are in motion, connecting George's aggressive blindness to Asagai's anticolonial aspirations. And in this scene they overshadow and overpower the dissatisfactions of the women around them.

Walter's feverish assessment of George's "difference" here is worth pausing over, for it offers us an instance of class differentiation within blackness. As a character, George recalls David McKemster in Gwendolyn Brooks's affect-driven 1953 novella *Maud Martha*: "Here were the socks, here was the haircut, *here were the shoes*. The educated smile, the slight bow, the faint imperious nod. He belonged to the world of the University."[53] George is perhaps a comment upon this character, who aspires to throw Vernon Parrington's *Main Currents in American Thought* around like a football, and who senses "a physical unhappiness" when he considers the black people who live west of the Midway: "Looking up in those kitchenette windows, where the lights were dirty through dirty glass—they *could* wash the windows—was not at all 'interesting' to him. . . . He knew it was a mess!"[54] Without overstating the parallels, it is important to note the centrality of kitchenette windows to the disdain David voices about working-class blacks, a disdain that registers as a feeling of physical malaise. Both *Maud Martha* and *Raisin* link the windows of kitchenette apartments on Chicago's South Side to the affective dissonance between mid-century black subjectivity and white middle-class ideals. Similarly, both texts depict intraracial class tensions by summoning the stereotype of the integrated middle-class black man. In Brooks we witness the identification of American exceptionalism within the college curriculum as instrumental to the character's shaping, a reference not specified regarding George. Nonetheless it is fair to say that both George and David McKemster represent a type that the college-educated and Chicago-raised Hansberry knew well and sparred with over questions of class, racial assimilation, gender equality, and anticolonialism.

In this sense, Walter's appraisal of George reads as an articulation of such sparring, and as Walter's attempt to establish difference in the face of a fated racial parallelism. Walter's assessment marks a somewhat desperate attempt to identify the ways in which George is inferior to Walter, based on a normative measurement of working-class manliness—running a mill or a factory. At the same time, it pronounces Walter's anxious sense of inferiority—coded as superior knowledge—as he struggles to come up with a tangible index of what makes George's difference from him matter. Walter's class literacy is pointed: in a fashion that forecasts the kinds of attunements Pierre Bourdieu would later analyze in his work on distinction, Walter assesses George's pronunciations, his sensibilities, his courses, his gait, and, of course, his *shoes*.

But the play takes such distinctions a step further, highlighting their connections to corresponding emotional affect. Consider the work of

bitterness. It establishes a distance between bodies such that their difference is read off the surface: George's white shoes become a target for
Walter's homophobic rage. Likewise, Walter's spite (and his black dialect)
becomes a target for George's own superiority and disdain. And yet we
must recall that Walter's rage nonetheless *connects* these black men. Rage
simmers inside Walter, and at the same time the larger landscape of emotional reverberation points to fear as a driving force. After all, this is not
only the story of a black family's attempt to move into a white neighborhood in spite of the loathing of their would-be white neighbors. This is a
play that showcases the legacies of white fear of black bodies, and how
this fear contorts those who are objectified as such.

Frantz Fanon's *Black Skin White Masks* offers a point of reference here.
Fanon's extensive discussion of the statement, "Look, a Negro!" presents a
phenomenological entry point for understanding the ways blackness as an
externalized articulation of selfhood based purely on skin color seals
Walter—and George—into a crushing objecthood. Skin and feeling are
fused in this Fanonian moment into one. In the famous fifth chapter of
Black Skin White Masks, Fanon describes the process of epidermalization
wherein the skin is understood as no longer porous but rather made into
an objectified shell—what he identifies as a "suffocating reification."[55]
Such reification creates a sense of being in the world as a surface object
instead of a subject of diverse experiences, histories, and sensations. A
skin-based identity hardens over the complex affective experiences of difference, intersubjectivity, and living with difference, squeezing selfhood
into a Hegelian dialectic of self/other in which the "Negro" facilitates
perpetual white subjecthood. In her reading of Fanon, Hortense Spillers identifies this process of epidermalization as the signifying surface of
difference tied to coloniality, locating fear within the axiomatic lexicon
through which blackness was identified: "Look, a Negro, I'm scared!"[56]

Fear, of course, was not coincidentally the defining emotion of the
Cold War period. From early critical assessments such as John Lewis
Gaddis's *Strategies of Containment*, to later studies such as Kate Brown's
Plutopia, scholars have long agreed that fear of Soviet attack held the
United States captive—in culture and in politics—with a tenacious grip.[57]
I have discussed elsewhere how a perceived Soviet threat morphed into
an anxiety about those assigned as "others," and how slippages in categories of otherness (such as Soviet, communist, black, woman, gay) enabled
fear not only to move between signs, but also to attach itself to objects
historically associated with people.[58] In a different register, Sara Ahmed
allows us to expand on Fanon's identification of skin with fear. Ahmed

argues that: "A movement between signs is what allows others to be attributed with emotional value . . . an attribution that depends on a history
that 'sticks,' and which does not need to be declared. Fear does not reside
in a particular object or sign, and it is *this lack of residence* that allows
fear to slide across signs, and between bodies."[59] Ahmed's rereading of
Fanon is helpful for situating the ways in which the Youngers occupy
signs of blackness that are not static, but constantly reproduced. It is this
reproduction that creates the adhesion between blackness and fear, and
yet *Raisin* also challenges that reproduction.

As the character of Lindner demonstrates for us, the Youngers are
feared as a black family (determined visually) seeking to move into a segregated white neighborhood. However ephemerally, the Youngers inhabit
signs of blackness that the neighborhood association fears. Interestingly,
Hansberry has Walter perform some of these signs—black, male, furious.
And yet in performing them, Walter explodes the stereotype associated
with them, the culturally mandated connection between these signifiers
and "the angry black male." Over the course of the play, black male rage
shifts the sensation (by which I mean the anticipated audience response)
from fear to *pathos*.[60] So much so that Walter's story, his coming into
his manhood, becomes the central story grounding this narrative about
movement. In this sense, domesticity is detached from its more predictable feminine contours and shown to be centrally linked to Cold War
masculinity.

In *Raisin*, fear defies its emotional typecasting, recasting both Fanon's
account and its subsequent critical readings. For what if fear took up residence; what if it stuck, as it were, and refused the sliding scale between
signs and bodies? Taking up residence is of course the central issue of the
play: will they or will they not move into Clybourne Park? This fear im-
pacts every movement of the Younger family. Hansberry deploys Walter's
rage to document the ways in which rage enables misrecognition of the
other. And the play documents the Younger's family refusal to take up
residence in familiar signs, relics of past history that are trying doggedly
to stick to them in the present. At the end of the play, however, taking up
residence takes on greater stakes. As we witness through the character of
Lindner, "white flight" is a sensory experience; if only momentarily, the
Youngers seem to say "bring it on: fear us." *We will take up residence.*
In turning down Lindner's offer to buy back their claim, the Youngers
refuse the restriction of movement that would be associated with them
as the ominous object moving into a racially restricted neighborhood.
This refusal exposes the era's valorization of white expansion—and its si-

multaneous dependence on black containment—in order to sustain white suburban development.

This sort of dual motion is evident elsewhere in *Raisin*, particularly in regard to what Amy Kaplan has called "manifest domesticity," a notion I discussed in the introduction to this book. Manifest domesticity designates the women's sphere as a morally privileged site through which empiric expansion is not only condoned, but also authorized. Kaplan argues that an image of social unity both depends upon and sustains a vision of national expansion, creating what she calls an "empire of the affections."[61] In the linking of Walter and Asagai through an affective circuitry of threshold emotions wrought by the state of being between subject/object, *Raisin* refutes the binding of household and nation imagined by Kaplan. And the play further challenges the ideas of manifest domesticity by putting the men so centrally in the domestic space typically reserved for and conceptualized as the women's sphere.

One of Kaplan's key points is the contradictory motion between empiric expansion and the inspansion of the domestic sphere to exclude racial others, such that "homeland insecurities" become vital sentiments. She asks: "How does this struggle with foreignness within 'woman's sphere' shape the interiority of female subjectivity, the empire of the affections and the heart?"[62] But *Raisin* asks a different question: How does the struggle with foreignness within the women's sphere shape the interiority of *male* subjectivity? Walter's story is our answer. By refusing the place of object and by taking up ownership, however haltingly, Walter struggles through to claim uncertain territory. The ending of the play thus reverberates with anxious emotions—traced within the objects that surround those emotions. Nonresolvable tensions close the play.

The logic of expansion/inspansion is of course the same double motion that underwrites U.S. policy in Africa. When Walter says, "OCOMOGOSIAY! Do you hear, my black brothers!" (78), we hear the play using emotions and their resonances to show us the ideological connections between the attempted eviction of the Youngers from Clybourne Park and Nigerian independence movements. In refusing the logic of the border that would, through fear, establish them as other than national subjects, the Youngers take a stance—they put their bodies on the line. In precisely the way that Asagai proclaims they must, the Youngers assert that one cannot stand apart and move forward: "Before you can start talking about what is wrong with independence, get it!" The play teaches us that the motherboard of emotions on display here—even and especially those emotions as banal as domestic ones—connects the United States to a parallel colonial circuitry.

At the same time, the play also reminds us that this connectivity is not some phony racial essentialism: "Black brother, hell," George retorts to Walter's beckoning call. These links are the affective filaments that surge from structural parallels to put mid-century African Americans in correspondence with their Nigerian counterparts. In rejecting intraracial solidarity, however, George cannot shake the fact that Lindner would reaffirm their commonality; he would make the same proposal to George that he has made to the Youngers.

Finally, the affective proof of Walter's masculinity is his refusal of racialized emotional typecasting. By the end of the play, he is no longer the angry black father, but rather the strong and proud black patriarch. While the play's misinterpretation by some audiences in 1959 may make us wonder why the affective proof of Walter's performance was less than adequate to his family's story in 1959, we might consider this very misreading—a disappearing act of social relations and power structures—a lesson unto itself. Perhaps the attenuating fantasy of familial identification across difference provided the most accessible and therefore most satisfying read. The question for contemporary audiences is how such misreadings of the social lives of emotions in *Raisin* continue to serve as racialized shorthands today. Hansberry's rendering of the kitchen as central to this oversight reminds us that we must work through the Cold War logics of the kitchen in order to refute the fantasy of historical progression and its related affective racial conditioning.

[5]

SELLING THE HOMELAND: *SILK STOCKINGS*,
STILYAGI, AND STYLE

Nixon [hearing jazz music]: "I don't like jazz music."
Khrushchev: "I don't like it either."
Nixon: "But my girls like it." —exchange from the kitchen debate[1]

ALTHOUGH IT ENJOYED CRITICAL popularity upon its release in 1957, the musical film *Silk Stockings* has been lost in the shuffle of U.S. Cold War artifacts. Most of the figures associated with the film—Fred Astaire, Billy Wilder, and Cole Porter, to name a few—enjoy iconic status in the arts. But their parts in the film remain obscure reference points in careers that look elsewhere for significance. Nevertheless, *Silk Stockings* brought together a remarkable constellation of mid-century artists who created a film that is not only lovely and entertaining, but also comments in intriguing ways on many of the major tropes and ideas percolating in the Cold War kitchen. In leading us to reconsider how gender and sexuality were mobilized in the service of economic imperatives, the film reveals how fraught the use of cultural objects as mechanisms of persuasion was in the 1950s. Like the Eames's *Glimpses of the USA*, *Silk Stockings* exposes the fracture lines of consensus culture through an engagement with the persuasive tactics of attraction, desire, and envy. Unlike the texts discussed in earlier chapters of this book, however, *Silk Stockings* broadcasts an awareness of itself as making a claim for the primacy of pop culture—fashion, music, and the movies—in waging a Cold War against the Soviet Union. Together, the film's collaborators tapped into U.S. anxieties about the shaping of subjectivity through emergent technologies, and about the ability of Western cultural forms to attract and change minds behind the Iron Curtain.

Propelled by the popularity of its 1955 Broadway version, as well as critical praise—the *New York Times*' Bosley Crowther selected it as a film of the year—*Silk Stockings* enjoyed great success at the box office.[2] During its initial release the film made over $4 million, and it became the

largest grossing musical film to date at Radio City Music Hall. The film
was nominated for two Golden Globe awards, including best musical and
best actress. Like *An American in Paris* (1951) and *Kismet* (1955), the
film meditates upon its routing through international venues and offers
commentary on the movement of American culture.

Most obviously, the film recalls David Riesman's satiric essay of 1951,
"The Nylon War," the sociologist's fictional account of undermining
communism through a battalion of American cultural objects. Riesman's
spoof has now become a popular reference point in suggesting the direction U.S. policy would take as the decade moved on, and Riesman
himself is often cited as prophetic. To be sure, "The Nylon War" captured
an ethos, an American perception of the widening gap between quotidian
existence in the Soviet Union and the United States. Describing what he
called "operation abundance"—an aerial offensive dropping everything
from Tampax to toasters—Riesman promoted, "an idea of disarming
simplicity: that if allowed to sample the riches of America, the Russian
people would not long tolerate masters who gave them tanks and spies
instead of vacuum cleaners and beauty parlors."[3] Riesman's focus on
women's undergarments as exemplary of the cultural differences between
East and West purposefully confused gender and sexuality with economic
imperatives.[4] Riesman framed the U.S. economy as consumer oriented
and liberating for women, while downgrading the Soviet economy as
mired in a backwards utilitarianism that kept Soviet women trapped in
the past. In Riesman's fantasy, stockings represented the merits of a system that was not only robust but also endorsed fragility; the shapely
curve of a woman's leg would be protected by a culture that shielded her
from demanding physical tasks—anything that might snare her hose. On
the other hand, the woolen Soviet counterpart suggested drudgery and
gloom, the risks of life on a factory floor rather than the domestic ease of
a sparkling suburban home.[5]

The American National Exhibition in Moscow was held just a few
years after Riesman's spoof was published. Decades later, political scientist Joseph Nye would use the term "soft power" to describe the sort
of ideological persuasion that some in the Eisenhower administration
sought to achieve with ANEM. Using this concept to replace the related
terms of "propaganda" and "psychological warfare," Nye distinguishes
soft power from the hard power of nuclear bombs and military coercion,
defining it as persuasion by means of attraction and cooptation instead of
force.[6] Rather than using concrete strategies such as trade embargoes and
corporate pay-offs, soft power deploys more intangible tactics such as

values, belief systems, and culture, or—in the Eamesian rubric—a democratic state of mind. More recently, Riesman's fictional account of the
centrality of cultural objects to the victory over the Soviet bloc has been
reinterpreted by critics such as Walter Hixson, Victoria DeGrazia, and
Greg Castillo, who focus on the instrumentality of cultural persuasion
to U.S. Cold War strategies. Hixson's pioneering work suggests that soft
power was effective; DeGrazia and Castillo are more nuanced in their
assessments of success.[7] Nonetheless, the idea that goods embodied ideals
—and that Soviets would be lured by American products to renounce
the shackles of communism and embrace democracy—has become a
commonplace of historical accounts of the Cold War. And yet even in
Riesman's day, cultural objects were articulating complicated and vexed
trajectories. Although it would be inaccurate to say that Riesman's "operation abundance" was adapted into U.S. policy, it is significant that a
central object of his essay—nylons—is taken up with such energy by *Silk
Stockings*. Even as it advertised the splendors of consumption, the film
questioned the more general assumptions of capitalist triumph based on
the allure of objects over ideology.

While *Silk Stockings* was not shown in Russia at the time—its car-
toonish characterization of the Soviets would have been an obvious dis-
incentive—its engagement with Riesman's fable of abundance leads us
directly to the ways in which related avenues of soft power did reach
Soviet citizens. This occurred not just as the result of focused U.S. propaganda, but also more broadly, through jazz music, fashion, and a subculture youth movement known as the *stilyagi*, or "stylish ones." For this
reason, it's important to look more fully at the energies summoned by
the film and the permutations of soft power that its constellation of figures assembled in terms of style, direction, lyrics, music, and fashion. *Silk
Stockings* makes explicit the tropes about female sexuality and Cold War
cultural binaries that I've been discussing thus far. And like *The Bell Jar*,
A Raisin in the Sun, and *Like One of the Family*, it also makes explicit the
racial undercurrents within these forms. Seen in this way, *Silk Stockings*
not only addresses the links between the modes of attention and information flow that undergirded *Glimpses of the USA* and ANEM, but also
helps to reconfigure the oppositions used to read the axiomatic terms of
the Cold War kitchen—global polarity, racial hegemony, and the sexual
division of labor.

Critics have remarked on the film's textbook exposure of Soviet and
U.S. economic structures, as revealed in the transformation of the female
lead, Nina Yoschenko (played by Cyd Charisse), from drab commissar

into fashionable woman. These accounts focus on the transparency of the told tale: romance and consumption routed through female subjectivity so as to best represent the victory of commodity capitalism over dowdy totalitarianism. In her fine assessment of the film, Helen Laville writes, "the fulfillment of the narrative imperatives of the romance genre is expressed through the symbols of feminine fashion consumption as an expression of liberation."[8] In this guise, the film becomes a mouthpiece for patent Cold War truisms in sync with what I have been calling the logic of the Cold War kitchen: universal female emotions create the soft power to generate Technicolor happy endings.[9] But if *Silk Stockings* mobilizes an image of universal femininity as a wedge against Soviet drabness, it does so through a curious erasure of race, and hints at a deep awareness of this strategy in ways that require a careful look. *Silk Stockings* makes its signature transitions—from Soviet masculine female to U.S. feminine female, and from one economic system to another—through the absent figure of African American subjectivity. As we will see, the entire movie turns on these central and yet removed bodies. Recalling the evacuation of the mechanics of production at ANEM, such that techniques of compression enabled a message of Americanism to occlude social relations, this chapter looks more closely at a similar mechanics upon which *Silk Stockings* depends, and to which it ironically calls attention.

What does it mean to read race back into a film from which it has been erased? My argument is that it has a lot to do with form. *Silk Stockings* is first of all a Hollywood musical—a song-and-dance fantasy of heterosexual romance. Set in a city known for lovers—as Fred Astaire's character, Steve Canfield, reminds us, "Paris loves lovers"—the film instructs us that happy endings are the result of chirpy couplings between men and women (no matter the age difference between them). But the film is also a musical about the making of a musical. In this sense it is engaged with—even self-conscious about—questions of cinematic form, reflecting how 1950s popular film was caught up in the movement between highbrow culture and middlebrow entertainment. At the center of these debates about anxieties over cultural form —and how these forms move when they go abroad—is the subsumed presence of African Americans and their contributions to music, dance, and style. Through its insistence on the various ways in which films as sensory texts come to have meaning for an audience—through technology, vision, sound, movement, and subjectivity shaping performance—*Silk Stockings* repeatedly draws on associations between modernity and emancipation. And yet the lessons it professes are also the self-same lessons the film forecloses.

As the late film critic Miriam Bratu Hansen has reminded us, the "sensorium" of filmic experience layers over narrative expectation and fulfillment. Hansen writes: "Hollywood film in relation to modernity may take cognitive, discursive, and narrativized forms, but it is crucially anchored in sensory mimetic identifications that are more often than not partial and excessive in relation to narrative comprehension."[10] While *Silk Stockings* seems to endorse the sexual liberation of its heroine, Nina, as part of the forward-moving engine of its technological prowess, the film also reveals that the cost of Nina's freedom is the sublimation of black bodies—both behind and across the Iron Curtain. This sublimation is registered across the sensorium—visually, aurally, affectively. Racial erasure is thus not only the enabler of discussions about female sexuality and the differences between mid-century high and low culture, it is also the enabler of the forces of modernity that in the film are aligned with Cold War consensus.

We can build on Hansen's notion of the sensorium to address "sensory mimetic identifications" in the film that the audience would have associated with black cultural forms such as jazz and dance. But, as Hansen cautions, these identifications were partial; audiences also could assign these forms to a different other—the Soviet. This kind of international identification—based either on race or oppression—was precisely the aim of American cultural diplomacy in the 1950s, and the reason many State Department goodwill tours featured jazz, which was associated with "freedom of expression." As I discuss below, in mobilizing the issues surrounding the era's attempts at cultural diplomacy—particularly in the Soviet Union—the film cautions against the assumed success of these endeavors. At the same time, *Silk Stockings* warns against reading these encounters against the grain, as places where celebratory identifications of oppressed peoples took place outside of politics.

By retrieving the presence of blackness that the film evokes, I suggest that *Silk Stockings* offers a critique of the humdrum storyline of the West's victory over the East as a fable of a woman's transformation through consumerism. In other words, while the film suggests that unleashed female sexuality is a threat to the Cold War consensus, by allowing this threat to be acknowledged—female sexuality as scary, inchoate, and inexorable—the film also recognizes the presence of other bodies necessary to the production and containment of that threat. Powering the ship of Cold War fantasies of female containment is racialized entertainment as commodity: the partially occluded labor of black cultural producers. Here my work is indebted to the insights of critics Michael Rogin and Eric Lott, who discuss white usurpation of black cultural forms as

the foundational story of popular American entertainment. While allowing that popular culture as a genre is defined by that which is borrowed,
Rogin claims that, "the four transformative moments in the history of
American film . . . organized themselves around the surplus symbolic
value of blacks."[11] Developing the idea of the cultural logic of blackface
as a way of understanding white desire for black forms, Eric Lott argues
that minstrelsy "opened to view the culture of the dispossessed while
simultaneously refusing the social legitimacy of its members," a process
he identifies as a "truly American combination of acknowledgment and
expropriation."[12] *Silk Stockings* does not include scenes of blackface minstrelsy per se, but its dependence on black cultural forms without attribution suggests a closely related kind of impersonation.

Lott's configuration of the pleasures of white spectatorship that guide
the spectacle of black minstrelsy enable us to identify not only the erotics
undergirding racial expropriation in the film, but also the economics. As
Lott notes, the repeated references to economic exchange in meetings between "racial representatives" suggest that "all accounts have been paid
in full" in these transactions. Such accounting, while certainly indicative
of theft of a cultural kind, also indicates "white guilt or anxiety around
minstrelsy as a figure for the plundering of black culture" that stems
"from slavery's unremunerated labor."[13] This anxiety lodges deep within
the economics of popular culture professed in *Silk Stockings* and is announced in such numbers as "Red Blues" and "The Ritz Roll and Rock."
Just as Carol Clover has argued that the film *Singin' in the Rain* (1952)
mobilizes an entire plot to "accomplish the forgetting of the 'efficient
expropriation of the cultural commodity 'blackness,'"[14] I propose that
Silk Stockings evokes black subjectivity as that which must be suppressed
in order to keep white femininity aligned, emancipated, and "free." The
musical enacts as it reveals the requisite subsumption of race within Cold
War narratives of progress: the liberal ruses of freedom accommodate
pernicious acts of symbolic and actual violence.[15] Considered on its own
merits, *Silk Stockings* is hardly a transformative cinematic masterpiece.
Unlike other films of its era and genre, however, *Silk Stockings* conjures
an historical past that the United States needed to subsume in order to
prove itself superior to the Soviet Union. And the film demonstrates how
the projected victory over the Soviet bloc—routed through cultural warfare or the "soft power" of entertainment—is inextricably indebted not
only to black cultural forms, but also to a systematic and persistent exclusion of African Americans from the entitlements of full citizenship.

In this sense the film offers us another version of American exceptionalism, a dependence on binaristic thinking that can only imagine the world from within two competing paradigms, American or Soviet. At the same time, the film troubles that Nelsonian dicta for mid-century design discussed in chapter 1, wherein the surface appeal of the object belies the machinery that powers it. Nelson's distaste for visible machinery created the penchant for streamlined surfaces, behind which the mechanics were hidden. *Silk Stockings* punctures the pretty surface of mid-century design, bursting forth with ruptures, just like Peggy Dayton splashing to the surface in one of her swimming stunts—nose plug and all.

Stocking Stuffers

Directed by Rouben Mamoulian, *Silk Stockings* is a musical remake of the 1939 film *Ninotchka*.[16] Adapted from the 1955 stage musical by George S. Kaufman, Leueen McGrath, and Abe Burrows, with songs composed by Cole Porter, the lead roles are played by Fred Astaire and Cyd Charisse. The plot follows the transformation of a Soviet commissar into a sleek Western woman through romantic attachment to an American man. In *Ninotchka*, the commissar is tempted to forsake her country for love. Although *Silk Stockings* borrows the outline of the earlier film, it tells a more layered tale that involves Hollywood, high fashion, and Cold War political high jinks. An American movie producer named Steve Canfield (played by Astaire) is in Paris to shoot a Hollywood version of *War and Peace*. When the Russian composer for that film, Peter Boroff, goes astray following a concert in Paris, three inept Soviet commissars—Brankov, Bibinski, and Ivanov—are sent to bring him back to Moscow. But they too become spellbound by Parisian luxury, and soon compromise their mission. The ultra-stern Nina Yoshenko (played by Charisse) is dispatched to retrieve them. Once in Paris, Yoshenko encounters Canfield. In spite of Nina's off-putting female masculinity, Steve falls for her.[17] He plies her with all the aspects of Western decadence: romance, high fashion, and champagne. Though she resists his temptations at first, Nina ultimately succumbs to Steve's advances. Offended by Steve's popularization of Boroff's classical compositions, however, Nina returns to Moscow. Back home, she and Boroff commiserate over what they left behind. Like Nina, Steve longs to be reunited and hatches a plan to get her out. Soon Nina is back in Paris, enjoying champagne at a Russian nightclub owned by the city's newest capitalists—Brankov, Bibinski, and Ivanov.

All of the major figures involved with *Silk Stockings* deserve recognition for their contributions to the film; each brought extensive experience

and an influential perspective. Rouben Mamoulian, the film's director, was
an Armenian raised in the former Soviet republic of Georgia. He received a
law degree from the State University in Moscow, where in the early 1920s
he also studied theater and acting with Stanislavsky at the prestigious
Moscow Art Theater. Uneasy with Bolshevism, Mamoulian emigrated to
the United States in 1926, where he joined the faculty at the Eastman
School of Music. From there he went on to direct Broadway shows, including Dubose Heywood's production of *Porgy* in 1927, noted for its
all-black cast. Mamoulian then directed three of the most popular shows
in the history of American musical theater: *Porgy and Bess* (1935), *Oklahoma!* (1943), and *Carousel* (1945). He is best remembered, however, for
his work on the 1931 film *Dr. Jekyll and Mr. Hyde*, perhaps his biggest
success. In his later film work, he was known for his innovative use of
color, camera tracking, and sound.[18] Described as independent-minded,
Mamoulian was a lifelong campaigner on behalf of directorial autonomy.
He helped to unionize directors in 1936, and his efforts to defend artistic
freedom resulted in his being investigated by the House Un-American
Activities Committee during the early 1950s.[19] After that investigation,
Mamoulian withdrew from Hollywood and focused on the stage, directing revivals of *Oklahoma!* and *Carousel*. Despite the former scrutiny of
his politics, he was asked by the State Department to direct a European
tour of *Oklahoma!* in 1955. Mamoulian was thus one of the so-called
cultural ambassadors who spread the U.S. message during the Cold War.
His last directorial job was on the film *Porgy and Bess*, a position from
which he was unceremoniously released after having shot several scenes.
(Otto Preminger took over and finished the film.) In 1982 he received a
lifetime achievement award from the Director's Guild.

Cole Porter wrote many popular songs of the 1930s, including "Let's Do
It," "Night and Day," and "I Get a Kick out of You." The musicals *Anything
Goes!* (1934) and *Kiss Me Kate* (1948) were his biggest Broadway suc-
cesses. Like Mamoulian, Porter expressed a late-career self-consciousness
in his contributions to *Silk Stockings*. His lyrics and music comment on
the anxieties of Cold War subjectivity as shaped through and constitutive
of the forms and discourses of consensus culture. *Silk Stockings* was the
last musical that Porter wrote for the stage, although he did compose a
number of new songs for the film in 1956.

The lead actor in *Silk Stockings*, Fred Astaire was arguably one of the
greatest jazz artists of the twentieth century. Like Mamoulian and Porter,
Astaire was best known for his work in the 1930s. (And, as was the case
with the director and the composer, *Silk Stockings* marked the end of

Astaire's film career.) His partnership with Ginger Rogers in a number of top-grossing films of the 1930s, including *The Gay Divorcee*, *Top Hat*, and *Shall We Dance*, made him a household name, associated with ballroom dancing and black-tie affairs. After leaving RKO Pictures, Astaire made a number of popular films in the 1940s and early 1950s in which he focused on innovative dance routines, of which the best known is "Puttin' on the Ritz." Astaire partnered with some of the era's favorite actresses, including Judy Garland, Leslie Caron, Rita Hayworth, and Audrey Hepburn. But his virtuoso dance performances were what characterized his fame.

Among these seasoned contributors, Cyd Charisse was the relative newcomer, having made her name opposite Gene Kelly in the final ballet sequence of *Singin' in the Rain* (1952). Trained in classical ballet, Charisse became MGM's principal female dancer in the 1950s, when she starred with Astaire in *The Band Wagon* (1953) and with Kelly in *Brigadoon* (1954). She was nicknamed "Legs," and her key assets were reportedly insured for over $5 million. Charisse was hand-picked for her role in *Silk Stockings*; because singing was not a strength, however, her voice was dubbed.[20] (Coincidentally, *Silk Stockings* was her last dancing role in film.)

Though he played a relatively small role in the film, the Hungarian-born Peter Lorre would have been instantly recognizable to the audiences of *Silk Stockings*. With his trademark voice, Lorre was famous for his roles in Warner Brothers films, including *The Maltese Falcon* (1941), *Casablanca* (1942), and *Arsenic and Old Lace* (1944).

How does all this star power converge on the film's Cold War themes? With Astaire's tap-dancing, the dance sequence "Red Blues," and the opening of a jazz bar by the Soviet commissars, the film repeatedly reminds us of the undercurrent of black themes and bodies within postwar Paris. At the same time, the film stages the belatedness of Russia's "arrival" as a great power in the Western account of historical progress. Winning over the Soviets to the pleasures of the West is all about the future: "We can never change the past, only the future," Steve tells Nina. And when one is in need of Western enlightenment, what better setting than the City of Light? Soviet backwardness—especially in matters of sexuality—cries out for the tutelage of the West. (The song "Chemical Reaction" describes Nina's mechanical approach to romance and pheromones.) Modernity and female emancipation were thus never a surer fit, and yet the cost of freedom, *Silk Stockings* reminds us, is very often the erasure of black subjectivity. Even in Paris, liberation must accommodate new forms of discipline. It's not Soviet Russia that the three commissars import to Paris, but the Russia of czarist days—the "good" old Russia of the pre-Soviet era, before women were liberated—when serfs were really serfs (and racism was legal). In this detail, Paris becomes the contact zone of American postwar fantasy.

Cole Porter's music recalls precisely this Paris, a place of pre-war memories. Porter's contributions expand the *Ninotchka* tale from the era of black-and-white film to that of stereophonic musical, while querying the apparent deflection from politics that soft cultural attacks were designed to sustain. If the *Ninotchka* story relies on the contiguity between heterosexual romance and consumer capitalism, then Porter's songs trouble an easy symmetry between the two. His lyrics open a space where ambivalence towards popular culture is also ambivalence towards compulsory sexual predilections.

Serving as a pivotal space for the meeting between East and West, Paris triangulates the East/West encounter, offering up its starry skyline as a background for Cold War rivalries. But Paris in 1953 isn't just a city of ephemeral dreams. It is also the Paris of postwar reconstruction and the Marshall Plan, a city rebuilt with U.S. resources to be "safe" from further totalitarian threat. In *Silk Stockings*, Paris is not only a seduction, a "pleasure city" as Steve calls it, but a luxurious stomping ground for U.S. affluence. In this light, Paris itself doesn't matter as much as the use of its urban venue; it's a showcase for the East/West split and the superiority of American exports—technology, culture, and cunning. If the Paris of *Silk Stockings* is a postwar pleasure city, it is so in an American guise: a place where bourgeois pastimes are uniformly positive and indulgence is good. As Dana Heller notes, "the postwar American love of Paris, as nationalized motion and emotion, derives out of a roving and raffish resistance to the burdens of historical consciousness. . . . a love thus compelled to perform and spectacularize its authenticity through narrative fantasies of the loss and recuperation of one's natural, self-governing romantic impulse, an impulse that tends to secure an image of the American nation-as-family," as savior and guardian.[21] Paris is not only a city that prompts a recovery of one's true self through the ephemera of love, it also best sets off and affirms indulgence, individualism, and selfishness as strengths against the repression, industry, labor, and dreariness of the Soviet Union—as if to say, the Soviets may have Sputnik and science, but we have Paris and romance! Indeed, Paris on the screen becomes a kind of American technological wonder—set in the gorgeous hues of Metrocolor, expanded in CinemaScope, and broadcast in stereophonic sound.

Silk Stockings imagines Paris, then, in a way that complicates the usual association of Paris as a contact zone. Vanessa Schwartz has argued that 1950s U.S. films set in France participated in a production of "Frenchness" that did not simply relay American ideology but created its own mid-century frame of meaning. These films, among which she includes *Silk Stockings*, "pay homage to France to celebrate film itself as an emblem of modern life. . . . At a moment when TV introduced grave concern for the future of filmgoing, these films reasserted the magic of the form. By self-consciously foregrounding matters of visual artifice, they advocated to filmmakers and audiences alike that entertainment could also be art."[22] Schwartz's argument illuminates the continuities between mass entertainment and culture in France and the United States, and demonstrates how these continuities upheld connections to the French Belle Époque—long the era of "high culture"—and the indebtedness of American cinema to its French origins.

However, such continuities also depended upon global hierarchies that many of these films underplayed. Throughout the first half of the twentieth century, African Americans enjoyed a social acceptance in Paris that they had not found in the United States. Particularly following World War I, Paris became a haven for many African American artists and intellectuals. Over 200,000 blacks came to Paris as workers and soldiers during World War I; after the armistice, many more flocked there to enjoy the lack of official segregation, if not unrestricted mobility.[23] As I discussed in *Beyond the Color Line and the Iron Curtain*, freedom of movement—for many black Americans—became synonymous with a national elsewhere.[24] For some, this elsewhere became France; for others, France was merely a stopover on the way to a more avowed racial equality in the Soviet Union. France's acceptance of African Americans was of course complex, given the history of French colonialism and the strident racism of France towards Africa. The experiences of African Americans in Paris were caught up in the circulation of jazz as an instrument of cultural exchange and as a racially marked commodity. Josephine Baker and Langston Hughes were celebrated even as French Africans were being detained, jailed, and deported.

During World War II, African American soldiers fought the "Double V" campaign—freedom abroad, freedom at home—to remind white Americans that, just as they fought shoulder to shoulder with white soldiers, they should be accorded equal status as citizens after the war. In France, African American soldiers mingled easily with white Europeans, establishing Paris as an interracial contact zone. As a setting for an American film, postwar Paris was therefore already marked as interracial; it was not only a playground for wealthy whites, but also a place of partial refuge for American blacks who sought to escape racial persecution at home.

Silk Stockings reminds us of the racial hybridity of Paris as a post-war setting through Porter's repeated allusions to and use of jazz forms in combination with Astaire's dance routines. Together these abundant citations of blackness weave a tale of the racially marked relationships between modernity and the Cold War consensus—recalling the logic of the Cold War kitchen. By summoning forms of music and dance identified with African American culture, the film reveals that its high/low entertainment anxiety is not simply about the status of the Hollywood musical, but also about the absences that are also recollected in scenes of entertainment (such as "Red Blues" and "The Ritz Roll and Rock") within the film.

As a setting, Paris showcases resurgent luxury, while at the same time demonstrating the limits of that racially exclusive fantasy. Silk stockings were particularly fetishized in the postwar period because of the rarity of silk during the war. Wartime rationing was due to a lull in silk production, the use of silk for parachutes, and the fact that before the war Japan was the leader of the global silk industry. Initial complaints about synthetic replacements like nylon boosted female interest in securing the real thing, which meant that such finery became associated with good times, wealth, bounty, and material comforts—all embodied in silk as a textile. But the film's eponymous object signals more than a rarefied commodity: because women wear this translucent material on their legs, women and sexuality come together in the object. Moreover, it is created to look natural, as if it didn't exist at all. As transformative transparent object, silk stockings enable a woman to be her better, her truer self. In spite of Cyd Charisse's sparkling youth and celebrity legs, the character she plays (Nina Yoshenko) is devised as the foil or the limit to all such bourgeois decadence. At eighteen, she "renounced all bourgeois pleasure" and fought on an anti-aircraft tank crew during the war. When we first meet her, she wears tightly belted suits in drab shades of gray and brown. She is, in a word, dull. In one early scene, Nina asks about stockings: "How can such a civilization survive where women are permitted to wear such things?" The movie's narrative lesson provides the answer, of course. But a corollary lesson is that female emancipation through fashion consumption is a complexly woven tale of liberation and modernity that depends upon the summoning and erasure of specifically racialized bodies.

When Nina shuts the door to her Parisian hotel suite, closes the blinds, and collapses the portrait of Lenin on her bedside table, she is preparing to be transformed from the outside-in. During her dance solo—a love song to stockings and lingerie—she is transformed. Upon donning silk stockings, all her views become different. She loses her accent, comes to love flowers, the air, the "scent" of springtime in Paris. Lingerie improves her mood, and her self-identification with finery completes her. The messages here are rote but bear repeating: (1) buying clothes makes women like themselves more and reveals who they really are, and (2) because women's properly dressed exteriors perfectly reflect who they are inside, women are commodities—they have nothing internal to them that cannot be showcased on the surface. Moreover, these facts are offered as universally true—they need no words—it's a solo dance here, not a "routine." The film's guiding credo—an American criticism of the unfeminine lives of Soviet women as the pivotal difference between East and West—seems to dictate the terms of Nina's seduction. That willingness to be seduced is the fatal flaw of Soviet women and, by extension, of all Soviets.

Later we learn, as Porter's lyrics put it, that without love, "a woman is pleasure unemployed," and "a man to a woman is her life." If these lyrics weren't winking at us so insistently, we might almost believe that the Cold War could be won through heterosexual bliss wrought through the logic of the kitchen: buying things to make women happy; buying women; making men happy. As Khrushchev notably said to Nixon, all of us are "for the ladies," aren't we?

Satin and Silk, Stalin and Silk

I consider that color on the screen must be used as an emotion.
—Rouben Mamoulian

The possibility that women's love of goods—especially if they are from Parisian fashion houses—threatens women's interest in men is suggested playfully by the movie's most dynamic character, Peggy Dayton. Played with robust wackiness by the irrepressible Janis Paige, Peggy is the film's true heroine. A scene-stealer at every turn, Peggy is the anti-Nina: louder than life, splashy, gung-ho, vibrantly indulging in every available decadence. With flaming red hair and emerald eyes, she mockingly turns a deaf ear to easy questions. When asked about the author of *War and Peace* by a reporter, she replies: "There's absolutely no truth to the rumors. We're just good friends." Peggy's prior roles as an Esther Williams clone—in fictional aquamusicals like *The Cowboy and the Mermaid*— have clogged her ears. She is constantly shaking her head and speaking over her companions. In this role, Peggy thwarts Nina's cool commissar. Whereas Nina is all business, Peggy is all fun—she uses her spunky sexuality as a resource (not as a means to "find herself"). As Peggy sings in her pitch-perfect ballad "Satin and Silk": "You can't expect a lady to exert that certain pull, if she's wearing flannel bloomers and her stockings are made of wool." Dayton's sexual playfulness reminds us that women's sexuality is an energy—a pull—that can and must be put to good use, channeled into arenas like culture (and musicals) lest it exert itself and wreak havoc. At the same time, the film laughs at the very idea that culture isn't politics. In fact *Silk Stockings* suggests that the right kind of culture makes the best politics. This is the Hollywood message Steve Canfield promotes, and the message that Nina buys hook, line, and sinker. For Steve, and the version of 1950s Hollywood represented in the film, culture is the front where the war can be fought best.[25]

But while ostensibly following the logic of the kitchen—in which commodities are liberating and women can be appealed to on the basis of universal emotions—the movie showcases no small degree of ambivalence about the politics behind a soft-power engagement with the Soviets. Both the screenplay and the lyrics seem uncertain about the culture they present. In fact, the film spends plenty of time parodying the state of American popular culture and commenting self-reflexively on its own pandering to that market. The early number "Stereophonic Sound," performed by Astaire and Paige, is a critique of American entertainment values. While the song is loud, colorful, and larger than life, it is also a lament about the days before TV cornered the screen market and forced film to compete with its easy access.[26] As Mamoulian's biographer, David Luhrssen, puts it: "reeling at the box office from the impact of TV, Hollywood in the mid-1950s turned to wide-screen, Technicolor spectacles to draw patrons from their living rooms and into theaters. Colorful adaptations of popular Broadway musicals became part of Hollywood's strategy to shore up sagging ticket sales."[27] The lyrics of "Stereophonic Sound" seem to ask: how can films attract an audience and continue to have meaning for them? By becoming bigger, brighter, and louder:

> Today to get the public to attend a picture show
> It's not enough to advertise a famous star they know
> If you want to get the crowds to come around
> You've got a have glorious Technicolor,
> Breathtaking Cinemascope and
> Stereophonic sound.

As Helen Laville notes, the Arthur Freed Unit at MGM that produced *Silk Stockings* was renowned for its genre-blending projects, and Freed's conception of the "filmusical" was, according to Gerald Mast, "a seamless weave of high art and low entertainment, the elegant European arts and the vital American arts, 'commerce but with class.'"[28] Commerce-driven culture is the butt of every joke in "Stereophonic Sound." Yet MGM was enacting just what it pilloried, allowing the form of the film (and its technologies) to be debunked even as it relied on them for the transmission of its message. Although Mamoulian was a devout advocate of color, the director was known to have derided CinemaScope as "the worst shape ever devised."[29] This kind of autocritique may have helped audiences to feel they were in on the wink, or it may have helped them to empathize with Astaire—who was clearly a man being beaten at his own game, as I discuss below. But perhaps most importantly, the film's self-criticism enabled questions about a compulsory link between technological innovation—the form through which the message was wrought—and female emancipation.

As a technological innovation in her own right, the character of Peggy Dayton is not merely a foil for Nina's capitulation to the studio system, she is also hyper visible. In this extreme visibility, Peggy takes on the burden of race, standing in for the film's racially absent bodies. This point is essential, and its omission has been the basis of the misreading of Peggy, and of the film in general. One critic calls Peggy "monstrous," stating that: "Dayton personifies the gimmick-ridden state of American cinema, which has abandoned all pretensions to artistic integrity in a bid for the lowest common denominator of public taste and interest."[30] But to read Peggy's character as the embodiment of a crass mass culture is to miss the larger point. Her "monstrosity" is the very failure or lie of the Cold War consensus. *Silk Stockings* is a romance of historical amnesia and a reminder of everything that Peggy's heightened, augmented presence helps to subsume. While race is pushed to the background, Peggy is forwarded not only as an excessively feminine character, but as the surplus "color" of the film. The film forces Dayton's sexuality upon us as lowbrow and tasteless—the embodiment of American popular culture run amok. Her aggressive sexual vernacular not only enables the elegance of Nina's dialect to hum along in comparison, it also renders a bitter sarcasm towards the fable of "silk stockings," as told by the movie's plot. Peggy's presence provokes the question we must ask of Nina: how much is the smooth victory of market capitalism connected to the sexuality of women and the subsumption of racial erasure?[31]

In her signature solo, "Satin and Silk," Peggy walks the French runway in an American striptease. As Peggy peels off her finery in front of a captive Boroff, she assembles and disassembles the assumptions about female sexuality with which Nina has been charged. On the one hand, a good striptease is all in a day's work; women's bodies are key assets in the commerce-driven machinations of Hollywood entertainment. On the other hand, she is an American on an international stage, making a case for the United States as the capital of the future. The emphasis on Western fashion as an indicator of modernity signals the backwardness of Russia. If all Soviet women could be as emancipated as Peggy—stripping freely in front of prostrate men, winning them over to the pleasures of the future—then the Cold War might be quickly won. The scene provides a light-hearted critique of the straitlaced coupling of modernity and emancipation. As Peggy sings, "It's strange what undergarments do / to convert a maiden's attitude. / If she's wearin' silk and satin / she's for pettin' and for pattin'." Drawing attention to this number as a scene of entertainment—both for Boroff and the film's audience—the film reminds us that terms like "freedom" and "emancipation" must be scrutinized when used in the service of commerce.

The Heritage of Her Sex: Christian Dior in Moscow

Modernity is a code and fashion is its emblem.   —Jean Baudrillard[32]

The use of fashion as a means to make the film's signature statement about the superiority of Western goods over Soviet artifacts puts a timely stamp on the film's reception in the United States. In June 1959, less than two years after *Silk Stockings* was released, the Parisian fashion house of Christian Dior would debut its fall collection in Moscow at the "Wings of the Soviet Air Club." Between ten and twelve thousand Soviets saw the show, most of them designers, young women related to party elites, and theater and movie celebrities. Like the American National Exhibition, which would open a few weeks later, the Dior show received a burst of interest from the U.S. media. *Life* magazine sent the photographer Howard Sochurek to cover the show and follow the Dior models through Moscow's premier department store, GUM. Sochurek took dozens of color photos, most of which juxtapose graceful Parisian models with Muscovites who look like they have just come in from the farm.[33] Following the logic that female liberation was equated with a fashion-forward Western modernity, Sochurek's photos depict dowdy Russian women alongside their sylphlike Parisian counterparts.

In one set of photos, the models literally loom over the Soviet women, who gaze up at them, as if in awe. These photos cast Soviet femininity as not only backwards, but also infantile. In figure 5.1, the French models enact the child's game "London Bridge" over the heads of a pair of Soviet women wearing headscarves. In figure 5.2, the models beckon playfully while a Russian woman reaches towards them, as if asking to be elevated to their level. In figure 5.3, a model with her back to the camera appears to "flash" a befuddled Russian onlooker. The model's coat opens to show a revealing neckline; we can only imagine what else is on display. Although these French and Russian women likely did not speak a common language, the visual vernacular of the U.S. magazine's images is clear. Soviet women lag behind their French counterparts in all ways— temporally, aesthetically, and politically—and they are eager to catch up. As *Life* commented: "For the Russians the biggest attraction was a team of twelve shapely Dior models from Paris who flew in to show off a million and a half dollar's worth of shapely fashions. Russian women, who are more used to the baggy babushka look, were enchanted. 'I've never seen anything so beautiful in my life,' they kept saying."[34] This "baggy babushka" perspective was echoed by Harrison Salisbury, the *New York Times* correspondent in Moscow from 1949 to 1954. Salisbury declared that "Neither puritanism nor emphasis on heavy industry is going to divert the Russian woman much longer from the heritage of her sex, the right and opportunity to look just as pretty as she wants to. . . . Moscow women literally fought for tickets."[35]

The acumen of Salisbury's account notwithstanding, Sochurek's photographs tell a more interesting story because they reveal an investment in making the narrative of Soviet backwardness affectively true for the American viewer. As I explored in relation to *The Bell Jar*, the desire to create a specific image of Soviet women's lives as dreary and hopeless was championed by U.S. government publications. One USIA pamphlet, titled "The Soviet Woman under Communism," depicts a generic Soviet named Nina Saitsev whose "life is an endless round of work and worry, of physical hardship and spiritual dejection. . . . [H]er long, bleak days of toil and hardship convince her that communism is death in life."[36] Government-sponsored narrative descriptions may have generated a bleak picture of life in the Soviet Union, but photographs like these brought visual affirmation—the dreariness of Soviet existence come to life in all its texture and affect—for an audience who could not travel there.

Conversely, the *Life* spread would have appalled most Soviets, whose sense of being *kul'turnyi* or "cultured" was of utmost importance. *Kul'turnost'*

FIGURE 5.1. Soviet women observe Dior models in Moscow's GUM department store. Photo by Howard Sochurek for *Life* magazine, July 6, 1959. Getty Images

FIGURE 5.2. Dior models beckon to a Soviet onlooker on the steps of GUM. Photo by Howard Sochurek for *Life* magazine, July 6, 1959. Getty Images

(culturedness) was a concern throughout the Soviet period, beginning soon after the revolution, when culture was a key part of shaping Soviet people and facilitating their economic development. As Catriona Kelly and David Shepherd explain, "the centrality of *kul'tura* and *kul'turnost'* to the post-1917 period is beyond any doubt: *kul'tura* was at the core of Soviet cultural policy, while *kul'turnost'* was of a semi-official order and referred to the realm of everyday practice."[37] As a concept and a practice, *kul'turnost'* was a civilizing mission, used to discipline Soviets by shaping their everyday behavior and elevating the lower strata to the level of the elite. At the same time *kul'turnost'* also created a way of coping with the

FIGURE 5.3. Soviet women gaze at Dior models in the halls of
GUM. Photo by Howard Sochurek for *Life* magazine, July 6,
1959. Getty Images

ideological quandary of Soviet consumerism. Historian Sheila Fitzpatrick
summarizes: "one of the great advantages of the concept of *kul'turnost'*
was that it offered a way of legitimizing what had once been thought of
as 'bourgeois' concerns about possessions and status: one treated them
as an aspect of *kul'tura.*"[38] In the post-Stalin era, *kul'turnost'* helped explain an emergent culture of production as linked to all kinds of self-
presentation, not the least of which was bodily hygiene and dress.

When the model in figure 5.3 flashes her décolletage at her Russian counterpart, we don't see admiration in the Russian woman's response. This is not longing, but wariness. The models are like people from another world—lovely, seductive, daring, breathtaking.[39] And although Soviet women lived in a climate of shortage and scarcity, they managed to dress themselves. The texture of these photos is repudiation as much as it is fascination. What kind of empowerment does the modernity of high fashion bestow upon women? True, these Soviet onlookers wear socks that bunch at their ankles, while the Dior models wear stockings with a trademark seam up the back of the leg, but has high fashion triggered female equality, or yet another realm of classification and captivity, a means of separating the elite from the plebeians while keeping all women confined? What kind of emancipatory discourse does *défilé* offer the standard Soviet woman?[40]

Americans visiting Russia in the 1950s were quick to pick up on the campaigns of *kul'turnost'* created to enforce the difference between acceptable and unacceptable behavior. Marguerite Higgins, a Pulitzer prize-winning writer for the *New York Herald Tribune*, noted in her 1955 exposé, *Red Plush and Black Bread*: "There is no doubt about many Russian ideas of what is *kulturni* or *nye kulturni*."[41] Like many reporters of that era, Higgins fell prey to typical U.S. stereotypes, writing that "in questions of taste and refinement, the Russian Communist state, like many new civilizations, suffers from a feeling of insecurity and from an inability to profit by comparison with more mature cultures outside the Iron Curtain. Many Soviet attempts at culture seem as heavy-handed and rough-hewn as the peasant stock to which so many Russians, including those in the city, are still so closely related."[42]

Higgins's description of the immature, peasant-stock Russian is echoed vividly in Sochurek's photographs. And yet, the photographs also prompt us to read against the obvious rhetorical strategy of placing Russians in a primitive past. Beneath their headscarves, these women cast gazes that express curiosity, befuddlement, perhaps even disdain. According to *Izvestia*, the Dior styles were too open and short, and would not compliment the Soviet figure. These comments and others like them trigger a now familiar and overwrought debate about Western standards of beauty and female agency. Instructive as this debate may be, the compelling piece of this antagonism lies elsewhere.

Another set of images from Sochurek's private collection of photos (figs. 5.4–5.8) plays on the racial rhetoric of Soviet difference from the West. Hegelian accounts of history in which Russians were displaced, lodged behind their European counterparts on history's conveyor belt, also suggested that Russians were not properly "white." These photos depict Russians as racially proximate to white Europeans but essentially different; the tacit social knowledge communicated is that the Soviets are of a different lineage, and background. Their "whiteness" is thus of a second order. Although the photos establish this difference emphatically, they also activate a response that is in excess of this social knowledge—they suggest that Soviets may not care about Western standards of judgment. With their arms crossed, the Soviet onlookers create a textural *frisson*. They appear defiant, even cynical, about the West and its claims to superiority. Moreover, this defiance suggests their weariness of the rhetorical twoness historically pressed upon them, as both related to the West and not especially Western. These photos rely on a social context in which the viewer understands herself to identify as Western, and therefore as superior to the subject drawn. With so many of the French models turned away from the viewer, the Soviet onlooker—and her reaction—is the focus: in this triangulation of gazes, we see the Soviet seeing the French, the French seeing the Soviet, and the Soviet seeing the U.S. camera. Much like *Silk Stockings*, in which the otherness of the Soviet is evoked as hyperbolic, the photos both encourage and query such judgment, creating the possibility for multiple paths of identification.

These photos recreate the mute social performance required of the Russian subject as double.[43] In this sense, Soviets are caught in a middle ground between East and West, a place of mediation and difference. These headscarf-wearing babushkas are made to serve up the image of an archaic, utilitarian femininity, while the Western femininity they observe luxuriates in finding itself through things. This composite sense of national identity—one which would have been familiar to Soviets as a thematic of Russian doubleness dating to nineteenth-century literary themes, but against which they would have reacted vehemently—is recuperated in the film, as I explain below.

To be fair, even Soviet bureaucrats did not consider the idea of Russian backwardness as purely fiction. The Dior visit had been arranged by the Soviet Chamber of Commerce after months of negotiations. Haute couture and its related luxuries were a key part of Khrushchev's thaw culture. As Harrison Salisbury noted,

> When all is said and done why did the Soviet government invite Dior to Moscow? Not just to give the daughters of the ministers and the rising young actresses a thrill. . . . No. Dior was brought in because the government wants to take the Russian woman out of her flowered print and give

FIGURE 5.4. Photo by Howard Sochurek of Dior models in Moscow. Courtesy of Tania Sochurek

FIGURE 5.5. Photo by Howard Sochurek of Russian woman observing Dior model in Moscow. Courtesy of Tania Sochurek

her a chance to look like her Western sisters. Why? Because, I would guess, the Russian woman wants to look like her Western sisters and the present Russian government can see no reason of policy why she should not.[44]

Salisbury's reductive conjecturing obscures the disparate routes of desire, identification, and refutation launched by the Parisian models in Moscow, directing his reader towards a single possible conclusion: Russian flowered-print backwardness. But Salisbury does identify correctly the confusion within Soviet policy that in part encouraged such conclusions.

FIGURE 5.6. Photo by Howard Sochurek of Soviets observing
Dior model in Moscow. Courtesy of Tania Sochurek

As I discussed in chapter 1, Khrushchev was not opposed to embracing
aspects of the West he felt the Soviets could use in order to outperform
their antagonists. Like all aspects of consumerism, fashion had to be "rational" and "cultured," not irrational and excessive as in the West. According to *Zhurnal Mod* (Fashion journal), the preeminent Soviet fashion
magazine from the period, the difference between socialist and bourgeois
fashion was function: "In order to create clothes in harmony with the
image of people of the socialist era, clothing designers must attentively

FIGURE 5.7. Photo by Howard Sochurek of Dior models in
Moscow. Courtesy of Tania Sochurek

analyze and observe their contemporaries and their life in all its various
dimensions, understanding the ideals, aspirations, and interests by which
the whole society lives, and finally they must absorb the spirit of our time,
of our era."[45] Although the emphasis may have been on function, the
notions of "spirit" and "aspiration" were sufficiently vague to be open to
interpretation, and likewise to bourgeois tendencies, creating an Emper-
or's Clothes kind of logic to the Soviet declaration of a "rational" haute
couture.

Khrushchev's embrace of what we might call the transnational circu-

FIGURE 5.8. Dior models attract attention at Moscow's GUM. Courtesy of Tania Sochurek

lation of fashion was also a re-embracing of Western models of beauty that had for decades served as standards for the Russian elite. Under the tsarist regime, the spoken language among the upper class had been French; Russian nobility sent their dressmakers to Paris to study the latest designs, or traveled to Paris themselves for fabric and fittings. The Paris-Moscow fashion trail was thus particularly sedimented with the historical riches of elitism and anti-provincialism depicted in Sochurek's photos.[46] Put on hiatus for the decades since the revolution—a productive period in fashion in its own right—this relationship reemerged alongside the new focus on *kul'tura*.

As the preeminent French designer, Dior had an esteemed role in Soviet fashion. In the 1950s, his "lily of the valley" skirts could be seen throughout Soviet fashion magazines. After Dior's death in 1957, a young Yves Saint Laurent took over the House of Dior and reinvented Dior's signature "New Look" by introducing the trapeze line—dresses that flared out from the shoulders downward. Dior's "look" appealed to the Soviets for its allegedly classic and neutral lines.[47] Soviet planners believed that Dior's basic patterns could be copied and recreated annually, thus lowering production costs and keeping a functional new look fresh for Soviet consumers. The very notion of a new "look," however, again suggests a visual vernacular, one that in this case conveyed contradictory messages. While Russian women could see these designs as sophisticated and modern (i.e., not Soviet), they also immediately registered that they would not find them on any local store shelves. Most of the fashions that showed up in big magazines like *Zhurnal Mod*, *Sovetskaia Zhenshchina* (Soviet woman), and *Rabotnitsa* (Woman worker), as well as in smaller pamphlets such as *Iskusstvo odevat'sia* (The art of dressing) and *moda i my* (Fashion and us) were not readily available—the equipment to produce them on a massive scale did not exist. As a result, women often tried to recreate these silhouettes on their own, with the basic assistance of the *Entsiklopediia domashnego khoziaistva* (The household encyclopedia), which was passed around from friend to friend and neighbor to neighbor as a kind of talismanic almanac.[48]

The focus on "look," or self-presentation, became so prevalent a part of Soviet female self-conception that in 1960 the journal *Rabotnitsa* started a column called "Posmotrite na sebia, pozhaluista!" (Look at yourself, please!). The imperative tense of the title suggests the compulsory accounting of the command. As Olga Gurova explains: "The column contained advice on taking care of the body, learning etiquette, and, in general, acquiring Soviet taste. Art critics, artists, designers from the House of Fashion were considered as experts and invited to provide comments on the topics."[49] The shaping of Soviet female subjectivity as a form of state authorized to-be-looked-at-ness contributed to an awareness of that same subjectivity as inferior, as less than *kul'turnyi* when compared with her Parisian counterparts, in spite of the fact that Soviet women were at the same time told that they were superwomen, superior to the decadent excesses of irrational consumerism typified by the West.

Given the antipathy in the public realm towards Western extravagance, not all the press about Dior's show was positive. The distinction between socialist "good taste" and bourgeois "extravagance" in fashion began to fray, creating a kind of doublespeak that called it excessive while at the same time quietly embracing it. On the one hand, party ideology claimed social justice for all; on the other hand, the Soviet system was spiked with material privileges for an elite few. (To be sure, the target audience for the Dior show was not the peasant stock of Sochurek's photographs.) In other words, while Soviet dogma proclaimed equality for the masses, Soviet officials strove to distinguish themselves from the masses by acquiring elite taste—and fashion was an easy route to acquire that taste. As Catriona Kelly and Vadim Volkov note, "the simplest and least demanding aspect of *kul'turnost'*, and the first to be associated with it, was dress."[50] A kind of vertical dissemination of taste followed Dior's visit to Moscow and, likewise, the visits of Soviet designers to Paris. The French cultural historian Larissa Zakharova writes: "Soviet designers had to adopt a double language. In public discourse they expressed the politically correct clichés regarding 'bourgeois fashion exaggerations,' but in internal reports they justified the need for regular visits to France by referring to the positive aspects of French haute couture that could nourish Soviet clothing design."[51]

The prevalence of double language was familiar territory for most Soviets, accustomed as they were to a variance between public discourse and private longings. And the simultaneity of these two powerful and interwoven cultural discourses contributed to what Russian philosopher Mikhail Epstein has called a "super signified"—the reality to which external life refers, but to which no one pays real allegiance.[52] The "as if" rhetoric of utopia made the nation feel different, a difference superimposed on the actual living conditions of everyday life—even as everyone was aware of the two simultaneously existing realities.[53] The long-standing dissonance between hearing one thing and understanding another opened up a visceral mode of attention in which meaning was dynamic—not binary, but both.

In the world of Soviet fashion, just as in the West, clothing was a social marker. Although early Soviet ideology denounced fashion as mired in class distinction (and instead advocated function and utility), Khrushchev's wife and daughter attended a Dior fashion show in Paris in 1960, legitimating such distinctions as "cultured" rather than "classist." The public self became linked to Soviet efficiency, which for decades had been calculated through a metric of *shortage*. But the rift between mass and elite selves expanded as the differentials between them increased—once there were goods to be had. The vanguard function of Soviet fashion became similar to its role in the West: the education of the masses. But it also suggested a vexed relationship between female advancement and modernity, as some women had access to advancement while others were made to dream of catching up. The emphasis on female dress produced and was produced by the intense gendering of Soviet subjects. At the same time, many women used dress as a means of negotiating the market. In spite of material scarcity, some relied on a remarkable resourcefulness to self-fashion their public selves such that the adaptation of Western goods or looks could be done in the service of Sovietness.[54]

Harrison Salisbury claimed that the influence of the 1959 Dior show on Muscovite fashion was direct and powerful: "Within a week or two you began to see girls on Gorky Street wearing imitations of the more simple Dior styles. Spike heels appeared, dreadfully expensive, in the House of Shoe Styles. The demand for sheer Western nylons became greater than ever."[55] Without discounting Salisbury's observations, we can use other measures for judging influence: by consulting, for example, the *Entsiklopedia domashnego khoziaistka*, a fashion source for all Soviets who sought specific patterns for dressmaking. The 1959 edition of the *Entsiklopedia* features only three basic dress patterns—dominated by flouncy skirts and bows. By 1966, Soviet taste had indeed changed. Borrowing from their French counterparts, the later edition of the *Entsiklopedia* shows multiple patterns in which silhouettes are narrow and streamlined, and one of the suits strongly resembles that worn by a Dior model in 1959. While Khrushchev's regime imported fashion in an effort to instill a higher degree of *kul'turnost'* in Soviet women, these same women responded by taking the form and making it Soviet, not in an effort to become Western per se, but in order to be more Soviet.

Silk Stockings exposes that vexed relationship more explicitly, playing on the idea of *kul'turnost'* while revealing fashion to be less associated with good taste than with selling things and making money. In *Silk Stockings*, women's liberation through things is both endorsed and ridiculed. Peggy Dayton's target on the runway is the classical composer Peter Boroff; she is supposed to win him over for Canfield's production of *War and Peace*, while at the same time winning him over for Western popular culture (and the viewers of *Silk Stockings*). In both cases winning means convincing him—through her feminine sexual wiles—of the validity of the commercialization of his music.[56] As the epitome of a *kul'turnyi chelovek*, Boroff reeks of good taste, and his reaction to the commodification of his piece "Ode to a Tractor" (into the show tune "Josephine") puts him over the edge. He is outraged by the popularization of classical music, calling it the "most insulting travesty on Russian culture." Canfield explains to him that, "In America we do this sort of thing all the time. We make popular songs out of the classics and millions of people enjoy them."

Film scholar Jane Feuer offers a rubric through which to understand Canfield's quip, explaining that the "central ideological project" of musicals was the defense of popular entertainment. She writes: "The narrative resolution of every musical involves bringing together the forces of entertainment with the forces opposed to entertainment. The synthesis achieved through the union of the romantic couple always involves a reconciliation of values associated on the one hand with rational cognitive thought. . . . and on the other hand the world of imagination, the world of freedom, impulse, spontaneity."[57] In *Silk Stockings*, this project is mapped onto the reconciliation of Soviet high culture and American popular entertainment. Although these cultural genres are fused with national differences, they receive their "resolution" through the instrumentality of the "Red Blues." This song is not simply a validation of Canfield's claim that high and low cultures can mix, but an acknowledgment of the invisibility of discussions of race within these conversations about cultural genres. In a sense, *Silk Stockings* mocks the central ideological project of the Hollywood musical as a fusion of classical and mass cultures, postponing resolution by conjuring race and identifying the instrumentality of popular culture as Cold War weapon.

As the lyrics of "Stereophonic Sound" remind us, filmic experience is often about sensation in excess of cognition. At the same time, this song demonstrates how a technologically enabled heightening of the senses has removed black people from visibility, while retaining the black cultural forms of motion and emotion that fuel the plot. *Silk Stockings* thus becomes much more than a simple story of women's universal femininity and Soviet susceptibility to market capitalism. The film is a large-scale allegory for the way Western modernity anchored itself to the suppression of black bodies, and of the ambivalences that must be covered over for that narrative to proceed. The film advocates choice and a diversity of options as the means for priming postwar subjectivity for democratic horizons; "Stereophonic Sound" in particular relays new ways of inhabiting spaces through access to new technologies, propounding its lessons by way of what Fred Turner called "surrounds." There are numerous surrounds presented both in the film and outside the film. From the catwalk in the fashion show to the theater refreshment line, from the dance floor to the box office lobby and, most essentially, to the city streets, Paris becomes an idealized choice among multiple options. These options, however, are constrained within an overarching binary, a twoness that overrides the seeming plethora of choices and any meaningful diversity.

From the moment she steps off the plane in Paris, Peggy Dayton is coupled with Peter Boroff. As Steve announces, if Boroff can write it, Peggy can turn it into a pop tune. Peggy's striptease is meant to tempt her designated partner, but theirs is an odd coupledom. Peggy is aggressive and performs a femininity that perverts its acceptable boundaries, while Boroff is backwards, belated, and must be won over to the American future. Together they are both off-center, and their queerness props up the legibility of Nina and Steve's heterosexual bliss. Titillated but reluctant, Boroff doesn't "go" for Peggy. He isn't the easily susceptible Soviet she makes him out to be (and thus some Soviets have proven less willing to be seduced than their reputation would argue). Boroff does go for jazz, however. In the end, he is more taken with jazz than with Peggy. (Apparently not all men are "for the ladies," nor do all follow the heterosexual mandate of the kitchen.)

Selling the Homeland

> Sevodgnia on tantzuet dzhaz, a zavtra rodinu prodast.
> (Today he dances to jazz, tomorrow he will sell his homeland.)
> —Russian proverb

When Boroff and Nina are sent back to Russia, Boroff confides that he has been seduced—not by Peggy, but by this "new form of music," jazz. He and Nina speak in hushed tones, conspiring behind a curtain, an allusion to the fact that, until 1957, American jazz had been officially condemned in the Soviet Union. It was only after the World Youth Festival, held in Moscow that year, that the ban on jazz had been lifted as part of the Khrushchev thaw.[58] From behind this curtain, Boroff and Nina break into the "Red Blues." The initial lyrics of this set piece could not be more straightforward and uninspired: "We've got the red blues" is repeated six times—marking it as distinct from Porter's other titillating, tongue-in-cheek lyrics. In terms of music and movement, however, the number is multifaceted. It starts as twelve-bar blues, a form that, as music historian Todd Decker explains, was "a progression at its barest using only three chords, the tonic (I), subdominant (IV), and the dominant (V)—[that] remained a viable musical form for popular musicians from the 1910s to the 1960s."[59] As Boroff plays around with this basic form, Nina begins to dance. But the routine really starts to move when male dancers file in, creating two groups who chant the lyrics in tandem.

As a dance number, "Red Blues" is based on music and movement. The traditional twelve-bar form modulates into jazzy harmonies; eventually, the blues are taken over by big band grandstanding. The dance movements combine folk, ballet, and jazz with what looks to a modern audience like breakdancing, with Nina at the center of a group of Russian men. Here we witness a version of what dance historian Susan Manning has called "metaphorical minstrelsy" when describing the performance of early twentieth century, white modern dance. Manning describes this as a practice through which white dancers choreographed movement metaphors by abstracting and personifying the existence of other racial groups.[60] A filmusical is not the same sort of project as modern dance, of course, but the concept of metaphorical minstrelsy can be helpful in understanding the use of movement to invoke race. The choreography in "Red Blues" uses jazz moves that signify racial hybridity at a far distance from the ballet school depicted in the movie's opening scenes.[61] So the film not only makes a musical reference to African American cultural forms, but also to black dance. Michael Rogin's work has been especially helpful in pointing out that blackface minstrelsy, as it had been previously practiced, came to an end during the postwar period's "embarrassment about racial subordination and stereotyping," alongside an agreement between the NAACP and Hollywood to improve representational practices. In its place, a sort of blackface "more broadly understood" continued, most notably through musical covers of black music by white performers. Rogin writes: "the theft of black music and performance styles energized 1950s popular culture."[62] *Silk Stockings* makes it clear that black dance was expropriated as well.

In "Red Blues," the racial references do not stop with blackness, however. The scene's abstracted movement is meant to represent both blackness and Russianness simultaneously. The dancers move between tap dance and Cossack jumping—squatting kicks right out of the Russian dancer routine in Tchaikovsky's *Nutcracker* ballet. These dance formations channel African American energy with a Russian flair; the dance is a combo of sorts. But no blacks are present. This scene thus becomes the film's most directly indirect citation of black cultural forms—themselves hybrid, mixed, open to modulation.[63]

As the title of the song indicates, the "Red Blues" are an amalgam. But by the end of the number, these blues are all Hollywood, as the scene uses all of the film's technological resources (bigger, brighter, louder) to deliver a blow-out, big band performance. As Nina is raised in the air by a circle of outstretched male arms, we witness that she has become the product of black cultural forms. The men around her offer their hybridized bodies as the raw materials for the production of her liberated white femininity. As the *New York Times* noted, "Miss Charisse unlimbers herself superbly with a gang of cutups doing 'The Red Blues.'"[64] Who has the right to sing the blues? Apparently even the Russians do: Russians who, by the logic of the Cold War kitchen, are clamoring for freedom, just like slaves. What better way to part the curtain?

As the original director of *Porgy*, Rouben Mamoulian was no stranger to African American contributions to U.S. cultural forms. Pearl Bailey, the actress he directed as Butterfly in *Porgy*, recalled that during an episode of infighting among the cast, Mamoulian "reminded everyone of the great contribution the Negro had made to America, giving the country its only original art: music."[65] Having been invited to direct the European tour of *Oklahoma!* alongside performances by Louis Armstrong and Dizzy Gillespie, Mamoulian also was well aware of the importance of cultural diplomacy to U.S. strategic aims against communism and, more importantly, of the reliance of these incursions on black musical forms. The U.S. popular press proclaimed this reliance quite boldly. A 1955 article in the *New York Times* claimed that the "United States has Secret Sonic Weapon—Jazz."[66] During the years following the Bolshevik revolution, popular dances such as the fox-trot and the tango were considered immoral and jazz was suppressed. The association with sexuality was explicit—even Maxim Gorky declaimed the eroticism of jazz—but by the 1930s the mistrust had eased. During the 1930s and 1940s, there were countless Soviet jazz musicians, with Leonid Utesov and Alexander Tsfasman among the best known. But after the war, jazz again came under attack. In 1948 Andrei Zhdanov, who was in charge of cultural policy under Stalin, ordered the arrest of jazz musicians and banned all saxophones. Jazz again went underground, and the Soviet government's contempt for jazz was played up in the West. Boroff's desire for jazz is thus an American send-up of the Soviet fear of jazz as cultural infiltration. At the same time, it also registers the desire of American white men for black cultural forms, for a mediation of blackface "more broadly understood." If Boroff's jazz romance ended there, we might close the chapter at this point, but Boroff's interest in jazz also points elsewhere—to the Soviet group of malcontents known as the *stilyagi*, who kept jazz alive throughout its formal denunciation by Soviet policy.[67]

Interlude: Stilyagi *Style*

During the post–World War II period, Soviet youths who imitated Western cultural modes came to be known pejoratively as the *stilyagi*—from *stil* meaning "style." These so-called "stylish ones" hailed from diverse backgrounds: some were children of the elite, some were orphaned by the war, many fell somewhere in between these two poles. They represented the era's alienated youth and, to the best of their abilities, dressed in a fashion they associated with the West. Known to use slang terms such as "guys," "dude," and "hang out," they called each other "Joe" or "Bob," and likewise referred to the wide avenues of Moscow and Leningrad as "Broadway," where they danced to jazz and "boogie voogie." Typically, the men could be identified by their long pants, narrow ties, and brightly colored shirts, and the women by garish skirts, high heels, and loud lipstick. When possible, they preferred Lucky Strikes and Camels to homegrown *papirosa* or unfiltered Soviet brands.[68]

The *stilyagi* sutured together these references through various means, including wartime connections, movies like *Tarzan* and *Sunset Serenade*, and limited access to newsprint depictions during lulls in anti-U.S. propaganda. The mass return of so-called "white" Russians from Europe after the war, along with the nascent Soviet program of sending sports groups abroad, resulted in new sources of both Western goods and first-hand information.[69] Restless Soviet youth, exhausted by wartime hardship and curious about the outside world, sought to copy and exchange these items, remaking their sense of this world in their own guise. Identifying the texture of this world beyond the border in things as disparate as clothing tags, cigarette boxes, jazz music, and the pages of glossy magazines like *Life* and *Look*, the *stilyagi* stitched together a version of the West that was premised on traces, both real and imaginary.

What started as a small subculture of youthful malcontents garnered growing condemnation from the government, although full-on repression did not begin until the 1950s. State-run papers like *Pravda* and *Izvestia* frequently published denunciations of the *stilyagi*, but it appears that they were considered a small and insignificant group of deviationists. One way in which this sense of insignificance was reinforced was through the pigeonholing of the *stilyagi* as uneducated, coarse, and soulless—not on a par with the Soviet youth who took culture, including Western culture, seriously. According to the contemporary press and some post-Soviet accounts, the *stilyagi* were dilettantes, while other youth groups were more sophisticated.[70] The *stilyagi* were patrolled by patriotic and well-disciplined Komsomols, party groups put on the street to monitor them and decry their bourgeois activities.

While existing scholarship on the *stilyagi* has tended to concur that they were a minor formation, I would like to consider this social group more carefully. The phenomenon of the *stilyagi* helps to elucidate the ways in which the logic of Nixon's kitchen was not simply repudiated, but repurposed. First, as a group based on style, the *stilyagi* have something to teach us about style as a mode of mid-century Soviet cultural uptake (thus recalling our discussion of the reception of ANEM). Second, through their engagement with underground jazz, the *stilyagi* help us to think through the production, circulation, and consumption of a related minor formation—the X-ray record. Finally, through their linking of style and the X-ray record, the *stilyagi* push us to contemplate important connections between global media and the shaping of Soviet self-conception during the Cold War. The *stilyagi* enable us to see how Soviet subjectivity was shaped through Western style and Western objects, far from a polarized or polarizing state-endorsed rhetoric of anti-Westernism. The disparagement of the *stilyagi* allowed the acceptance of a more mainstream adoption of Western aspect as compatible with what it meant to be a good Soviet. Operating as a kind of vilified but not formally prosecuted faction within larger state-sanctioned modes of behavior and dress, the *stilyagi* came to be an "internal external," a formation through which less extreme and more routine enunciations of Western proclivities could be sustained.[71]

During her 1954 trip to Russia, Marguerite Higgins noted that "Even Russia has its zoot-suiters, youngsters who lean to flared trousers and gaudy ties."[72] While Westerners may have been quick to identify *stilyagi* as evidence of the cultural undoing of Soviet ideology, the phenomenon of *stilyagi* was more complex—the youth involved were less pro-America than they were interested in escaping what dissident Vasily Aksyonov called the "the structures of our minutely controlled everyday lives."[73] The *stilyagi* thus not only embody paradoxes of Soviet socialist life, but also show how ideals of socialism, including creativity and collectivity, were irreducibly mixed with fear, alienation, and control. This kind of reading enables us to escape the overwrought binarisms of East/West, official/unofficial, sanctioned/repressed, and more importantly serves as a foundation from which to rebut historical accounts of the downfall of Soviet socialism through the forbidden or illicit incursion of Western culture. *Stilyagi* and the forms through which they identified are so interesting precisely because they show the ways that Westernness could be embraced as intimately Soviet. This suggests a different routing for *Silk Stockings* and its narrative of soft-power success for the West.

The well-loved and widely circulated humor magazine *Krokodil* frequently ran cartoons lampooning the *stilyagi* as lost youth—soulless and outcast. In one of the best-known iterations of the type, popular author Dmitri Belyaev wrote a satiric spoof that pointed out the fatuousness of the consumer-oriented *stilyagi* who aped the worst of Western consumerism.[74] Between 1950 and 1960 in the major news outlets—*Pravda*, *Izvestia*, and *Literaturnaia Gazeta*—the word *stilyagi* appeared hundreds of times in articles about youth culture, hooliganism, and societal parasitism, and in official polemics about morality and culture, or *kul'tura*. One headline from 1951 reads "Capitalism—the Enemy of Culture," and goes on to outline the ways in which the *stilyagi* embody everything the Soviet system opposed.

> To our shame people still exist among Soviet youth, who are infected by the vices of the past, spongers, who live an idea of romantic life. On the central streets of Moscow, Leningrad, Tbilisi, Erevan, and several other cities loiter young men with Tarzan haircuts [*tarzan'ie pricheski*], dressed up like parrots, so-called *stilyagi*. They do not work anywhere. They do not study, but spend their nights in restaurants and pester girls. What kind of people are they?[75]

And yet in associating this group of malcontents so directly with "style," Soviets touched upon some of the key tenets of style as a form, and these tenets help us to further scrutinize the marginalization of the *stilyagi*. Around the same time that the *stilyagi* were occupying the "broadways" of Leningrad and Moscow, art historian James Ackerman pointed out that style represents a tension between change and stability. In his seminal essay, "A Theory of Style," Ackerman wrote: "The virtue of the concept of style is that by defining *relationships* it makes various kinds of order out of what otherwise would be a vast continuum of self-sufficient products."[76] The *stilyagi* then, for all their fatuousness, may well have enabled continuity between Western accoutrement and Soviet sensibility. After all, all styles are semblances, built on appearances, a successful or not-so successful attempt at achieving a particular "look." In this sense, as Nelson Goodman and other key theorists have contended, "no fixed catalogue of the elemental properties of style can be compiled . . . we normally come to grasp style without being able to analyze it into component features."[77] As Goodman suggests, style is also a mode of perception, a way of interpreting an object, rather than a set of objective qualities perceived. Style is always about fluctuation, but it is also about restriction in that style is also the product of a limited set of options. It is this apprehension of style—what kind of people are they?—that helps to adduce my interest in the *stilyagi*. A cultural group excoriated for its aping of bourgeois life (in fact, *stilyagi* were frequently portrayed in print media as apes and monkeys), the *stilyagi* teach us less about consumerism and opposition than they do about the future of Sovietness. Centrally caught up in the many paradoxes of Soviet socialist life that defamed Western influences and attitudes as bourgeois while also, given the right context, lauded them as internationalist, the *stilyagi* enabled a kind of *positivity* in all their stylishness. Rather than embodying dissent, these figures helped articulate a possibility for Sovietness in tandem with the

West—borrowing from the West and moving forward full steam into the Soviet future.

Two posters drawn by the Leningrad collective of graphic satirists known as Boevoj Karandash, or the Battling Pencil, illustrate some of these tensions within official condemnation of the *stilyagi*. Boevoj Karandash was a collective of a dozen or so graphic artists and poets that formed in 1939, producing satiric posters during World War II and the postwar period. Their signature emblem was a painter's palette with a rifle alongside a pencil, sharpened to look like a bayonet. (After the war, the rifle was removed.) They were the most popular graphic artists during the war, with printings of their propaganda posters reaching into the several thousands. These posters would have been seen in public spaces such as school hallways, cafeterias, post offices, subway stations, and underground crossings, as well as outside museums and concert halls. Their presence helped to shape civic life and the public perception of official Sovietness, while at the same time accommodating multiple, simultaneous unofficial readings.

In "Soul for Sale" (see fig. 5.9), the figure is not really a body at all, but rather a paper-doll cutout, different pieces of rubbish pasted together and made to look fashionable. The shirt is newsprint, while the pants emphasize hand-made stitching—well-known marks of fake and poorly approximated versions of that beloved Western symbol: blue jeans. A couple of garish ties emblazoned with "Made in the USA," one with a scantily clad woman, hang from one arm, while letters postmarked "USA" are held close to the chest—or where the heart would be, if the degenerate figure had a heart. The feet are akimbo, almost pigeon-toed in their apparent lack of coordination, a point that is visually consistent with the gap between legs and feet. The argyle socks and pointy shoes are not attached to the figure they are supposedly supporting; rather, they are posed as if afterthoughts. Similarly, the headless phantom wears a hanger (or the hanger wears the phantom). The suggestive hook where a head should be not only implies emptiness—a readiness to be hung in any vapid ideological closet—but also bespeaks a certain kind of violence. This empty shell is held together by its cut-up parts, a recycled thing draped over a hanger. The poem reads, "Here are the leftover pieces of clothing from different countries / À la New York, à la Paris / For him and those like him / It is to spit on self-honor / When anticipating the gain!" While the condemnation may ring loud and clear, it is important to recall that Khrushchev and his daughter attended the 1960 Christian Dior show in Paris. Soviet readers would have been aware of this fact and

FIGURE 5.9. Boevoj Karandash, "Soul for Sale," 1961.

accepted it as not incongruent with the poster's ideological denunciation of the West and its fashions.

Another poster by the same group is even more pointed about the degeneracy inherent in Western influence. In this print, titled "In Their Circle" (see fig. 5.10), the verse reads, "[You] have to be an enemy to yourself / to suffer in such a circle / voluntary tortures / are a trick of rock-and-roll." With a record label that reads "Bugy-vugy, made in Barakhalka," this image pillories the music favored by the *stilyagi*, pictured here as three comical couples. (Barakhalka, one of the *stilyagi*'s favorite hangouts, was a flea market where illegal goods were traded.) Among those black-market goods were

FIGURE 5.10. Boevoj Karandash, "In Their Circle," 1956.

recordings made on old plastic X-rays, known as "jazz on the bones" or
"jazz on the ribs." (In figs. 5.11 and 5.12, the lighter areas correspond
with the images of bones.) While of poor quality, these recordings made
jazz available in a period when Soviets had to cozy up to their short-
wave radios in hopes of catching a minute or two of Willis Conover's
famous show, *Music USA*, on Voice of America. During that period, the
saying *segodnia on tantzuet dzhaz, a zavtra rodinu prodast* (today he
dances to jazz, tomorrow he will sell his homeland) captured the sense
of betrayal the *stilyagi* evoked.[78] The proximity of jazz and disloyalty is
especially telling. Even after Khrushchev's thaw began, jazz continued to

FIGURES 5.11 AND 5.12. Examples of Soviet x-ray records, or "jazz on the bones." Paul Heartfield / X-Ray Audio Project (www.x-rayaudio.squarespace.com)

be condemned officially (Khrushchev famously quipped that it gave him gas), though by then it had widespread popular appeal.

The technological leap of using X-ray plastic as a surface for printing records was allegedly dreamed up by a jazz-loving medical student. Whatever its true derivation, this innovation correlates with nascent discussions of cultural circulation: the appropriation of an American form eerily pressed onto a Soviet likeness. As the music critic Artemy Troitsky explains, "These were actual X-ray plates—chest cavities, spinal cords, broken bones—rounded at the edges with scissors, with a small hole in the center and grooves that were barely visible on the surface . . . they were the cheapest and most readily available source of necessary plastic."[79]

In a culture of scarcity, the bounty of used X-rays speaks to various kinds of discrepancies—including, most prominently, an emphasis on science and the technologization of the Soviet body concurrent with perpetually empty shelves. As a mode of creativity, however, these homemade gramophone records were not simple reproductions of American recordings. Instead, the ingenuity and imagination of their form implicitly distanced these discs from the materialism of the bourgeois classes that the "voluntary tortures" of American music purportedly represented. These records could be both artifacts of the official enemy and internally celebrated for their genius and creativity.

The external/internal instability that I used to describe the *stilyagi* extends to X-ray records and their engagement with the question of intimacy. In providing the basis for these new grooves, the apparitional outlines of anonymous Soviet bodies—from chest cavities to split clavicles—also created new possibilities for inhabiting Sovietness. What we witness is a reshaping not only of the listeners (the *stilyagi* and other "enemies to themselves"), but also of the nameless bones and crevices of the Soviet public upon which this music was etched. This new form of media permanently shifted the sense of Soviet postwar subjectivity, as evidenced by the anonymous, spectral images of Soviet internality on these X-rays grooved with black American music. Through the incursions of jazz and bebop, Russian selfhood became both more Western and also stylized differently, as indelibly Soviet. Being Soviet was about these new grooves in which official and unofficial discourse were mutually and intimately embedded.

If this image of jazz represents what Soviet anthropologist Alexei Yurchak might call a kind of Soviet futurity, it is also important to remember that American jazz was an art form deeply embedded with questions of marginalization, opposition, and resistance to norms of U.S. subjectivity. The fact that its Soviet iteration was both figuratively and materially pressed onto the internal images of nameless citizens so as to become legible to youthful malcontents further complicates the divisions of East and West, black and white, Soviet and American. While Soviets were encouraged to hear in jazz the music of internationalism—of the working peoples of the world—they also were able to recreate this music in their own likeness, so to speak, through the X-ray record. The racial component of jazz was radically altered and reinterpreted to the point of negation, such that there could be no contradiction between norms of Russian white supremacy and the championing of bebop. The X-ray records elicit notions of structural oppression and resistance in their very grooves, blurring all kinds of lines between bodies, borders, and time.[80] In this way the X-ray record animates the undead of the past, as well as the symbolic orders through which politics can become erased.

To put it differently, the X-ray is a figure for memory. It is an imprint of a particular body, captured at a particular moment in time. But an X-ray is not just any imprint, but an imprint of a body's intimate interior, the internality of the body exposed, externalized—for all to see. In the process of this externalization, the X-ray also loses a bit of its individuality. It is a picture of the body's skeletal commonality, separated from the particularities with which we have come to associate identity—fingerprints, eye color, height, weight, and, importantly, skin color. In fact, the X-ray is a kind of refusal of epidermalization. The skinning process of the X-ray makes it easy to forget that the bodies behind this music were held within skin that was not Russian and, for the most part, not white. Erasing the gendered racialization of the bodies memorialized in sound, these samizdat gramophone recordings could not portray the bodies conducting and performing the music. The X-ray record enables and perhaps even requires a disavowal of the racial recording on which it is based. Thus the playing of black jazz music on these discs in the Soviet Union calls attention to the artificial border between "us" and "them" in the multiple moments in which the edges literally blur through the seductive grooves of sound.[81]

While the jazz tours of American musicians were widely popular with Soviets, what these performances conveyed was rarely a simplistic notion of black oppositional consciousness. Remaking jazz to suit themselves, and often to distance themselves from the "negry," Soviet listeners could revel in style, technical innovation, as well as in the perpetuity of their state (not its undoing through cultural diplomacy). One historian has dubbed the radio program *Music USA* as "probably the most effective propaganda coup in [U.S.] history."[82] However, it would be wrong to believe that U.S. jazz begat the downfall of the Soviet empire. Nor should the cultural diplomacy typically associated with Western overtures towards the Soviet bloc be credited with the historical narrative of Soviet undoing. Rather, these overtures may have helped form the basis of a distinctively shaped Soviet public, fashioned through recycled culture and bootlegged versions of a future yet to come.

Jazz and its sibling insurgent—rock and roll—would eventually become facts of Soviet life. By the late 1950s, jazz was not only permitted in the Soviet Union, it also had found a vibrant and widespread audience. The mainstreaming of jazz and the admiration for American objects, however, were not synonymous with a championing of U.S. foreign policy or claims of democratic superiority. As a lived experience, Soviet communism did not sustain binary divisions between political systems, official and unofficial, nor public and private. As the *stilyagi* and the X-ray record teach us, when Western objects and ideas circulated in the Soviet world, they were taken up and remade in a guise that was uniquely Soviet—and perhaps unrecognizable to the spaces and places from which those objects hailed.[83]

Evidence of this kind of partial uptake is accommodated, in a different way, by the character of Boroff in *Silk Stockings*. Through the uneven juxtaposition of Soviet malcontents and African American cultural forms, the film suggests that we should not be too quick to pinpoint cross-racial identifications as moments for a celebratory dissident discourse of any kind. When *Porgy and Bess* debuted in Moscow in 1951, there was celebration to be sure; likewise when Paul Robeson made his triumphant return to perform there in 1958. While Russians may have grooved to the tunes of some African American performers in the 1950s, however, their large-scale embrace of racial difference was limited and prone to hypocrisy.[84] Denying U.S. claims of jazz as a "distinctly American art form," Soviets felt that jazz was equally their own, a form of music that had percolated in the folk music of the Caucasus, been performed publicly as early as the 1920s, and become embedded in the soul of Russian (dissident) culture.

Thinking through these permutations of Soviet jazz enables us to see Boroff as another version of the cultural emissary. Like the musicians who fronted the U.S. State Department–sponsored tours of American jazz,[85] Boroff could be considered a cultural ambassador of jazz. He returns to Russia adamant that he will not compromise his high musical standards for the pop-trash penned by Peggy. But he admits his romance with jazz, such that the cultural debate between "high" and "low" culture is mediated by jazz. Boroff becomes not only a convert to the popular, but also a proselytizer. In other words, his (Soviet) anti-elitism requires elitist foundations.

But what might Boroff's decision to commercialize his music say about American perceptions of Soviet weakness in terms of cultural production and exchange? From the perspective of cultural diplomacy, Soviet culture is assumed to be a weak front, easily penetrated and won over to the innovations and diversity of U.S. cultural forms. And yet in *Silk Stockings*, this penetration comes about through a black cultural form based in what historian Penny Von Eschen identifies as an oppositional consciousness. In her study of state-sponsored jazz tours during the Cold War, Von Eschen contends that, "If there is anything that can be learned from the tours, it is that audiences never confused or conflated their love of jazz and American popular culture with an acceptance of American foreign policy." Von Eschen argues that, beginning in the late 1950s and continuing until 1970, the use of African Americans as cultural ambassadors served not only to project images of U.S. racial harmony abroad (in spite of inequities at home), but also allowed these emissaries to use international stages to work "in the breaks" between official doctrine and their affective impact on the audience. She contends that jazz as cultural product was always about an oppositional consciousness and not about the superiority of U.S. democracy. It was with this minoritized oppositional consciousness that audiences abroad—particularly those in Africa, Asia, and Eastern Europe—identified.

Released during the same period when the jazz ambassadors were tooting their horns around the globe, *Silk Stockings* reiterates this interpretation of cultural diplomacy while satirizing it at the same time. If Boroff takes a liking to jazz because he senses in it an oppositional consciousness that gives him leave to abandon his classical routes (read Russia) and embrace the new world of mass entertainment (read America), in the end this consciousness is less oppositional than it is commercial. Boroff brings the consciousness of this music back to Russia, where it is transformed into a viable commercial opportunity in the big band number that the "Red Blues" becomes. Boroff is then emancipated from Russia to Paris, where he will use this cultural form to make a profit. In this sense, Boroff's trajectory suggests the success of State Department goodwill tours—the achievement of soft power—not the pull of an oppositional consciousness across the Iron Curtain. We cannot read jazz in *Silk Stockings* outside the political strategies meant to contain it, but rather must see and hear it as part of the commerce-driven culture that the film embodies and pillories at the same time. The film uses black cultural forms as shifters between high and low, classical music and mass entertainment, technically alleging that the "Red Blues" are about Boroff and Nina stuck back in Russia. But the "Red Blues" really are about the suppressed racial injustice at the center of the progressive American myth of emancipation and equality for all. With no African Americans present, it is as if the movie wants to claim the powers of oppositional consciousness for the oppressed peoples of the Soviet bloc while directly suppressing the presence of minority Americans.[86] Incorporating new-comers such as Boroff, Brankov, Bibinski, and Ivanov into the Western fold is accompanied by denying blacks full equality. The movie's ambiva-lence towards its alleged message returns in the film's final number, "The Ritz Roll and Rock."

Winking at Elvis

> The real target of Communist newspapers are the boys and girls who go for Western-style hot jazz.   —Marguerite Higgins[87]

> We should make dance serve some important dramatic purpose. So let us think of Astaire's and Charisse's dancing as one of the most vital and emotional factors in advancing the story. . . . The Dance here becomes the climactic factor which resolves the whole story.   —Rouben Mamoulian[88]

At first glance a viewer might mistake the final dance routine of *Silk Stockings* for a classic Astaire number: the top hat, the tux, the cane in hand. Astaire appears ready to sweep across the floor with Charisse at his side. But with the first pulse of the musical accompaniment, the viewer quickly realizes that something else is going on. This is an intentional misrecognition: "The Ritz Roll and Rock" is all about Elvis, and the fact that Steve Canfield (like Astaire) has been eclipsed by a genre that will outdo him. If you can't beat Elvis, join him, the title of the song seems to joke. The attempt to put the "Ritz" back into the wildly popular phenom-enon of rock and roll is a feeble one, however, and the routine ends up being more a parody of rock and roll than a desire to emulate it.[89]

Music historian Todd Decker points out that Astaire's performance makes particular sense considering that Elvis would shoot "Jailhouse Rock" on the same soundstage a few months later. Decker writes, "'The Ritz Roll and Rock' was an attempt to remain relevant, with the twelve bar blues being one element of popular music continuity Astaire could hang onto."[90] Elvis was clearly the inspiration for this number, which was added to the movie production at the last minute, along with a male chorus reminiscent of Busby Berkeley. Given Astaire's tight control over all of his dance scenes, however, it would be wrong to see this number as Hollywood hailing new forms.[91] As Decker's comment about the twelve-bar blues makes clear, this was just a new spin on an old form. Given Astaire's penchant to keep things the same—which is to say, not to be swayed by new cultural forms in spite of his character's claims to the contrary—why might he have agreed to this number in the first place?

"The Ritz Roll and Rock" not only debunks rock and roll, it also stakes a claim for getting back to the romanticism of the 1930s, the Fred and Ginger days. In this sense, the musical number reiterates its own paradox: pandering to the crowd to make a buck, while acknowledging its nostalgic preference for a bygone era before the technology to pander in such a robust manner was possible. This was also an era when the racial genealogies of American dance were less proximate, less pressing, and perhaps more easily denied.[92] Like Nina's transformation, Boroff's capitulation to Western ways establishes that, in *Silk Stockings*, freedom and modernity are linked only in their instantiation of new forms of discipline based on outdated and corrupt patterns. And these corrupt patterns are no more evident than in this final number. During the heyday of the studio era, strict codes against interracialism kept black actors and dancers off screen while white actors dominated. The limitations faced by African American actors during the studio era and into the 1950s are described fluidly by Jill Watts in her biography of Hattie McDaniel, the first African American woman to win an Oscar: "Black characters became props, manipulated by white filmmakers to signal specific messages regarding white social position and racial ideology."[93]

Astaire's relationship to dance and music is informed by racial ideology that kept black actors, musicians, and dancers largely absent.[94] And in "The Ritz Roll and Rock," he reiterates this distancing by trying to contain the energy of Elvis, by putting the class—or the *kul'turnyi*—back into the popular. Elvis's energy can be read as sexual, racial, subversive—certainly it was felt as all of the above. Instead of embracing these energies, however, Astaire splits the distance between new and old, and comes up short between them. One reviewer wrote: "Mr. Astaire, too, has a bright solo (with chorus) to a new song, 'The Ritz Roll and Rock,' which, while synthetic, is not as inconsistent as it sounds."[95] In his meditation on Astaire's indebtedness to black cultural forms, Stanley Cavell argues that

Astaire's use of black dance is far from bald appropriation but rather part of a "painful and potentially deadly irony of the white praise of a black culture whose very terms of praise it has appropriated." Cavell notes that, in fact, Astaire owes his deepest identity as a dancer "to the genius of black dancing."[96] In *Silk Stockings*, Astaire abandons Elvis (who was a racially citational figure in his own right), and returns to the comfort of the twelve-bar blues. This return is hardly a sign of praise, but rather one of pressing futility. At the end of the number, when Steve stomps on his top hat, we witness not only a crushing of the past, but also an odd squashing of Astaire's trademark, his on-screen masculinity. In fact, there has been an eerie disconnect between Nina and Steve throughout this Parisian romance. Their entire courtship feels forced. (Astaire was reportedly concerned about being too old to play the romantic lead opposite Charisse.) On screen, their twenty-two-year age difference translated into a visible tension, despite the aura of authentic feeling promoted by the film's technological innovations. In the finale, we witness improvisation with the appearance of spontaneity. Astaire's closing gesture is the decimation of an outdated masculinity—the shriveled top hat serves as a reminder of what he once was, or at least what his on-screen presence once was. *Silk Stockings* was Astaire's final filmusical; "The Ritz Roll and Rock" was his final Hollywood studio-era solo.

This parting homage to Astaire's career obscures the film's putative message, that innovation itself equals Americanism. As Steve says to Nina after his performance: "I couldn't get in, so I got you out." On the surface, American know-how and self-reliance have won the day, as Steve subverts the vast bureaucracy, stupidity, and buffoonery of the Soviets to rescue Nina. But the abundant scenes and citations of blackness weave a forgotten tale of the racially marked relationships between modernity and Cold War consensus—the logic of the Cold War kitchen. Through a summoning of black forms of music and dance in support of the film's central object of femininity, the film's anxiety about high versus low cultural forms becomes not just about the Hollywood musical, but about most U.S. movies of this era, as determined by the absence of the presence they formally rely upon, their generating discourses of movement and sound—as recalled in numbers like "Red Blues" and "The Ritz Roll and Rock." Moreover, the film's preoccupation with the idea of persuasion by culture, and with technology's role in soft-power success, showcases just how indebted to the forced absence of oppositional bodies this victory was.

With Paris painted as the new America, the film's Soviet characters become Russians of the old guard: capitalists of the worst sort—property owners of a cosmopolitan jazz bar.[97] For happy couples like Nina and Steve, the message is that we can celebrate the past as vanguard of the future. But what we actually witness is the hidden presence of African Americans in a romantic narrative of the triumphs of capitalism, a narrative in which the proper production of white femininity depends upon a visually absent black masculinity whose hybridized body is nonetheless conjured to produce the heroine (Nina) as properly Americanized. *Silk Stockings* wages black negation as a necessary corollary not only to white femininity, but also to the naturalization and Westernization of Eastern European emigrés. A similar pattern would be repeated in U.S. immigration during the 1960s, as white, Eastern Europeans took refuge in the West while Africans and racially marked others were pushed to the margins.[98] At the same time, *Silk Stockings* was an end point for nearly all involved, and as such can be read as signaling the end of an era. If Hollywood was preoccupied with fusing high culture and a popular medium during the postwar period, *Silk Stockings* reveals the utility of racial formations to the proposal, promise, and future of that fusion.

EPILOGUE: A KITCHEN IN HISTORY

JUDGING BY THE POPULARITY of mid-century aesthetics, design, and cultural references in the early twenty-first century, the Cold War will have staying power. From the U.S. penchant for *Mad Men* and *The Americans* to the return of the fedora and the bar-cart, Cold War proclivities are embraced today with an almost gleeful abandon. Beyond the fantasies of white supremacy, patriarchal privilege, and streamlined environments, what these tendencies reveal is that the mentalities of the Cold War remain with us. In various facets and fictions, the Cold War returns symptomatically, disclosing what remains to be resolved in the present.

During the 1950s and early 1960s, the United States depended upon the binary distinction between West and East in order to shore up a version of itself as exceptional. This dichotomy also served to disavow the violences rendered in the name of democratic freedom during this period, what Donald Pease identifies as the abandoning of the ideals of democracy in favor of the idea of those ideals. As Rey Chow has argued in the case of China, the dualism between communism and capitalism enabled a forgetting of the systematic oppressions built constitutionally into the creed of American freedom, and at the root of its democracy. The cultural artifacts of the Cold War kitchen reveal these tensions. *Glimpses of the USA* offered a multimedia environment that augured the power of choice to sway mass individualism in the age of the Internet. The General Electric kitchen provided a stage for the terms of affective conditioning that characterized ANEM's designs. Writers like Childress, Plath, and Hansberry deployed different ideas of communication—the fomenting of a collective consciousness triggered by a shared sense of oppression, what Lenin might have called radical agitation, to coincide with current material conditions.

As we have seen throughout this book, various articulations of the kitchen return us to the fictions of commodities as liberating and of universal womanhood, and the occlusions of minority voices and diverse ways of being. I would like to close the book with a photo of the kitchen that throws these assumptions even further off-kilter. The way of being in the world staged in Moscow was radically challenged in the years that followed 1959, so much so that by the early 1960s, an epistemological break in the logic of the kitchen begins to become apparent.

On November 23, 1963, *Life* photographer Allan Grant and correspondent Tommy Thompson arrived in Irving, Texas, at the home of Ruth Paine. They were looking for Marina Oswald, whose husband Lee Harvey Oswald was the prime suspect in the assassination of President John F. Kennedy. Arriving at the Paines' the morning after the assassination, Grant and Thompson found Ruth, Marina, and Marina's mother-in-law Marguerite going about their daily rituals. (The Oswalds had a toddler, June, and a one-month-old baby, Rachel.) Although the photo essay eventually published in *Life* featured pictures of Jackie Kennedy—with just one smaller photo of Marina and June, and another of Marguerite— Grant took several photographs of the women tending to their chores in Paine's kitchen. The photo pictured here (fig. E.1) offers a means of concluding *The Racial Imaginary of the Cold War Kitchen*.

Juxtaposed with the canonical image of Nixon and Khrushchev in the Moscow kitchen, this photo marks the splintering of an historical moment, and the unraveling of Nixon's rhetoric. The Cold War frame of dichotomous thinking can no longer hold the kitchen in the same way. With young June at what Roland Barthes would call the picture's punctum—that aspect of the photo that holds our attention—and the three women arranged around her in a triangle, the photo offers a revealing moment: women at work, plowing through their daily drudgery.[1] Here we see the underside of history, a Russian and two Americans—all mothers—stitching together the quotidian threads of life in a small Texas town. Even when presidents are shot, there are still meals to be made and diapers to be changed. Of course this was not just any day, and these were not just any women. But the rupture here is less about historical events than it is about the framing of them. This kitchen scene, like the events it is trying to grasp, is in disarray.

In several obvious ways, the photo breaks with an idealized image of kitchen life and the housewife this kitchen was supposed to support.

FIGURE E.1. Marguerite Oswald, Ruth Paine, June Oswald, and Marina Oswald in Mrs. Paine's kitchen. Photo by Allan Grant for *Life* magazine, November 23, 1963. Courtesy of Allan Grant Productions

In place of gleaming surfaces and a well-coiffed, apron-clad woman in heels, it reveals working-class womanhood. Paine's kitchen is no miracle kitchen. There's a six-pack of Tab on the counter, a sweater hung to dry over the door of an open cupboard, a newspaper with the day's headline partially obscured. Things are out of place and disordered, not because of historical events, but because this is maternal temporality, its day-to-day mode. The room is marked by a clutter of appliances that may be labor-saving, but also are inconvenient and in the way. Out of focus, but poised at the front of the image, is an iron—hot or not, it appears ready for someone to use it. This photo disrupts the smooth functioning of the ideas espoused at ANEM, an event that marked the politically opportune promotion of private spaces for public consumption. The apparatuses of work and its messiness are thrown into the foreground by Grant's photo. This is an extension of the emphasized publicness of a woman's work-space in Nixon's kitchen, an extension that also emphasizes the changing terms of political culture and its emphasis on the public consumption of private individuals through rhetorics of verbal and visual intimacy. To be sure, photojournalism emerged in the mid-century as a tool not only of public figures who sought to control their image, but also as a medium through which private individuals could achieve (or be subjected to) publicity. Marguerite Oswald would fall into both of these categories.

This photo is especially interesting considering the notoriety that followed Marina and Marguerite. Marguerite, in particular, was derided by the public and an irritant to the Warren Commission.[2] Such scorn was captured with critical aplomb by Jean Stafford in her profile of Marguerite, which was commissioned by *McCall's* and later published as *A Mother in History*. That book provides a record of the three days Stafford spent with Marguerite Oswald at her home outside Houston in May 1965.[3]

The title of Stafford's book flags as eccentric Oswald's deviance from expected norms of motherhood: namely maternal selflessness and keeping quiet about public affairs. Her belief that she has something to say about history immediately marks Oswald as "off." Thus, while *A Mother in History* calls attention to the relationship between mother and son, it also names a relationship between mother and author. If Stafford disapproved of Oswald (which she certainly did), she disapproved even more strongly of her version of motherhood. At odds with all expectations, Marguerite proclaimed an eccentric working-class motherhood, repositioning it at the center of national discussions of the maternal. Recalling the vernacular intellectualism of Mildred in *Like One of the Family*, and the positioning of black women as the vanguard of black radicalism, Marguerite's elocutions summoned the inanities—and the traumas—of women's Cold War containment. With statements like "I would say that the Oswald family was actually an average American family," and "I'm a mother in history I'm all over the world," Marguerite proclaimed an itinerant motherhood that shattered the fictions of the U.S. housewife.[4] Her scandalous declarations had a splintering effect, so much so that Jean Stafford had to take refuge in a migraine.

But in linking herself to history and its mechanisms of record in this determined way, Marguerite Oswald indicated the faltering sweep of dichotomous thinking and Cold War containment. Her penchant for notoriety—for going public—both brought together and rendered asunder the Cold War links among patriotism, internationalism, and motherhood. Proclaiming her voice as an essential component of the public conversation about "the American way of life," Marguerite establishes herself as the other mother. In so doing, she unwittingly takes up the space of the racialized other foreclosed in the Moscow kitchen, reminding Stafford's readers of their own, intimate relationships with the working class.[5] In this way, Marguerite recalls not only Mildred, but also the ghostess in the Kitchen Aid advertisement. The haunting trace of labor in the latter is aggressively foregrounded in Marguerite's performance of herself as representatively maligned mother: "Now let's have some defense of Lee Harvey Oswald and his mother!"

Perhaps more than any other public figure, Marguerite Oswald calls up the breach in Cold War protocols of behavior and ways of being. Whereas the Eameses sought to use ANEM to render a message of democratic choice, to move people into the future by way of technological flow, Oswald's bristling non-sequiturs point to irresolvable tensions and discontinuities within those smooth systems of communication. As a ghostess of the kitchen, she summons the energies of those who labor without attribution and calls for some recognition: "I need money to carry on the campaign against the campaign against me, and as a mother, I think I deserve it!"[6] Egotistical and self-congratulatory, she is also now largely forgotten, hovering at history's margins, and outside the carefully measured operation of the public's image of respectable maternity.

The image of this kind of deviant motherhood is reinforced by the photo of Marguerite that was published in *Life*.[7] Marguerite was incensed that this photo had caught her with her stockings rolled down below her knees. This presentation of motherhood appeared worn and drab. Wearing her nurse's uniform, Marguerite looked like a caretaker, in charge of the affective labors of the household. In this role of the domestic, the photo frames her as pitiful, an outcast, hardly a match for the carefully controlled and sublimely maternal Jackie Kennedy, who appeared on the next page.[8] The published image of Marina Oswald, on the other hand, with the baby on her lap, manages to capture some of motherhood's heroism. Marina is pitiable, not pitiful, like Marguerite.

Unlike the photos that appeared in *Life*, Grant's photo of three women and two children play across the thresholds of the kitchen's domestic, international, and maternal aspects and their mid-century publicity. This photo indicates that the myths in which women have been housed since the 1950s have lost their grip. The Paines were in the midst of a divorce, Marina had been beaten by her husband, and Marguerite was a divorcée and a working mother who had blithely placed her boys in foster care. Through an inversion of public and private space, the photo quite pointedly reveals the insufficiency of prior fictions of Cold War womanhood—international and domestic—at the site of the kitchen.

If we can apprehend the dwindling appeal of mid-century kitchen fictions, then why are we surrounded by a continued desire for their seeming simplicity? The push-button kitchen of ANEM has become the smart house of today.[9] Texts like *The Bell Jar, Like One of the Family, A Week Like Any Other, A Raisin in the Sun,* and *Silk Stockings* warn us away from, as Esther Greenwood might put it, "pretending not to notice" the histories lodged within physical spaces. These texts advise us to return to the kitchen, as a site where disavowals continue to take root. A kitchen is more than just the room where all converge at a party, it is a creation deeply embedded within material and physical histories. The kitchen is likewise the space in which global polarities, racial hegemonies, and the sexual division of labor must be confronted. The more we try to ignore them, the more these histories and their contrary energies will demand to engage us.

ACKNOWLEDGMENTS

Many debts are owed to the people who made this book possible. Most of the writing was done on borrowed time, carved out of nap times, early mornings, and during "play dates" which, in the course of the book's formation, have grown into "hang outs." Other parts were conceived on trails, when the solitude necessary to think was indebted to caregivers, whose sister-wife dedication came to define the phrase "affective labor": Aga Lechocinska, Elisangela Santett, Claudine McGregor, Dana DeAno, Kate Wrobel, Becky Kremin, Kim Barbaro, and Amanda Bryant. Before this was a book it was a seed of an idea born of a community of now dispersed colleagues: Kathy Psomiades, Ewa Ziarek, Krzys Ziarek, Graham Hammill, Glenn Hendler, Jim Collins, and Valerie Sayers.

At Northwestern I have been lucky to have the support of two schools, the School of Communication and Weinberg College. I am grateful to the former dean of Weinberg, Sarah Mangelsdorf, and the Office of the Provost, Dan Linzer, for providing funding for research and writing time; and to the dean of the School of Communication, Barbara O'Keefe, for supporting me in Rhetoric and Public Culture, where I am surrounded by a stimulating intellectual environment with Dilip Gaonkar, Robert Hariman, Jan Radway, Angela Ray, David Zarefsky, Jasmine Cobb, C. Riley Snorton, Ellen Wartella, Eszter Hargittai, James Schwoch, Darren Gergle, Pablo Boczkowski, Kathleen Galvin, Irving Rein, and Liz Gerber. In addition to these colleagues other sounding boards and friends at Northwestern have helped to bring the book into being: critical thanks for the wisdom and humor of Susan Manning, Ramon Rivera-Servera, E. Patrick Johnson, Shalini Shankar, Hamid Naficy, Deborah Tolchinsky, Miriam Petty, Martha Biondi, Mary Finn, Reg Gibbons, Laurie Shannon, Harris Feinsod, Rebecca Johnson, Carl Smith, Betsy Erkkila, Julia Stern, Jay Grossman, Andrew Wachtel, and Susan McReynolds. At Northwestern I have also had the good fortune to work with an outstanding group of students in seminars, independent studies, workshops, qualifying exams, dissertations, and senior theses. Many of these students were majors in the Program in American Studies, a program I had the honor of directing over most of the years this book was written. The imprint of our discussions and debates is reflected here. These pages also have benefitted from the graduate student talents of Jill Bugajski, Lauren DeLaCruz, Dave Molina, Leigh Meredith, Elisabeth Ross, Tommy Rousse, and Patrick Wade. Their exceptional minds have made this a better book. I continue to benefit from the inspiration and rich scholarly examples of Hazel Carby, Lisa Lowe, Bill Maxwell, Katerina Clark, Donald Pease, Brent Edwards, and Jonathan Flatley, who have all helped this book to be a better version of itself.

More proximate audiences also have been key interlocutors. Portions were presented at workshops and seminars, most notably at the Stanford Humanities Center, Harvard's Davis Center for Russian and Eurasian Studies, the Literature Department at UCSD, Slavic and Comparative Literature at UC Berkeley, the Newberry Library, Dartmouth's Summer Institute on American Studies, the Department of Comparative Literature at UCLA, and Northwestern's American Cultures Colloquium. Earlier versions of some parts of the manuscript have appeared in print elsewhere. A portion of chapter 2 was published as "The Radical Imaginary of *The Bell Jar*," *Novel* 38.1 (fall 2004): 21–40. A version of chapter 3 appeared as "Alice Childress, Natalia Baranskaya, and the Speakin' Place of Cold War Womanhood," in *Globalizing American Studies,* co-edited by Brian T. Edwards and Dilip Parameshwar Gaonkar (Chicago: University of Chicago Press, 2011), 135–52. Two paragraphs of the epilogue appeared in "Between Mother and History: Jean Stafford, Marguerite Oswald, and U.S. Cold War Women's Citizenship," *differences* 13.3 (2003): 83–120. I am grateful to these publications for allowing me to incorporate the work here, but mostly to their engaged editors, whose feedback helped me to hone my thinking about the Cold War kitchen and its others: Nancy Armstrong, Elizabeth Weed, Brian Edwards, and Dilip Goankar.

Archivists at the National Archives in College Park and in the Library of Congress, notably Barbara Natanson in the Prints and Photographs Division, encouraged me to keep digging; and Tania Sochurek shared with me her personal files of her time as a guide at the American National Exhibition. Likewise, Anne Sullivan, who is pictured next to Khrushchev in the iconic photo in this book's preface, let me pick her brain about that Moscow July of 1959.

Especial thanks to Dartmouth College Press, especially for the encouragement of Richard Pult and the exemplary copyediting of Peter Fong; to

Donald Pease, the series editor, a steadfast supporter of my work; and to Alan Nadel, whose generous reading of an early draft pushed me to think more deeply about the book.

Throughout the process, the wizardry of my departments' administrative supporters—Natasha Dennison, Shatoria Lunsford, and Sharron Shepard—has kept me smiling. And my late-arriving research assistants, Alissa Shapiro and Adri Kascor, helped me through key stages of inquiry.

Family members made writing possible in distinctive ways. My sisters, Pamela and Elizabeth, have woven distance into expansive quilts of connection. My parents, Joseph L. Baldwin and Mary Burt Blume, who may be disappointed that I gave up tennis to learn Russian, continue to be steadfast fans.

Mostly, I am grateful to Ollie, Pia, Theo, and Charlotte, who make life's meaning meaningful, and endow each day with new ways of asking, "why?" Finally, this book owes much to many people, but none more so than to Brian Edwards, to whom this book is dedicated, with love, admiration, and respect, along with our four BES.

NOTES

Preface

1. Joseph Stalin would later claim "A nation is a historically evolved, stable community of language, territory, economic life, and psychological make-up manifested in a community of culture." *Marxism and the National Question: Selected Writings and Speeches* (New York: International Publishers, 1942), 12.

2. Kate A. Baldwin, *Beyond the Color Line and the Iron Curtain: Reading Encounters between Black and Red, 1922–1963* (Durham, NC: Duke University Press, 2002).

3. William B. Davis, "How Negroes Live in Russia," *Ebony*, January 1, 1960, 65.

4. Davis names Garnett in "How Negroes Live in Russia," 66. Walter Hixson names Herb Miller in *Parting the Curtain: Propaganda, Culture, and the Cold War, 1945–61* (New York: Palgrave Macmillan, 1997), 196.

5. In fact, W.E.B. Du Bois had been in Moscow just the previous winter to discuss Khrushchev's support for the creation of an African studies institute. In 1959, Du Bois was awarded the Lenin Peace Prize, which Paul Robeson had received in 1953, along with Howard Fast.

6. According to Joy Carew, State Department notes reveal that Eisenhower was especially perplexed over the choice of African Americans as guides, as the specifications included Russian fluency—an attribute not typically associated with blacks in the 1950s—as well as "well educated and of good appearance." The notes state: "The president's desire to meet with the guides [in person] stemmed in no small part 'because he was curious as to why four Negroes should have studied Russian well enough to act as interpreters.' . . . 'I would just like to ask a question first of the four Negroes here. How did you happen to get interested in Russian?'" See Joy Carew, *Blacks, Reds, and Russians: Sojourners in Search of the Soviet Promise* (New Brunswick: Rutgers University Press), 190.

7. Davis, "How Negroes Live in Russia," 69, 71.

8. Ibid., 73, 68.

9. See Cedric Robinson, Penny Von Eschen, Brenda Gayle Plummer, Nikil Pal Singh, Mary Helen Washington, Brent Hayes Edwards, Robin D. G. Kelly, and William Maxwell, among others.

10. Hixson, *Parting the Curtain*, 172.

11. See Hixson, *Parting the Curtain*, 172; and Carew, *Blacks, Reds and Russians*, 190.

12. This report can be found in the Nixon archives; John R. Thomas, "Report on

Service with the American Exhibition in Moscow," Rand Corporation, P-1859, March 15, 1960.

13. This recalls the parallel interest of Langton Hughes in Soviet Central Asia in the early 1930s, and his comparisons between the U.S. South and the Soviet south in his Soviet-published pamphlet, *A Negro Looks at Soviet Central Asia*, which I discuss in chapter 2 of *Beyond the Color Line and the Iron Curtain*.

14. "The development of cultures national in form and socialist in content is necessary for the purpose of their ultimate fusion into one General culture, socialist as to form and content, and expressed in one general language." I. V. Stalin, *Marxism and the National Question* [1934] (New York: International Publishers, 1942), 34. There is a vast body of scholarship on the national question in the Soviet Union, including Richard Pipes, *The Formation of the Soviet Union: Communism and Nationalism* (Cambridge: Harvard University Press, 1997); Ronald Grigor Suny, *The Revenge of the Past: Nationalism, Revolution, and the Collapse of the Soviet Union* (Stanford: Stanford University Press, 1993); Yuri Slezkine, "The USSR as Communal Apartment, or How a Socialist State Promoted Ethnic Particularism," *Slavic Review* 53.2 (1994): 414–52; and Francine Hirsch, *Empire of Nations: Ethnographic Knowledge and the Making of the Soviet Union* (Ithaca: Cornell University Press, 2005).

Introduction: Cold War Hot Kitchen

1. Michel de Certeau, "Plat du Jour," in M. de Certeau, L. Giard, and P. Mayol, *The Practice of Everyday Life, Volume II: Living and Cooking* (Minneapolis: University of Minnesota Press, 1998), 171.

2. McClellan was also the former president of the National Association of Manufacturers.

3. Charles and Ray Eames developed their plywood chair, or Lounge Chair Wood (LCW), as it was popularly known, in the mid-1940s in an effort to create a streamlined, single-shell chair that could be easily reproduced. Although the chair ultimately was built from two main pieces—seat and backrest—its form still boasted a simplicity and transparency in its parts. It was the LCW that first caught the eye of George Nelson, who was then design director for the furniture company Herman Miller. Nelson urged his company to hire the Eames Office as design consultants and in 1946 Herman Miller began to produce the Eameses' full range of plywood furniture, a collaboration that continues today.

4. Together these attractions made up what the design team dubbed the "information machine," a name that came to be synonymous with the dome. For an excellent discussion of RAMAC in Moscow, see James Schwoch, *Global TV: New Media and the Cold War, 1946–69* (Urbana: University of Illinois Press, 2009). I am very grateful to Jim for sharing with me some of his research on ANEM.

5. An extended report on the site planning for ANEM is offered by Robert Zion in his article, "Russian Rigor: Site-Planning the Moscow Exhibition," *Landscape Architecture* 50.3 (spring 1960): 164–69; 197–98. For an analysis of the art exhibit in the context of cultural diplomacy, see Marilyn Kushner, "Exhibiting Art at the American National Exhibition in Moscow, 1959," *Journal of Cold War Studies* 4.1 (winter 2002): 6–26. For an illuminating discussion of "The Family of Man," and the political

and cultural contexts in which it emerged, see Eric J. Sandeen, *Picturing an Exhibition: "The Family of Man" and 1950s America* (Albuquerque: University of New Mexico Press, 1995). Fred Turner offers a recent reappraisal of the show as heterogeneously appealing to its audience in "*The Family of Man* and the Politics of Attention in Cold War America," *Public Culture* 24.1 (2012): 55–84; and *The Democratic Surround: Multimedia and American Liberalism from World War II to the Psychedelic Sixties* (Chicago: University of Chicago Press, 2013), discussed below.

6. While all U.S. reports bear interest, see "Ivan Takes a Look at American Life: Photo Report from Moscow," *US News and World Report*, August 10, 1959, 40–50. For a detailed description of the event from a contemporary perspective, see Walter L. Hixson, *Parting the Curtain: Propaganda, Culture and the Cold War, 1945–1961* (New York: St. Martin's, 1996). Because the exhibition was the first "weapon" launched into enemy territory, care was taken to promote its success at home. As the Soviet press wryly noted, dozens of U.S. journalists were sent along to cover Nixon's visit; *Literaturnaia Gazeta*, 28 July 1959, 2. *Time, Life, Newsweek, US News and World Report*, and the *New York Times* all carried multiple articles and photo essays documenting ANEM's success.

7. Following historian Kenneth Osgood, scholars Ned O'Gorman and Kevin Hamilton describe "Atoms for Peace" as "'the largest and most concerted propaganda campaign' of the early Cold War, which entailed a deliberate long-term effort on behalf of the US government to ease fears about the destructive power of atomic science and persuade publics that, as Eisenhower told the UN on December 8, 1953, atomic weapons might be 'put into the hands of those who will know how to strip its military casing and adapt it to the arts of peace.'" See "At the Interface: The Loaded Rhetorical Gestures of Nuclear Legitimacy and Illegitimacy," *Communication and Critical/Cultural Studies* 8.1 (March 2011): 41–66.

8. Sandeen, *Picturing an Exhibition*, 128.

9. "Better to See Once," *Time*, August 3, 1959, 16.

10. As Donald Pease notes, "During the Cold War, the discourse of American exceptionalism had legitimated America's dominance within a dichotomized world order by supplying the rationale for America's moral superiority to Russian communism. Throughout the Cold War, US dominance was sustained through the US's representation of itself as an exception to the rules through which it regulated the rest of the global order." (Donald Pease, "Re-thinking 'American Studies after US Exceptionalism,'" *American Literary History* 21.1 (2009): 19–27; first published online September 29, 2008, doi:10.1093/alh/ajno55.

11. See Brian Edwards, "Pre-posterous Encounters: Interrupting American Studies with the (Post)Colonial, or Casablanca in the American Century," *Comparative Studies of South Asia, Africa and the Middle East* 23.1–2 (2003): 70–86.

12. Brian Edwards and Dilip Goankar, eds., *Globalizing American Studies* (Chicago: University of Chicago Press, 2010), 23.

13. See "Humanity's Critical Path, from Weaponry to Livingry," in Buckminster Fuller, *Critical Path* (New York: St. Martin's, 1983).

14. As Karal Marling notes, "The latest in kitchen consumerism stood for the basic tenets of the American way of life. Freedom. Freedom from drudgery for the house-

wife. And democracy, the opportunity to choose the very best model from the limitless assortment of colors, features and prices the free market had to offer." Marling, *As Seen On TV: The Visual Culture of Everyday Life in the 1950s* (Cambridge: Harvard University Press, 1994), 243.

15. "The Two Worlds: A Day-Long Debate," *New York Times*, July 25, 1959, 1.

16. The Russian term for "housewife" is *khoziajka*, but it is a term that signals more "host" than housewife. A seldom-used word, *domokhoziajka*, more closely approximates the American housewife, but is in fact just an iteration of "home" (*domo*) before "host."

17. As Ruth Oldenziel and Karin Zachmann point out in their collection, *Cold War Kitchen*, there was one woman at the kitchen exhibition. The American guide Lois Epstein demonstrated to visitors how a typical U.S. housewife might make use of the kitchen (2). *Cold War Kitchen: Americanization, Technology, and European Users* (Cambridge: MIT Press, 2009).

18. "Better to See Once," *Time*, August 3, 1959, 15.

19. Every U.S. president from Eisenhower through Obama has subsequently declared the third week in July as "Captive Nations Week."

20. Indeed since John Steinbeck toured a war-ravaged Russia in 1947 with the photographer Robert Capa in search of what he termed the "great other side of politics— There must, he wrote, be a private life of the Russian people" the sense that a capitalist attitude towards women was universal provided an enduring model. Steinbeck's search detailed an inability of postwar America to fathom Russia without invoking femininity as a battleground. Like other texts by equally left-leaning authors such as Marguerite Higgins, Margaret Bourke White and Ella Winter, Steinbeck's *Russian Journal* is actively engaged in teaching a new postwar Americanness in which "the Russian woman" is used to help determine a binary relationship between the U.S. and the U.S.S.R. The fascination with Soviet femininity became especially fashionable in the late 1950s, when numerous articles in the *New York Times*, *Life*, and *Newsweek*, and elsewhere showcased the dreary attempts of Russians to be real, which is to say consumer-oriented, women. I take up this fascination in more detail in my discussion of envy in Chapter one. See John Steinbeck, *A Russian Journal*, with photos by Robert Capa (New York: Viking Press, 1948).

21. Max Frankel, "Premier Taunts American Visitor," *New York Times*, July 24, 1959, 1.

22. USIA Office of Research and Analysis, RG 306, Records Relating to the American National Exhibition, Moscow, 1957–59, box 11, National Archives and Records Administration (NARA). Also cited in Susan Reid, "'Our Kitchen is Just as Good'": Soviet Responses to the American National Exhibition in Moscow, 1959," in Oldenziel and Zachmann's collection, *Cold War Kitchen*, 103.

23. Kaplan explains, "If domesticity plays a key role in imagining the nation as home, then women, positioned at the center of the home, play a major role in defining the contours of the nation and its shifting borders with the foreign." Amy Kaplan, "Manifest Domesticity," *American Literature* 70.3 (1998): 582.

24. Trudier Harris, *From Mammies to Militants: Domestics in Black American Literature* (Philadelphia: Temple University Press, 1982).

25. Although his theories about information flow were influential on the ANEM design team, Norbert Wiener's opinions about American exceptionalism were surprisingly overlooked. In his widely read *The Human Use of Human Beings* (New York: Doubleday, 1954), Wiener notes that "Most of us in the United States prefer to live in a moderately loose social community in which the blocks to communication among individuals and classes are not too great. I will not say that this ideal of communication is attained in the United States. *Until white supremacy ceases to belong to the creed of a large part of the country it will be an ideal from which we fall short*" (50, emphasis added). Wiener is similarly critical of some of the foundational myths of Americanism, for example, that of the frontier ("to the average American, progress means the winning of the West"), manifest destiny, and slavery ("the existence of new lands encouraged an attitude not unlike that of Alice's Mad Tea Party. When the tea and cakes were exhausted at one seat, the natural thing for the Mad Hatter and the March Hare was to move on and occupy the next seat" (46). At the same time his thoughts about the forced removal of native peoples are less forthcoming. He does not name the racial genocide that took place with westward expansion, noting instead that "the development of the United States took place against the background of the empty land that always lay further to the West" (43).

26. Some of the most influential readings of the kitchen debate can be found in Elaine Tyler May's study of women's culture during the early Cold War period, *Homeward Bound: American Families in the Cold War Era* (New York: Basic, 1991); Walter Hixson's *Parting the Curtain: Propaganda, Culture and The Cold War* (New York: Palgrave, 1997); Karal Marling's *As Seen on TV: The Visual Culture of Everyday Life in the 1950s* (Cambridge: Harvard University Press, 1996); Beatriz Colomina's *Domesticity at War* (Cambridge: MIT Press, 2007); Victoria De Grazia's *Irresistible Empire: America's Advance through Twentieth-Century Europe* (New York: Belknap Press, 2006; Greg Castillo's *Cold War on the Home Front: The Soft Power of Midcentury Design* (Minneapolis: University of Minnesota Press, 2010); *Cold War Hothouses: Inventing Postwar Culture, from Cockpit to Playboy*, edited by Beatriz Colomina, Ann Marie Brennan, and Jeannie Kim (Princeton: Princeton Architectural Press, 2004); and Susan Reid's pioneering archival work in her several articles on Soviet domesticity, including "Our Kitchen Is Just as Good," in Oldenziel and Zachmann's collection, *Cold War Kitchen*, 83–112.

27. Oldenziel and Zachmann, eds., *Cold War Kitchen*, 1.

28. Nelson, *Problems of Design* (Whitney, 1957), 6.

29. Numerous texts have been instrumental to my thinking here, including Paul Edwards, *The Closed World: Computers and the Politics of Discourse in Cold War America* (Cambridge: MIT Press, 1996), Jennifer Light, *From Warfare to Welfare: Defense Intellectuals and Urban Problems in Cold War America* (Baltimore: Johns Hopkins University Press, 2003; 2005) and James Schwoch, *Global TV: New Media and the Cold War, 1946–69* (Urbana: University of Illinois Press, 2009).

30. See, for example, their short film, *Powers of Ten*.

31. These products then became exchangeable units, which ideally would allow a consumer's resulting exploitation to be eventually motivated from within.

32. Donald Pease, *The New American Exceptionalism* (Minneapolis: University of Minnesota Press, 2010).

33. "Report on American Exhibition in Moscow," USIA Office of Research and Analysis Report P-47–59, 28 September 1959, RG 306, Records Relating to the American National Exhibition, Moscow, 1957–59, box 7, NARA, p. 15.

34. Max Frankel, "American Exhibition Put Ideas of U.S. Across, Analyst Finds," *The New York Times*, September 5, 1959, 3.

35. This pattern diverged from the theory of information flow that influenced Nelson and the Eameses in their exhibition design: Claude Shannon and Warren Weaver's *The Mathematical Theory of Communication* (Urbana: University of Illinois Press, 1949), which established the idea of measuring information processing between sender and recipient through speed and noise. Thematized by the Eameses in *Glimpses* as compression, this theory of communication is not in evidence in the USIA's declaration of success as calculated in communication units.

36. According to the USIA report on ANEM: "there was exaggeration in the *Time* article saying the Exhibit had 'wowed' Moscow. It didn't. There was exaggeration in the *Herald Tribune* editorial describing the Exhibit as a 'smash hit.' It wasn't." The report continues: "Slightly more than half of the overheard comments were negative." "Report on American Exhibition in Moscow," USIA Office of Research and Analysis Report P-47–59, 28 September 1959, pp. 1, 3.

37. Like many large-scale Soviet exhibitions, ANEM had guest books—open, blank books in which visitors were asked to record their impressions. Housed in the National Archive in Washington, D.C., these books are not reliable sources of what people actually thought. Some visitors with a favorable opinion might have felt more inclined to write, while others might have felt pressured to write critically of the exhibit, or to withhold their opinions entirely.

38. The guest books must be considered in the context of a highly chaperoned and controlled exhibition experience, in which Soviet visitors were led through the displays by Russian-speaking U.S. guides. For a vivid portrait of how Soviets were escorted through the exhibit, see *The Official Training Book for Guides at the American National Exhibition in Moscow, 1959*, prepared by Dorothy E. Tuttle (Washington, D.C.: USIA, 1959). For an extended discussion of how to read the guest books as historical documents, see Susan Reid, "Who Will Beat Whom? Soviet Popular Reception of the American National Exhibition in Moscow, 1959," *Kritika: Explorations in Russian and Eurasian History* 9.4 (fall 2008): 855–904.

39. Turner writes: "In theory they would integrate the variety of what they saw and heard into their own, individuated experiences. This integration would rehearse the political process of knitting oneself into a diverse and highly individuated society. Ideally visitors would see themselves not simply as part of a national mass, but as individual human beings among others, united as Americans across their many differences." *The Democratic Surround: Multimedia and American Liberalism from World War II to the Psychedelic Sixties* (Chicago: University of Chicago Press, 2013), 5.

40. Turner, *The Democratic Surround*, 6.

41. Ibid., 8.

42. Like Khrushchev, many Soviets remained dubious about the superiority of U.S

products. Commented one visitor to ANEM, "And this is one of the greatest nations? I feel sorry for the Americans. . . . Does your life really consist of only kitchens?" "Report on American Exhibition in Moscow," 27.

43. This critical move recalls the argument of Dilip Gaonkar and Beth Povinelli in *Public Culture*, in which they call for a move away from the virtuoso close reading long characteristic of cultural studies, toward a more vigilant attention to the forms through which cultural textuality comes into being. "Technologies of Public Forms: Circulation, Transfiguration, Recognition," *Public Culture* 15.3 (2003): 385–398.

44. Vaughn Rasberry, "'Now Describing You': James Baldwin and Cold War Liberalism," in Cora Kaplan and Bill Schwarz, eds., *James Baldwin: American and Beyond* (Ann Arbor: University of Michigan Press, 2011), 84–105.

Chapter 1: Envy and Other Warm Guns

1. The seventy-five American guides at ANEM received the following instructions in their *Official Training Book*: "At regular intervals, the lights of the Dome will dim. At that time, direct your attention to the ceiling where seven 20x30 foot screens are suspended over the truss structure. Projected on them will be sound motion pictures showing various aspects of American life and culture. Commentary will explain the scenes as they are flashed in sequence or, sometimes for special impact, all at once" (19). But even Dorothy Tuttle, the woman who prepared this training book, had not seen the film before ANEM opened.

2. Owen Gingerich, "A Conversation with Charles Eames," *American Scholar* 46.3 (summer 1977): 333.

3. As reported in the *New York Times*, "Vice President Nixon will be the highest ranking official to visit the Soviet Union since President Franklin D. Roosevelt attended the Yalta conference with Stalin and Churchill early in 1945." Max Frankel, "Soviet 'Contest' Awaiting Nixon," *New York Times*, July 27, 1959, 6.

4. As noted in the *Official Training Book*, "The first official United States exhibition to be held in the Soviet Union, it means combining the best talents and displays of American Government and private industry and organizations to place before the Russian people a realistic 'image of America,' [with] all efforts geared to the following objective: 'to increase understanding by the people of the Soviet Union of the American people, the land in which Americans live, and the broad range of American life, including American progress in the fields of science, technology, and culture'" (9).

5. Turner, "*The Family of Man* and the Politics of Attention in Cold War America," *Public Culture* 24.1: 256.

6. Iconography used to depict Nazis during the war was often used, without variation, to depict Soviets in the postwar period. See Jill Bugajski, "Totalitarian Aesthetics and the Democratic Imagination in the United States 1937–47," Ph.D. diss., Northwestern University, 2014.

7. George Nelson, "Designer's Comments and Extracts from a 'Log' on the American National Exhibition," *Industrial Design* 6.4 (April 1959): 47.

8. Wiener, *The Human Use of Human Beings*, 131–36. See also Fred Turner's summary in *The Democratic Surround*, 254–56.

9. Robert Zion, "Russian Rigor: Site-Planning the Moscow Exhibition," *Landscape Architecture* 50.3 (spring 1960): 164–69; 197–98. Zion reports surprise at the Soviets' differently conditioned mode of subjectivity, particularly in their relationship to nature and ecological well-being. In his essay about site-planning for the exhibition, he notes with admiration the way Russians treated their trees. "Large birch trees were transplanted in full leaf in mid-July, which is considered very bad horticulture practice; the fact that there were no losses is attributable to the great regard which Russians have for trees. This was reflected in their techniques of planting, as well as in their almost loving post-planting care. . . . So great is the Russian love of trees that we were not allowed to destroy any tree; any tree in the way of the exhibit had to be transplanted" (167). And again, "The Russian respect for trees, although a constant irritant to us, was nevertheless most impressive. Even the smallest sapling was considered worth saving. [Their method] is much too costly for general use by us capitalists. . . . Actually the least typical aspect of the [single tract] house was that the imaginary Long Island builder had spared any trees at all!" (197–98). "[E]ven at considerable risk of being labeled 'pink' or 'punk,'" Zion insists on noting this attitude and its manifestations in "a million small but observable ways" (198).

10. The concept of possessiveness as a mode of being is linked irrefutably to processes of racialization by George Lipsitz in his groundbreaking book, *The Possessive Investment in Whiteness* (Philadelphia: Temple University Press, 1998).

11. Nelson, "Designer's Comments and Extracts from a 'Log' on the American National Exhibition," 51. Charles Eames was in the process of developing a theory of design as communication such that information became more of a product than the material object. This idea hearkened back to Shannon and Weaver's *The Mathematical Theory of Communication*. In his later account of the exhibit, Jack Masey recalled that, "The Eameses' seven-screen film used the most cutting edged media techniques of the mid-twentieth century. . . . [It] presaged a transformation from design as being product-related to design as information-based. This shift of emphasis anticipated the wider economic shifts of what was later to be called the 'information revolution' in which services began to replace manufacturing as the base economic model, and the potential of information systems to define and create markets began to be explored." Jack Masey and Conway Lloyd Morgan, *Cold War Confrontations: US Exhibitions and Their Role in the Cultural Cold War* (Zurich: Lars Muller Publishers, 2008), 167.

12. Nelson, "Designer's Comments and Extracts from a 'Log' on the American National Exhibition," 48.

13. Frankel, "Soviet 'Contest' Awaiting Nixon," 6.

14. "Exhibit Opens in Moscow," *The Wall Street Journal*, July 26, 1959, 2.

15. Eames Collection, Library of Congress; Nelson, "Designer's Comments and Extracts from a 'Log' on the American National Exhibition," 53.

16. Masey and Morgan, *Cold War Confrontations*, 166.

17. Max Frankel, "Image of America at Issue in Soviet," *New York Times*, August 22, 1959, 8. Frankel erroneously identified the composer: it was Elmer Bernstein (see note 47 below). Later, the same article noted that the film, "offers thousands of glimpses of everyday American life at an amazingly rapid pace. Geared to a sin-

gle soundtrack are seven films that simultaneously illustrate a single point on seven screens."

18. Tuttle, *Official Training Book for Guides*, 12. See also *New York Times*, "US Guides Star at Moscow Fair," August 15, 1959, 1. This profile of the American guides off-handedly refers to the twenty-seven women among the seventy-five guides, but does not mention the four who were African Americans. In fact, none of the U.S. press coverage discusses the presence of these African American guides in Moscow. A year later *Ebony* magazine published a feature called "How Negroes Live in Russia" (January 1, 1960: 65–73). Written by one of the guides, William "Bill" Davis, the article chronicles living conditions for about twenty Soviet citizens of Black American extraction, and discusses the experiences of these Afro-Russians at ANEM. In the piece, Davis names only one other African American guide at ANEM, Norris Garnett, but does mention that there were four African American models that worked at various stations throughout the exhibit. (Hixson names Herb Miller as an additional African American guide.) Given the importance of Paul Robeson's 1958 concert in Moscow, it is likely that these guides were asked many questions about the relationship between the standard of living presented by the exhibition and racism in the United States. For more on the Russian-speaking American guides at ANEM and at other American exhibitions in the Soviet Union, see Tomas Tolvais, "Cold War Bridge-Building: US Exchange Exhibits and Their Reception in the Soviet Union, 1959–67," *Journal of Cold War Studies*, 12.4 (fall 2010): 3–31. Tolvais mentions but does not analyze the gender and race of the guides. Joy Carew provides a corrective to this general oversight, with her historical account of Davis's trip to Moscow and service at ANEM, in *Blacks, Reds and Russians: Sojourners in Search of the Soviet Promise* (New Brunswick: Rutgers University Press, 2008), 190–98.

19. *New York Herald Tribune*, March 11, 1959.

20. Marshall McLuhan, *Understanding Media: The Extensions of Man* (New York: Mentor, 1964).

21. See Beatriz Colomina, "Enclosed by Images: The Eameses Multimedia Architecture," *Grey Room* 2 (winter 2001): 6–29, and *Domesticity at War*; also Turner, *The Democratic Surround*.

22. Quoted in Masey and Morgan, *Cold War Confrontations*, 214.

23. Frankel, "Image of America at Issue," 8.

24. Showing how the Eameses used technologies developed during World War II, Beatriz Colomina connects the militarism of war to the portraits of domesticity in *Glimpses* and argues that the film should be read as the debut of a media space that foreshadows that of the Internet. As Colomina explains, "in fact we find ourselves in a space that can only be apprehended with the high technology of telescopes, zoom lenses, airplanes, night vision cameras. . . . the relationship between the images reenacts the operation of the technologies." "Enclosed by Images," *Grey Room* 2, 11. While her assessment of the Eameses's work at ANEM and elsewhere is illuminating, Colomina does not take the Soviet response into account.

25. Nelson, *Problems of Design*, 6.

26. Nelson may have been extrapolating from Wiener's notion of kinaesthesia,

through which he underscores the role of muscle memory in the processing of information. "Man is immersed in a world which he perceives through his sense organs.
Information that he receives is co-ordinated through his brain and nervous system
until, after the proper process of storage, collation and selection, it emerges through
effector organs, generally his muscles. These in turn act on the external world, and also
react on the central nervous system through receptor organs such as the end organs
of kinaesthesia; and the information received by the kinaesthetic organs is combined
with his already accumulated store of information to influence future action." Wiener uses this theory to develop his notion of automation feedback, arguing that for
any system to function well it must be furnished with results from its prior actions,
"sensory members which are actuated by motor members and perform the function
of *tell-tales* or *monitors*." Their performed action on the outer world and not their
intended action is reported back to the central regulatory apparatus. See "Cybernetics
and Society," in *The Human Use of Human Beings*, 17 and 24.

27. "Art X = The Georgia Experiment," *Industrial Design*, October 1954, 16. See
also, "A Designer with a Special Interest in Communication," *New York Times*, September 3, 1959.

28. Masey and Morgan, *Cold War Confrontations*, 179.

29. Nelson, "Designer's Comments and Extracts from a 'Log' on the American
National Exhibition," 54.

30. Stanley Abercrombie, *George Nelson: The Design of Modern Design* (Cambridge: MIT Press, 1995), 176.

31. For a rigorous and illustrative reading of Nelson's penchant for modern design
with invisible machinery, see Lynn Spigel, "Object Lessons for the Media Home: From
Storagewall to Invisible Design," *Public Culture* 24.3 (2012): 535–76.

32. See Miriam Hansen on "vernacular modernism" in "The Mass Production of
the Senses: Classical Cinema as Vernacular Modernism," *Modernism/Modernity* 6.2
(1999): 59–77.

33. Tuttle, *Official Training Book for Guides*, 19.

34. Ibid., 88.

35. See chapter 3's discussion of the "miracle kitchen" as a cage. Also see Castillo,
Cold War on the Home Front, 164–67.

36. Here I am indebted to Donald Pease's work on American exceptionalism, and
his claim that, "The Cold War ushered in an era when many of the ideals of America
were limited in order to protect the idea of the ideals of America." *The New American
Exceptionalism* (Minneapolis: University of Minnesota Press, 2009), 14.

37. U.S. Embassy, "Six Weeks in Sokolniki Park: Celebrating the 50th Anniversary
of the American National Exhibition in Moscow" (Moscow: U.S. Embassy, 2010), 32.

38. It was of course possible to visit the pavilion without visiting the dome, but
based on the records we have of how Soviets moved through the exhibition, this would
have been highly unusual. The deluge of objects may have invoked desire, disgust,
boredom, or all of the above, as the encounter with them was less scripted. Worried
that Americans would be seen as shallow consumerists, two consultants suggested that
the Nelson team reduce the emphasis on abundance.

39. Masey and Morgan, *Cold War Confrontations*, 182.

40. See Laura U. Marks, *Touch: Sensuous Theory and Multisensory Media* (Minneapolis: University of Minnesota Press, 2002).

41. "Glimpses of the USA," Working Script, The Work of Charles and Ray Eames, Manuscript Division, Box 202, Library of Congress, Washington, D.C.

42. Northrop Frye offers a breakdown of narrative topoi in *Anatomy of Criticism: Four Essays* (Princeton: Princeton University Press, 1957).

43. "Report on American Exhibition in Moscow," 10.

44. Sandeen, *Picturing an Exhibition*, 125, 142. For a recent reappraisal of the show as heterogeneously appealing to its audience, see Fred Turner "The Family of Man and the Politics of Attention in Cold War America," *Public Culture* 24: 1 (Winter 2012) 55–84.

45. See note 16 in the introduction. On July 11, 1959, the Soviet paper *Izvestia* initiated a new page devoted to "House and Family," featuring stories and images of women in their various duties as wage-earners and homemakers.

46. "Glimpses of the USA," Working Script, The Work of Charles and Ray Eames, Manuscript Division, Box 202, Library of Congress, Washington, D.C.; also quoted in Colomina, "Enclosed by Images," 12.

47. Although erroneously reported in the press as having been composed by Leonard Bernstein, the score was actually written by Elmer Bernstein, who wrote popular scores for movies such as *The Magnificent Seven*, *To Kill a Mockingbird*, and *Thoroughly Modern Millie*. Although not related to one another, the Bernsteins had proximate debuts in Moscow, which may have added to the confusion about the score's provenance. At the end of the fair, Leonard Bernstein, the son of Ukrainian Jews, traveled to Moscow for the first time with the New York Philharmonic, where he performed Dmitri Shostakovich's Fifth Symphony in the presence of the composer. Much was made of this debut and the exchange between Bernstein and Shostakovich in the Soviet and U.S. press.

48. On the other hand, the apparatus that creates this visual space is itself a form of technology (film), so an emotional recalibration must occur in both venues.

49. Given the emphasis on female labor in *Glimpses*, we might wonder about the Eameses' relationship to feminism. Ray's perceived secondary status, as wife to the more famous Charles, is eerily evident in the debut of the Eames lounge chair on NBC's *Arlene Francis Home Show* in 1956. In this episode, Ray stands deferentially in the background while Charles conducts a demonstration. (The original footage is available on YouTube, in two parts.) Nevertheless, Ray's creative contributions to the Eames office were equal to those of Charles.

50. Like the United States, the Soviet Union was a racially diverse nation, made up of federated republics based loosely on nationality. These territories had been the colonial holdings of Russia under the czar. While the Soviet project relinquished the claims of colonial ownership, the racial presumptions of white superiority over colored peoples remained largely entrenched. See Yuri Slezkine, "The USSR as Communal Apartment, or How a Socialist State Promoted Ethnic Particularism," *Slavic Review* 53.2 (summer 1994): 449; and Grigor Suny, *The Soviet Experiment: Russia, the USSR, and the Successor States* (Oxford University Press, 2010). As I have stated elsewhere, Soviet interpretation of their interventions, particularly in the Central Asian repub-

lics, as by definition "anti-imperialist" is problematic. For an illuminating account of the Soviet project of nation-making in Central Asia, see Francine Hirsch, *Empire of Nations: Ethnographic Knowledge and the Making of the Soviet Union* (Ithaca: Cornell University Press, 2005). For an especially insightful account of the project of Soviet unveiling in Uzbekistan, see Marianne Kamp, *The New Woman in Uzbekistan: Islam, Modernity, and Unveiling under Communism* (Seattle: University of Washington Press), 2006. See also Vera Tolz, who reveals the ways early Russian Orientologists reconfigured the ways knowledge about the East was created (anticipating and indirectly contributing to Edward Said's landmark study, *Orientalism*) in *Russia's Own Orient: The Politics of Identity and Oriental Studies in Late Imperial and Early Soviet Periods* (New York: Oxford University Press, 2011).

51. For my extended analysis of Du Bois's assessment of Soviet involvement in the outcome of Brown v. Board, see *Beyond the Color Line and the Iron Curtain: Reading Encounters between Black and Red, 1922–1963* (Durham, NC: Duke University Press, 2002). See also, Thomas Borstelmann, *The Cold War and the Color Line* (Cambridge: Harvard University Press, 2003).

52. See John R. Thomas, "Report on Service with the American Exhibition in Moscow," Rand Corporation, P-1859, March 15, 1960; and William Davis, "How Negroes Live in Russia," *Ebony*, January 1, 1960, 65–73.

53. In addition to Thurmond, forty-one fashion editors signed a letter protesting the mixing of black and whites at the staged wedding. These collective objections were successful, and officials removed the integrated scenes from the fashion show; Hixson, *Parting the Curtain*, 172. Fortunately, Fusco's photos of these scenes remain.

54. Walter Hixson states that the Nobles were engaged to be married at the time of ANEM. Joy Carew likewise notes that they were either engaged to be married or already married. See Hixson, *Parting the Curtain*, 172; and Carew, *Blacks, Reds and Russians*, 190.

55. Images of nightlife appear amid throngs of city dwellers: cabaret in Vegas, the opera *Don Carlo*, a still from *A Raisin in the Sun*, and Marilyn Monroe blowing a kiss in *Some Like It Hot*.

56. Robinson writes, "The development, organization, and expansion of capitalist society pursued essentially racial directions, so too did social ideology." *Black Marxism and the Making of the Black Radical Tradition* (Chapel Hill: University of North Carolina Press, 1983), 2; see also 9–43.

57. See note 50 above.

58. Pat Kirkham attributes the choice to Ray Eames, who wanted to close with something sentimental, noting that others wanted to end the film with a jetliner taking off, "to symbolize progress and the drawing together of different peoples in the global village that some saw as the inevitable result of high-speed air travel and other technologies." *Charles and Ray Eames: Designers of the Twentieth Century* (Cambridge: MIT Press, 1998), 323–24.

59. Masey and Morgan, *Cold War Confrontations*, 182.

60. Charles Eames to the *Imperial Valley Press*, El Centro, CA, September 10, 1959 (Eames Office File, Venice, CA).

61. "Soviet Comment Offered," *New York Times*, August 1, 1959, 24.

62. Norman Winston to Leonard Gross, "Six Things Mikoyan Envied Most in America," *This Week Magazine*, March 29, 1959, 4–7. In a profile in *Time*, Winston declared that "American businessmen must now take the role of the businessmen-diplomats of 50 years ago." The article continues: "Few men practice their preachments with more determined zeal than the author of those words, Norman Kenneth Winston, 59, an impish-faced, meticulously dressed man who ranks among the world's biggest builders (more than 20,000 houses and apartments worth $300 million), runs so many construction and real estate companies (more than 100) that he has lost count, manages a huge personal fortune ($40 million)—and still finds time to hustle continuously from continent to continent as envoy extraordinaire." "The Businessman-Diplomat," *Time*, July 27, 1959; accessed online at www.time.com/time/magazine/article/0,9171,864783,00.html.

63. Leyda notes, "One striking aspect of Khrushchev's unexpected attack on the 'personality cult' is that the only art repeatedly cited as misused to enhance the Stalin idolization is the art of cinema." Jay Leyda, *KINO: A History of the Russian and Soviet Film* (Princeton, NJ: Princeton University Press, 1983), 399.

64. Jeffrey Brooks, *Thank you, Comrade Stalin! Soviet Public Culture From Revolution to Cold War* (Princeton, NJ: Princeton University Press, 2001), 240.

65. Ilya Ehrenburg's *The Thaw* came out in 1954, for example, and Vladimir Dundintsev's *Not By Bread Alone* in 1956.

66. Julian Graffy, "'But Where Is Your Happiness Alevtina Ivanovna?': New Debates about Happiness in the Soviet Films of 1956," in Marina Balina and Evgeny Dobrenko, eds., *Petrified Utopia: Happiness Soviet Style* (London: Anthem Press, 2009), 233; 223.

67. "Who Will Beat Whom?" appears in *Kritika* 9.4 (fall 2008): 855–904; and "Our Kitchen Is Just as Good" in Oldenziel and Zachmann, eds., *Cold War Kitchen*, 83–112.

68. "Report on American Exhibition in Moscow," 2.

69. USIA Office of Research and Analysis, RG 306, Records Relating to the American National Exhibition, Moscow, 1957–59, box 11, National Archives and Records Administration (NARA). Also cited in Reid, "Our Kitchen Is Just as Good," 102.

70. Unless otherwise noted, all quotes are from the Records of the Office of Exhibits (RG 306.5.4, NARA). Many but not all are also cited in Reid, "Who Will Beat Whom?"

71. The first report on the exhibition vigorously pursues the question of ANEM's impact: "Was its success moderate or great? The answer depends on the aspect you are looking at. In sheer popularity or extent of approval its success was, I think, only moderate and somewhat equivocal." ("Report on American Exhibition in Moscow," 1). "If we learned anything about the Soviet public it is that they want to be amazed and impressed by the technically best things we have" ("Report on American Exhibition in Moscow," 6). "The most reliable criteria of popularity probably were the two that have the least favorable verdict: reports of guides and overheard comments . . . slightly more than half of overheard comments were negative." ("Report on American Exhibition in Moscow," 3).

72. Marietta Shaginian, "Razmyshleniia na amerikanskoi vystavke," *Izvestia*, August 23, 1959, 5. (Also cited in Reid, "Who Will Beat Whom?")

73. Ibid.

74. In the later 1950s, Khrushchev emphasized broadening socialist democracy so that woman's needs could be addressed in the public sphere, and not in the confines of the insular home. The Soviet project increased mechanization in the collective arenas outlined by Shaginian above, building communal laundries, dining facilities, crèches, and so on.

75. See Reid's "Who Will Beat Whom?" and "Our Kitchen Is Just as Good."

76. Interestingly, Reid refers to the U.S. kitchen as a "segregated" space, but does not discuss race or the racial dynamics of the Cold War kitchen; "Who Will Beat Whom?"

77. Here I differ from Reid and some cultural critics who follow her, such as Castillo and Colomina, who see in envy a kind of transparent admiration and desire, and therefore a tactic that was successfully deployed by the ANEM developers. Rather, I see envy as taken up antagonistically by the Soviets, revealing the obsessive reassertion of U.S. material dominance as a kind of harassment.

78. Sara Ahmed, *The Promise of Happiness* (Durham, NC: Duke University Press, 2010), 42.

79. Ahmed, *The Promise of Happiness*, 168.

80. Either in acknowledgment of U.S. developers' tactics, or in imitation of them, Khrushchev insisted that a counter exhibit be staged adjacent to ANEM. Although the Soviet exhibit drew many fewer visitors than ANEM, its message was clear: we can use the strategies of capitalist mass production for a glorious Soviet future.

81. Winston to Leonard Gross, "Six Things Mikoyan Envied Most in America," *This Week Magazine*, March 29, 1959, 4.

82. "Speech of N.C. Khrushchev on the Opening in Moscow of the American National Exhibition," *Pravda*, July 25, 1959, 1–2.

83. Colomina, "Enclosed by Images," 9.

84. A few days earlier, the *New York Times* published a picture of Pat Nixon with Ashken Mikoyan and Nina Khrushchev in which Nixon is gazing at Mikoyan with apparent longing. "Diplomat in High Heels," July 28, 1959, 11.

85. Castillo writes, "Khrushchev's address revealed that a 'politics of envy' had infected Soviet planning," citing Reid's article "Our Kitchen Is Just as Good" as the origin of the phrase; *Cold War on the Home Front*, 169.

86. Sianne Ngai, *Ugly Feelings* (Cambridge: Harvard University Press, 2005), 129.

87. It is important to recall here the difference between U.S. media accounts and those recorded by the USIA in their official report on the exhibition.

88. Ngai, *Ugly Feelings*, 130.

89. "Ivan Takes a Look at American Life: Photo Report from Moscow," *US News and World Report*, August 10, 1959, 40.

90. In his post-kitchen exchange with Nixon, Khrushchev announced, "In another seven years we will be on the same level as America. When we catch up with you, while passing you, we will wave to you." Transcript of exchange between Nixon and Khrushchev in Moscow, published in *Pravda*, July 25, 1959, 2.

91. Melanie Klein, "A Study of Envy and Gratitude" [1956], *The Selected Melanie Klein*, ed. Juliet Mitchell (New York: The Free Press, 1986), 212.

92. See Ngai's eloquent formulation of this dynamic, to which I am indebted, in *Ugly Feelings*, 162–63 and 379n43.

93. Yuri Olesha's popular novel, *Zavist* (*Envy*), was published in 1927. In the story, Nikolai Kavalerov, an aimless wanderer, is taken in by Andrei Babichev, a people's commissar. Together Nikolai and Andrei's brother Ivan plan a "conspiracy of feelings," to return Russia to its pre-communist order. Their plans are foiled, and they die in shame. The book was read widely in the Soviet Union as a condemnation of bourgeois feelings, although Kavalerov's plaintive calls for compassion and individuality are more complex. Regardless of our contemporary insights into Olesha's work, "envy" was an emotion widely associated in the Soviet Union with capitalism's mechanisms, and Khrushchev would have been aware of the literary connotations of the term with which he described his response to ANEM.

94. Castillo writes, "At a moment of enormous self-confidence, the Kremlin deliberately parted the iron curtain in the USSR's national interest." See *Cold War on the Home Front*, 160–64.

95. Osgood Caruthers, "US Fair Whetting Russians' Curiosity," *New York Times*, July 12, 1959, E4.

96. Allen L. Otten, "Russians Eagerly Tour US Exhibit Despite Cool Official Attitude," *Wall Street Journal*, July 28, 1959, 16.

97. Susan E. Reid, "Women in the Home," in *Women in the Khrushchev Era*, ed. Melanie Ilic, Susan E. Reid, Lynne Attwood (London: Palgrave, 2004), 157. See also Susan E. Reid, "Cold War in the Kitchen: Gender and the De-Stalinization of Consumer Taste in the Soviet Union under Khrushchev," *Slavic Review* 61.2 (summer 2002): 211–52.

98. Max Frankel, who covered Moscow for the *New York Times* from 1956 to 1959, wrote extensively about the Third Party Program's emphasis on industry and production. "The constantly growing demands of the population were not being met. Check the best foreign models. Redesign everything. Reduce the weight of metal beds and motorcycles and use the materials to increase production. Let there be electric coffee makers and teapots with heat regulators. More watches with sweep second hands. Wider angle television screens. More enamel ware—white enamel ware. New stain removers. Soap powders. And no more of those fringed silk lampshades!" Max Frankel, "The Russian Customer is Sometimes Right," *New York Times*, November 29, 1959, Sunday magazine, 21–23.

99. *Kratkaia entsiklopediia domashnego khoziaistva*, ed. A. I. Revin, et al. (Moscow: Gosudarstvennoe Nauchnoe Izdatel'stvo "Bol'shaia Sovetskaia Entziklopediia," 1959), 2 toma; and *Kratkaia entsiklopediia domashnego khoziaistva v odnom tome*, ed. A. I. Revin, et al. (Moscow: Izdatel'stvo "Sovetskaia Entziklopediia," 1966).

100. See Reid, "Cold War in the Kitchen."

101. For an excellent assessment of the Soviet use of advertising to condition subjectivity, see Randi Cox, "All this Can Be Yours," in *The Landscape of Stalinism: The Art and Ideology of Soviet Space*, ed. Evgeny Dobrenko and Eric Naiman (Seattle: University of Washington Press, 2003), 125–62. See also Harrison E. Salisbury, *To Moscow and Beyond* (New York: Harpers, 1964) and Marguerite Higgins, *Red Plush and Black Bread* (New York: Doubleday, 1955).

Chapter 2: Reframing the Cold War Kitchen

1. Nikita Khrushchev, *The Great Mission of Literature and Art* (Moscow: Progress Publishers, 1964), 69.

2. Sylvia Plath, *Letters Home: Correspondence 1950–1963* (New York: Harper-Collins, 1992), 477.

3. Diane Middlebrook, *Her Husband: Hughes and Plath—A Marriage* (New York: Viking 2003).

4. Images of Plath or her books often appear in popular media. The female protagonist in the movie *Ten Things I Hate about You* (dir. Gil Junger, 1999) reads *The Bell Jar*; in an episode of *The Gilmore Girls* TV series, the show's heroine reads Plath's diaries. The popularity of the Ryan Adams song "Sylvia Plath" also testifies to youth culture's ongoing obsession with her.

5. Lois Ames, "Sylvia Plath: A Biographical Note," *The Bell Jar* (New York: Harper-Collins, 1999), 262. See also Janet McCann, ed., *Critical Insights: The Bell Jar* (Pasadena, CA: Salem Press, 2010).

6. Christopher Lehmann-Haupt, "An American Edition—At Last," *New York Times*, April 16, 1971, 35.

7. Jacqueline Rose is the exception when it comes to critical exegesis on Plath. Rose writes, "at the point where it [the story of the fig tree in *The Bell Jar*] is still linked to its cultural origins, it signifies not plurality but difference, and the difference not of the sexes, but of race. This is, I would suggest, with all the force of its specific historical reference, one of the crucial subtexts of Plath's fiction writing, and indeed of the whole of her work." *The Haunting of Sylvia Plath* (Cambridge: Harvard University Press, 1993), 204.

8. As Gayatri Spivak has written, "Literature contains the element of surprising the historical. But it is also true that a literary text produces the effect of being inevitable—indeed one might argue that that effect is what provokes reading, as transgression of the text. . . . The representation, seeming inevitable, asks for transgressive readings." *Death of a Discipline* (New York: Columbia University Press, 2003), 55. Many studies of *The Bell Jar* read the novel as a progressive tale, a "rite of passage"; Michael Davidson, *Guys Like Us: Citing Masculinity in Cold War Poetics* (Chicago: University of Chicago Press, 2004), 184. One study contends that "the American girl is *The Bell Jar*'s topic"; Tracy Brain, *The Other Sylvia Plath* (New York: Longman, 2001), 63. As *The Bell Jar* instructs us, however, "the American girl" is not only a dangerous fiction, she is a racialized one. Moreover, there are other gendered fictions complicit with that of the alleged American girl in the 1950s: if she is a fiction to be exposed, the exposure reveals that fiction's dependency on other forms of gendering as well as supplemental relationships to the state.

9. Much criticism on the crucial links between race and the Cold War has emerged in recent years. While this list is by no means exhaustive, important interventions include Hixson's *Parting the Curtain*; Gayle Plummer, *Rising Wind: Black Americans and US Foreign Affairs, 1935–1960* (Chapel Hill: University of North Carolina Press, 1996); Penny Von Eschen, *Race Against Empire: Black Americans and Anticolonialism, 1937–1957* (Chapel Hill: University of North Carolina Press, 1997), and *Satchmo Blows Up the World* (Cambridge: Harvard University Press, 2004); Thomas

Bortelsmann, *The Cold War and the Color Line* (Cambridge: Harvard University Press, 2002); Kate Baldwin, *The Cold War and the Color Line: Reading Encounters between Black and Red, 1922–63* (Durham, NC: Duke University Press, 2002); Martha Biondi, *To Stand and Fight* (Cambridge: Harvard University Press, 2003); Nikhil Pal Singh, *Black Is a Country* (Cambridge: Harvard University Press, 2004); and Mary Helen Washington, *The Other Blacklist: The African American Literary Left and the 1950s* (New York: Columbia University Press, 2014).

10. *The Bell Jar* suggests that there are at least two sides to a fascination with U.S. Cold War femininity—a U.S. side and a Soviet side. And it's the disjuncture between these sides—the deception—that the book gestures towards as an aperture for rethinking the category of "woman." I elaborate on this disjuncture later in the chapter with a discussion of Nixon and Khrushchev's encounter in Moscow, but for now I want to continue to stress the text's disorientation of the multiple pasts upon which it draws.

11. For example, the use of the term "psychological warfare" to describe U.S. State Department tactics during the Khrushchev thaw could be productively compared to the use of correlative strategies Plath describes as deployed to keep women confined.

12. Davidson, *Guys Like Us*, 186.

13. See Alan Nadel, *Containment Culture* (Durham, NC: Duke University Press, 1995); Stephen Whitfield, *The Culture of the Cold War* (Baltimore: Johns Hopkins University Press, 1996); Donald Pease, *The New American Exceptionalism* (Minneapolis: University of Minnesota Press, 2009).

14. See my elaboration of this relationship in "Between Mother and History: Jean Stafford, Marguerite Oswald, and US Cold War Women's Citizenship," *differences* 13.3 (2003): 83–120.

15. The novel concludes with Esther feeling pulled by marionette strings, "guiding myself by them, as by a magical thread," as she enters the interrogation room. *The Bell Jar* (1963; repr., New York: Harper-Collins, 1999), 244.

16. The section begins, "I still have the makeup kit they gave me . . . I use the lipsticks now and then, and last week I cut the plastic starfish off the sunglasses case for the baby to play with." *The Bell Jar*, 3.

17. See Marie Ashe, "The Bell Jar and the Ghost of Ethel Rosenberg," in *Secret Agents: The Rosenbergs, McCarthyism and 50s America*, ed. R. Walkowitz and M. Garber (New York: Routledge, 1995), 215–34.

18. "Sentencing of Ethel Rosenberg," April 5, 1951; http://www.fjc.gov/history/home.nsf/page/tu_rosenberg_doc_4.html.

19. On July 18, 1950, the day after her husband was arrested by the FBI on a charge of conspiracy to commit espionage, Ethel invited New York reporters into her home. A series of photos was taken, including one of Ethel drying dishes near her kitchen sink. Although this photo was never published, it is widely available on the Internet and has become one of the most familiar images of her. At the time, *The New York Journal American* decided to publish a different photo of Ethel, a cropped close-up. Any further attempt to portray Ethel as a devoted housewife was undercut by the mug shots that would follow a month later, after her arrest.

20. Ross also notes that even if their Jewishness was articulated in "politically secular and Americanized terms," Jewishness in the era was "still massively identified

in the public mind with unpatriotic behavior." Andrew Ross, *No Respect: Intellectuals and Popular Culture* (New York: Routledge, 1989), 20–21.

21. Plath, *The Bell Jar*, 75.

22. "Six Things Mikoyan Envied Most in America," 4.

23. "The Two Worlds: A Day-Long Debate." *New York Times*, July 25, 1959, 1.

24. Deborah Nelson, *Pursuing Privacy in Cold War America* (Chicago: University of Chicago Press, 2002), 80.

25. As I discuss in chapter 1, by ceding to pressure to cut these scenes from the fashion show, the exhibition's producers created an opportunity for the Soviet press. Ideological exploit notwithstanding, the archive of these scenes, as photographed by Paul Fusco for *Look*, deserves close attention. They suggest a visual narrative of interracialism that was ironically absented when the event was scrapped. This scene of unstable presence/absence conjures similarly unstable dichotomies of the hostess of the Cold War kitchen, discussed in chapter 3.

26. "Better to See Once," *Time*, August 3, 1959, 15.

27. Ibid. [emphasis added].

28. For common U.S. stereotyping of the Soviet woman see Thomas P. Whitney, "S-x in the Soviet Union," *New York Times*, January 1, 1956, 43–44; and Harrison Salisbury, "Allure, Milady? Try Spirit of Red Moscow," *New York Times*, March 3, 1954, 1–2. According to Whitney, "Sex with a capital S could very easily distract citizens from the 'building of communism.'"

29. "The Iron Curtain Look Is Here!" *Life*, 1952; accessed at The Literature and Culture of the American 1950s, www.writing.upenn.edu/~afilreis/50s/iron-curtain .html. Apparently Plath's own "gams" were featured in a student newspaper in Cambridge when she was studying there on a Fulbright in 1955.

30. Davidson, *Guys Like Us*, 184.

31. Alan Nadel, note to author.

32. See Spivak, *Death of a Discipline*.

33. For an interesting corollary that takes the art of failure in a tangential direction, see Judith Halberstam, *The Queer Art of Failure* (Durham, NC: Duke University Press, 2011).

34. It is unclear if Esther prefers this world-at-a-distance pose, or if the text derides her naïve solipsism which sees "freedom" as escape from a body trapped in its Cold War contradictions. (In the next line, she recites the things she can't do—such as cook, sew, and clean, those mainstays of Cold War femininity.) Noting that Plath underlined this sentence in her copy of Cleanth Brooks's *The Well Wrought Urn*—"The lovers, in rejecting life actually win to the most intense life"—one critic argues that writing was "'the enduring immanence' Plath sought to create," thinking that through writing she would be ushered into a better life, one "most intense." Langdon Hammer, "Plath's Lives," *Representations* 75 (summer 2001): 77–78. But I wonder if we could read this link between Plath's doodlings and *The Bell Jar* otherwise. *The Bell Jar* portrays being removed from the world, engulfed in a "huge silence," in an ambiguous light in which cynicism about the urge to disengage from the world is equally apparent.

35. See Steven Lee, *The Ethnic Avant-Garde* (New York: Columbia University Press, 2015).

36. It is worth noting that Plath wrote her senior thesis on the figure of the double in Dostoevsky.

37. See Dale Peterson, *Up from Bondage: The Literatures of Russian and African American Soul* (Durham, NC: Duke University Press, 2000), which discusses in detail the way Hegel's account of history marginalized Russians and excluded Africans. See also Tolz, *Russia's Own Orient.*

38. Recall that Esther is concerned that Buddy is living a "double life," one that enables him to be an upstanding medical student, poised to marry well, and at the same time maintain a private sexual life, encapsulated in his affair with a waitress.

39. Mary Buckley, "The Woman Question in the Contemporary Soviet Union," in *Promissory Notes: Women in the Transition to Socialism,* ed. Sonia Kruks, Rayna Rapp, and Marilyn B. Young (New York: Monthly Review Press, 1989), 251–81.

40. Mikhail Epstein, *After the Future: The Paradoxes of Postmodernism and Contemporary Russian Culture,* trans and ed. A. Miller-Pogacar (Amherst: University of Massachusetts Press, 1995), 155.

41. See, for example, Barbara Evans Clements, Barbara Alpern Engel, and Christine D. Worobec, *Russia's Women: Accommodation, Resistance, Transformation* (Berkeley: University of California Press, 1991).

42. See Catriona Kelly and David Shepherd, eds., *Constructing Russian Culture in the Age of Revolution: 1881–1940* (New York: Oxford University Press, 1998), esp. 256–291; and Lynne Atwood, "Gender Angst in Russian Society and Cinema in the Post-Stalin Era," in *Russian Cultural Studies,* ed. Catriona Kelly and David Shepherd (New York: Oxford University Press, 1998), 352–68.

43. K. A. Simmons, "Zhenskaia Proza and the New Generation of Women Writers," *Slovo: A Journal of Contemporary Soviet and East European Affairs* 3.1 (May 1990): 66–78.

44. As I explore in chapter 3, Baranskaya's 1969 *Nedelia kak nedelia (A Week Like Any Other)* takes up the tensions between a national dream—the double as a messianic figure—and the everyday—the feminine banal—portraying a kind of female doubling that resists exclusivity. Navigating female selfhood in *A Week Like Any Other* requires contending not only with the false iconography of Soviet womanhood as good mother/good worker, but also with the impossibility of ever being able to account for the doubleness within that doubleness.

45. Quoted in Frances Stonor Saunders, *Who Paid the Piper? The CIA and the Cultural Cold War* (London: Granta Books, 1999), 20.

46. Before delivering her kick, Esther moves to a place where no one can see her actions below the waist. She doesn't kick him in the groin—that would be too obvious —and perhaps create too much of a connection between the orderly and Esther, who sits at the "crotch of the tree" in the fig-tree scene. After receiving a kick in the calf, the orderly rolls his eyes at Esther, playing the role of accommodating a white woman's antics.

47. Saunders, *Who Paid the Piper?,* 4.

48. These others are referenced through numerous racial and ethnic images throughout the novel and include the "big, smudgy-eyed Chinese woman staring idiotically into my face" (Esther's own reflection in the elevator after her food poisoning; 18); "the face in the mirror [that] looked like a sick Indian" (Esther's appearance the

night after her attack; 112); the Jewish man in the fig story (55); Mrs. Tomolillo, the Italian American woman Esther witnesses giving birth and then (falsely) identifies in the asylum (66); Marco, the Peruvian who assaults Esther (103); Dodo Conway, Esther's fecund Catholic neighbor (116); and the dark-skinned Doctor "Pancreas" (179).

49. "Today American women are awakening to the fact that they have been sold into virtual slavery by a lie invented and marketed by men. One book has named that lie and told women what to do about it," claims the back cover of *The Feminine Mystique* (1963; repr., New York: Dell, 1983), underscoring the links between civil rights and women's rights, however unwittingly.

50. Norma Alcaron, Caren Kaplan, and Minoo Moallem, "Introduction: Between Woman and Nation," in *Between Woman and Nation: Nationalisms, Transnational Feminisms and the State* (Durham, NC: Duke University Press, 1999), 13.

Chapter 3: Alice Childress, Natalya Baranskaya, and the Conditions of Cold War Womanhood

1. "Wives Kept Quiet at Dacha Dinner," *New York Times*, July 28, 1959, 1.

2. Hayot, "Against Periodization; or, On Institutional Time," *New Literary History* 42.4 (autumn 2011): 747. Hayot suggests new periods organized around times that "cross or combine with our existing ones," and "cross national boundaries and borrow for their logic some non-national principle of social or cultural coherence."

3. Ibid.

4. The first page of *Freedom* featured Paul Robeson's column, "My Story"; other pieces often followed up on his column.

5. These installments are not presented chronologically, however, and in many ways they leave the form of the monthly behind them. (For example, absent is the polyphonic discursive space of the magazine, in which articles are juxtaposed with advertisements, photographs, op-eds, and letters.) See Mary Helen Washington, *The Other Blacklist*, esp. 140–47.

6. My thinking here is influenced by a variety of theories of the public sphere, particularly the relationship between discursive spaces such as newspapers or magazines and their various reading publics. See especially Jurgen Habermas, *The Structural Transformation of the Public Sphere* (Cambridge: MIT Press, 1991); Benedict Anderson, *Imagined Communities* (London: Verso, 1991); Nancy Fraser, "Rethinking the Public Sphere," *Social Text* 25/26 (1990): 56–80; C. Squires, "Rethinking the Black Public Sphere: An Alternative Vocabulary for Multiple Public Spheres," *Communication Theory* 12.4 (November 2002): 446–68; Michael Warner, "Publics and Counterpublics," *Public Culture* 14.1 (winter 2002): 49–90.

7. Natalya Baranskaya, *Nedelia kak nedelia* [A week like any other], *Novyi Mir* 11 (1969): 23–55. [Unless otherwise noted, all page references are to this edition.] *Novyi Mir* has been described as "the most prestigious and politically independent journal of its day." Baranskaya's story was initially translated into English by *Redbook* magazine as part of a women's novel series. See Natalya Baranskaya, "The Alarm Clock in the Cupboard," trans. Beatrice Stillman, *Redbook Magazine*, March 1971, 179–201.

8. Alice Childress, *Like One of the Family: Conversations from a Domestic's Life* (Boston: Beacon, 1986), 37.

9. Alice Childress, *Selected Plays*, ed. Kathy A. Perkins (Evanston, IL: Northwestern University Press, 2011).

10. Ibid., x.

11. "Florence," *Masses and Mainstream* 3 (October 1950): 34–47.

12. Hilton Als provided an eloquent summary of Childress's work on the occasion of the production of *Trouble in Mind* at Washington's Arena stage in 2011. See "Black and Blue," *New Yorker* 87.31 (2011): 132–33.

13. See in particular her essay, "A Candle in a Gale Wind," in *Black Women Writers (1950–1980): A Critical Evaluation*, ed. Mari Evans (New York: Doubleday/Anchor, 1984), 111–16. Interestingly, Childress identified the audience she imagined in her early career in an essay titled "For a Negro Theater," published in *Masses and Mainstream* 4 (February 1951): 61–64; and reprinted as "For a Strong Negro People's Theater" in the *Daily Worker*, February 16, 1951, 11. This essay makes clear that she was never fully comfortable with leftist discourse, and her discomfort became clearer as time went on. See Washington, *The Other Blacklist*, for a full elaboration of these nuances.

14. Martha Biondi, *To Stand and Fight: The Struggle for Civil Rights in Postwar New York City* (Cambridge: Harvard University Press, 2003), 265.

15. Washington, *The Other Blacklist*, 131.

16. In this sense, it does not matter if Childress was a member of the Communist Party at the time; indeed, such summations of left-oriented writers have frequently led to an easy dissociation of cultural producers from their other political alliances and affiliations, the institutions as well as the cultural fields in which they worked. It is precisely this center-periphery bias that Michael Denning undoes so brilliantly in *The Cultural Front*, where he writes that this kind of narrative "leads to a remarkably inadequate understanding of the depth and breadth of the social movement, as well as a disproportionate emphasis on central Party leaders, an over-reading of the significance of pronouncements in Communist Party journals, and, in some cases, a search for the Moscow gold that kept it all running." Denning, *The Cultural Front* (London: Verso, 1998), xviii. Alan Wald makes a similar point in his discussion of the black literary left, noting that "what is more memorable than formal membership in the Party is that, for Black writers, the publications, clubs, and committees that were at least in part created by Party members, and with Party support, constituted principal venues in which many Black writers came together to formulate ideas, share writings, make contacts, and develop perspectives that sustained their future creative work." *Exiles from a Future Time: The Forging of the Mid-Twentieth-Century Left* (Chapel Hill: University of North Carolina Press, 2002), 267.

17. The novel's title was shortened from a column Childress published in *Freedom* in April 1952: "She's Like One of the Family: A Conversation from Life." This was the first and only time Childress used this title as part of her "Conversation" columns.

18. Mildred's selfhood thus speaks not so much *beyond* as *alongside* prevailing notions of double consciousness as articulated in Du Bois's famous description of black American selfhood. She offers us a means of investigating how black women might be made to experience differently the constraints of this cultural nationalism. For a very different take on Mildred's location in the kitchen, see Sonya Lancaster, "Too

Many Cooks: Contested Authority in the Kitchen," *The Southern Literary Journal* 38.2 (spring 2006): 113–30.

19. Elizabeth Brown-Guillory, "Like One of the Family," in *The Concise Oxford Companion to African American Literature*, ed. William L. Andrews, Frances Smith Foster, and Trudier Harris (New York: Oxford University Press, 2001), 258. See also Brown-Guillory, "Images of Blacks in Plays by Black Women," *Phylon* 47.3 (1986): 230–37. Excellent, comprehensive histories of black women's radicalism in the twentieth century can be found in Dayo Gore's *Radicalism at the Crossroads: African American Activists in the Cold War* (New York: NYU Press, 2011), and Erik McDuffie's *Sojourning for Freedom: Black Women, American Communism, and the Making of Black Left Feminism* (Durham, NC: Duke University Press, 2011). Farah Jasmine Griffin's *Harlem Nocturne: Women Artists and Progressive Politics during World War II* (New York: Perseus, 2013) provides a luminous portrait of the wartime politics and creative output of three key figures—Pearl Primus, Ann Petry, and Mary Lou Williams—whose left-accented activities in New York City overlapped with Childress's.

20. Mary Helen Washington attributes the formation of Mildred's character to Jones's essay, which identified women of color, and in particular Negro women, as the most vulnerable to labor and at the same time overlooked in leftist theorizations of labor issues (*The Other Blacklist*, 143–44).

21. Jones quoted in Carol Boyce Davies, *Left of Karl Marx: The Political Life of Black Communist Claudia Jones* (Durham, NC: Duke University Press, 2007), 40.

22. By 1949 Hughes had stepped back from many of his earlier pronouncements about the Soviet Union. But his interest in the Soviet project of unveiling offered an interesting counterpoint to notions of black modernity being formulated in the US in the 1930s. See my essay "Variegated Hughes: Revisiting Langston Hughes in Soviet Central Asia," *Russian Review*, forthcoming.

23. Davies, *Left of Karl Marx*, xxxii. See also Biondi, *To Stand and Fight*, which argues that many black women fled domestic labor to find jobs in venues that were opened to them during the war, such as the garment industry and telecommunications (25).

24. Harris, "Introduction" to Childress, *Like One of the Family*, xxiii. See also Trudier Harris, *From Mammies to Militants: Domestics in Black American Literature* (Philadelphia: Temple University Press, 1982).

25. See especially the chapter titled "Hands," in which Mildred offers a Marxist theorization of labor. "Everyone who works is a servant," Mildred begins then, noting the way material objects bear within them the trace of the labor that produced them, continues: "Marge, you can take any article and trace it back like that and you'll see the power and beauty of laboring hands. . . . Find the story, Marge, behind the lettuce and tomato sandwich, your pots and pans, the linoleum on the floor, your dishes, the bottle of nail polish, your stove, the electric light, books, cigarettes, boxes, the floor we're standin' on, this brick building. . . . . Why you could just go on through all the rest of time singin' the praises of hands. . . . When working folks get together it should be with the highest respect for one another because it is the work of their hands that keeps the world alive and kickin'" (63).

26. Washington, *The Other Blacklist*, 141, 297n.

27. In this section Mildred recounts a scene with a drunk black man on the bus. Although her friend Berniece wants to move to another car to avoid association with him, Mildred refuses. She explodes: "this man ain't no reflection on me whatsoever. Where did you get that crazy talk about proving yourself? Why if only the races that had no drunks in them was allowed to have rights, why nobody in the country could vote" (130).

28. Robert Hariman and John Lucaites, *No Caption Needed: Iconic Photographs, Public Culture and Liberal Democracy* (Chicago: University of Chicago Press, 2007), 9.

29. As discussed in previous chapters, Nixon's claim that marketplace diversity liberates women also necessarily highlights women's captivity in the kitchen.

30. See Lizabeth Cohen, *A Consumer's Republic: The Politics of Mass Consumption in Postwar America* (New York: Vintage, 2003).

31. Nadel, note to author. I remain grateful for this very helpful suggestion.

32. Michael Warner, *Publics and Counterpublics* (New York: Zone Books, 2005), 49.

33. Marge is also the name of Florence's sister in Childress's earlier play, "Florence."

34. This dialogic structure recalls the "call and response" form familiar to African American literature.

35. The structure of address in Childress's Mildred columns might be useful as a way of thinking through the collectivity created by shared emotion in a Leninist-inspired black radical newspaper. In an essay published in 1901, Lenin wrote, "A newspaper is not only a collective propagandist and a collective agitator, it is also a collective organiser." And later, in "What is to Be Done?," Lenin described the possibilities of the newspaper to help the worker feel the necessity for action: "Why do the Russian workers still manifest little revolutionary activity in response to the brutal treatment of the people by the police, the persecution of religious sects, the flogging of peasants, the outrageous censorship, the torture of soldiers, the persecution of the most innocent cultural undertakings, etc.? Is it because the 'economic struggle' does not 'stimulate' them to this, because such activity does not 'promise palpable results,' because it produces little that is 'positive?' We must blame ourselves, our lagging behind the mass movement, for still being unable to organise sufficiently wide, striking, and rapid exposures of all the shameful outrages. When we do that (and we must and can do it), the most backward worker will understand, *or will feel*, that the students and religious sects, the peasants and the authors are being abused and outraged by those same dark forces that are oppressing and crushing him at every step of his life. *Feeling that, he himself will be filled with an irresistible desire to react*" [final emphases added]. V. I. Lenin, "Where to Begin?" (originally published in *Iskra* 4, May 1901) and "What Is to Be Done?" In *Collected Works of Lenin*, vol. 5 (Moscow: Foreign Languages Publishing House, 1961), 23, 414. For an account of the potential for revolutionary counter moods, to which I am much indebted, see Jonathan Flatley, "How a Revolutionary Counter Mood is Made," *New Literary History* 43.3 (summer 2012) 503–25.

36. Books by Boyce-Davies, Gore, McDuffie, and Washington mark major steps forward in correcting the absence of black women in histories of black radicalism. Their work owes a debt (as does my own) to the path-breaking work of Alan Wald

on the literary left. See, especially, *Exiles from a Future Time: the Forging of the Mid-Twentieth Century Literary Left* (Chapel Hill: University of North Carolina Press, 2002).

37. Mildred responds to this differential in a chapter titled "Sometimes I Feel so Sorry," in which Mildred tells Marge, "You oughta hear Mrs. B . . . moanin' and groanin' about her troubles" (89).

38. By reminding us that the kitchen is the room in the white home most frequently occupied by people of color, the novel foregrounds the idea that a speaker's authority is connected to the place from which she speaks. One scene in particular elaborates the distinctive demarcations of space within U.S. domesticity. In a conversation titled "The Health Card," Mildred recounts to Marge the story of Mrs. Jones, whose hovering between the kitchen and living room causes Mildred concern, "I looks up and there she was in the doorway, lookin' kind of strained around the gills. First she stuttered and then she stammered and after beatin' all around the bush she comes out with, 'Do you have a health card, Mildred?'" (42–43). Not one to be caught off guard, Mildred responds by asking to see not only Mrs. Jones's health card but also that of her husband and each of her three children. As Mildred explains, "since I have to handle laundry and make beds, you know." Mrs. Jones pointedly backs out of the kitchen, scurries to the library where her husband waits, and then returns with the news that Mildred need not bring a health card after all. Mildred's response "I looked up real casual kind-of and said, 'on second thought, you folks look real clean too" (43). The kitchen vacillates here between Mildred's authority and the authority of her employer that resides, along with Mr. Jones, in the living room. Rather than submit to humiliation, erasure, a life without value to which the kitchen proper would assign her, Mildred claims that space as her own. Partly undermining Mrs. Jones's authority to segregate and discriminate against her as apart from the family, Mildred assumes equal human standing with her employer. Although the chapter ends with a ricocheting of smiles between Mrs. Jones and Mildred, this is not a moment of interracial solidarity. Rather, the unevenness of the exchange and its multiple levels of incommensurability—of communication and miscommunication—are emphasized.

39. With its title and the intimate coupling of Mildred and Marge, the novel sets itself up in a sphere of female fiction. And yet, the novel teaches us that femininity, as conceived in terms of the family, is typically a concept or metaphor for emotional constancy. See Lauren Berlant, *The Female Complaint* (Chicago: University of Chicago Press, 2008).

40. Baranskaya's subsequently published collections include, *Otritsatel'naia zhizel': Rasskazy, malen'kie povesti* (Moscow: Molodaia gvardiia, 1977); *Zhenshchina s zontikom: povest' i rasskazy* (Moscow: Sovremennik, 1981); *Portret, podarennyi drugu: ocherki I rasskazy o Pushkine* (Leningrad: Lenizdat, 1982); and *Den' pominoveniia: roman, povest'* (Moscow: Sovetskii pisatel', 1989).

41. Helen Goscilo notes that: "According to state ideology and popular belief, through exercising her childbearing capabilities, a woman not only realizes her 'natural (biological) function,' but simultaneously forges links with the mythical socialist future, a future which Soviets invariably posit in the optimistic belief that whatever lies ahead by definition must be better than the dismal present." Helen Goscilo, ed.,

Fruits of Her Plume: Essays on Contemporary Russian Women's Culture (Armonk, NY: M.E. Sharpe, 1993), xxi.

42. Benjamin M. Sutcliffe, *The Prose of Life: Russian Women Writers from Khrushchev to Putin* (Madison: University of Wisconsin Press, 2009), 40.

43. Helen Goscilo, ed. *Balancing Acts: Contemporary Stories by Russian Women* (Bloomington: Indiana University Press, 1989), 324.

44. See Susan Kay, "A Woman's Work," *Irish Slavonic Studies* 8 (1987): 115–26; K. A. Simmons, "*Zhenskaia Proza* and the New Generation of Women Writers," *Slovo: A Journal of Contemporary Soviet and East European Affairs* 3.1 (May 1990): 66–78; and Sutcliffe, *The Prose of Life*.

45. See studies from the 1980s like Arlie Hochschild and Anne Machung, *The Second Shift* (New York: Penguin, 2003). It should be noted, however, that Baranskaya was no feminist. She critiqued the movement and dissociated herself from it. See Pieta Monks's interview with Natalya Baranskaya in *Writing Lives: Conversations between Women Writers*, ed. Mary Chamberlain (London: Virago, 1988), 34.

46. Maria Mies, *Patriarchy and Accumulation on a World Scale* (New York: Third World Books, 1998), 181.

47. Baranskaya, *Nedelia kak nedelia*, 30. Unless otherwise noted, translations from the Russian are my own.

48. Mies, *Patriarchy and Accumulation*, 181.

49. See Berlant, *The Female Complaint*.

50. Edward Brown, *Russian Literature Since the Revolution* (Cambridge: Harvard University Press, 1982), 320.

51. Baranskaya, *Nedelia kak nedelia*, 43.

52. Lahusen, "'Leaving Paradise' and *Perestroika*: *A Week Like Any Other* and *Memorial Day* by Natal'ia Baranskaia," in Helen Goscilo, ed., *Fruits of Her Plume*, 211.

53. Ray Stokes, "Plastics and the New Society: The German Democratic Republic in the 1950s and 60s," in *Style and Socialism: Modernity and Material Culture in Post-War Eastern Europe*, ed. Susan E. Reid and David Crowley (Oxford: Berg, 2000), 75.

54. Alexei Yurchak discusses the circulation of ideas about the West in late Soviet society in his groundbreaking study, *Everything was Forever, Until It Was No More* (Princeton: Princeton University Press, 2005). See especially "Imaginary West: The Elsewhere of Late Socialism," 158–206, which I take up in more detail in chapter 5.

55. In one English version, this is incorrectly translated as "the American presidency." See Natalya Baranskaya, "A Week Like Any Other Week," trans. E. Lehrman, *The Massachusetts Review* (autumn 1974): 699. The Russian text reads, "Razve my ne govorili o prokurore Garrisone?" (52). The difference is key, as it indicates the specificity of the (rejected) topic of conversation.

56. For a brilliant reading of this period of Soviet consumption, see Reid, "Cold War in the Kitchen."

57. Baranskaya, *Nedelia kak nedelia*, 47. As I note in chapter 2, there is no word for "privacy" in Russian. The longing for the "private" in Baranskaya's text is available to the extent that its violations reinvent the search. At one point in the story, it seems that Olga finds more freedom on the street with her coworkers than she does in the seclusion of her home.

58. Martha Rosler, "Some Observations on Women as Subjects in Russia," in *After Perestroika: Kitchenmaids or Stateswomen?* (New York: Independent Curators, 1994), 1–20.

59. Natalya Baranskaya, *Nedelia kak nedelia*, ed. Lora Paperno, Natalie Roklina, and Richard Leed (Columbus, OH: Slavica Publishers, 1983), 56.

60. See Lynn Abbot and Doug Seroff, eds., *Out of Sight: The Rise of African American Popular Music, 1889–1895* (Jackson: University of Mississippi Press, 2003), 308–9, for the fascinating history of the Hampton Institute Folk-Lore Society's pathbreaking "Folk-Lore and Ethnology" column, in which this early report of the hullygully was cited.

61. The routings of African American musical formations through the Soviet Union are taken up more fully in my discussion of jazz and the *stilyagi* in chapter 5.

Chapter 4: Lorraine Hansberry and the Social Life of Emotions

1. "The Negro Writer and His Roots: Towards a New Romanticism," *The Black Scholar* 12.2 (March/April 1981): 5.

2. Eve Kosofsky Sedgwick, *Touching Feeling: Affect, Pedagogy, Performativity* (Durham: Duke University Press, 2003), 13.

3. *Freedom*, September, 1951, 1. While unattributed, the gendered terms of this description have always bothered me, and brought to mind a staff of men dependent upon women to do work they deem beneath them. This connotation underscores the importance of Hansberry's and Childress's preoccupations with the affective labors often relegated to women, even within an environment as allegedly supportive of women as that of *Freedom*. The partially recuperating gesture of a headshot of Hansberry and more laudatory commentary follows: "Miss Hansberry is a native of Chicago, studied journalism and art at the U. of Guadalajara and the U. of Wisconsin, and has lived in New York for more than a year. She manages, with all the things mentioned above, to sing in the Harlem Youth Chorus and take a leading part in the progressive activities of young people in the world's largest Negro community." For examples of the range of Hansberry's prolific journalism in *Freedom*, see Hansberry (with Stan Steiner), "Cry for Colonial Freedom Jolts Phony Youth Meet," *Freedom*, September 1951, 6; "Women Voice Demands in Capital Sojourn," *Freedom*, October 1951, 6; "Negroes Cast in Same Old Roles in TV Shows," *Freedom*, June 1951, 7; "Egyptian People Fight for Freedom," *Freedom*, March, 1952, 3; "Student Killing Exposes NYU Bias," *Freedom*, June 1952, 5; "Kenya's Kikuyu: A Peaceful People Wage Heroic Struggle against British," *Freedom*, December 1952, 3.

4. The fact that *Raisin in the Sun* includes a Nigerian anticolonialist showcases Hansberry's concern for linking contemporaneous domestic and international issues. At the time of the play's opening, Nigeria, the largest colony still officially part of the British commonwealth, was on the verge of independence. Hansberry would have been well aware of the timing of this momentous event, as it was widely covered not only in *Freedom* but in the mainstream press as well. See "Nigeria to Get Independence on Oct. 1, 1960," *Daily Defender*, October 27, 1958, A9. Moreover, Hansberry was mentored by her uncle William Leo Hansberry, a professor of African history at Howard University and close ally of Nigerian anticolonialist Nnamdi Azikiwe; Rich-

ard Iton, *In Search of the Black Fantastic: Politics and Popular Culture in the Post-Civil Rights Era* (New York: Oxford, 2008), 64.

5. "The Negro Writer and His Roots: Toward a New Romanticism," *The Black Scholar* (March–April 1981): 6. Although Hansberry delivered this lecture at the first Congress of Negro Writers at the American Society of African Culture in New York in March 1959, her talk was not included in the selected papers published by the society in 1960.

6. A characteristic critique of the play can be found in Harold Cruse, *The Crisis of the Negro Intellectual: A Historical Analysis of the Failure of Black Leadership* (New York: NYR Books, 1967), 267–84.

7. One reviewer commented, "It's a show about people, white or colored. . . . I see 'A Raisin in the Sun' as part of the general culture of the US." George Murray, "'Raisin in Sun' Terrific Theater," *Chicago American*, February 27, 1959, 19. Another review claimed that the play was about "human beings, who happen to be Negroes." Sydney J. Harris, "Sydney Harris Reviews: *A Raisin in the Sun*," *Chicago Daily News*, February 11, 1959, 39. See Hansberry's response to the varied reviews in Hansberry, "Willie Loman, Walter Younger, and He Who Must Live," *The Village Voice*, August 12, 1959, 7–8. For an extended engagement with the play's reception, see Robin Bernstein, "Inventing a Fishbowl: White Supremacy and The Critical Reception of 'A Raisin in the Sun,'" *Modern Drama* 42.1 (1999): 16–27.

8. Lillian Ross, The Talk of the Town, "Playwright," *The New Yorker*, May 9, 1959, 33.

9. Iton, *In Search of the Black Fantastic*, 67.

10. Ibid.

11. Taking up the idea of transnationalism, Fanon Che Wilkins asserts the geopolitics of racial oppression and colonial domination evident in the play. Wilkins provides a fine elaboration of the ways in which Hansberry's critical nationalism has been omitted from much scholarship on *Raisin*. Put back in the context of Bandung, the removal of Paul Robeson's passport, and the trial of W.E.B. Du Bois as a foreign agent, the play comes alive—breaking open conversations still to be had, what Iton might call the "intratextual dissonance lying just below the play's surface" (68). Wilkins, "Beyond Bandung: The Critical Nationalism of Lorraine Hansberry, 1950–1965," *Radical History Review* 95 (spring 2006): 191–210. See also Cheryl Higashida, who argues that "Hansberry must be read within a transatlantic conversation with writers who intimately shaped her understanding of diasporic blackness and anticolonial struggle," in "To Be(come) Young, Gay, and Black: Lorraine Hansberry's Existentialist Routes to Anticolonialism," *American Quarterly* 60.4 (December 2008): 919.

12. Lorraine Hansberry, "Alice Childress' Acting Brightens A Fine Off-Broadway Theatre Piece," *Freedom*, October 1953, 7.

13. See, for example, Peter Stearns's discussion of the human need for emotional outlets in *American Cool: Constructing a Twentieth-Century Emotional Style* (New York: NYU Press, 1994). While illuminating the relationship between middle-class leisure and emotions, Stearns takes for granted that there is a common range of emotions among all humans and that the capacity for these emotions sits deep within the psyche, either waiting for indulgence or suffering under suppression.

14. Jonathan Flatley, *Affective Mapping* (Cambridge: Harvard University Press, 2008).

15. By using the term "affective" in this way, I am referring to the space of bodily experience and perception, the ways in which elements of experience are taken in and refracted less by belief than by the ways these experiences are felt.

16. Here I am thinking of the work of Sara Ahmed who has argued that "rather than seeing emotions as psychological dispositions, we need to consider how they work, in concrete and particular ways, to mediate the relationship between the psychic and the social, and between the individual and the collective. " See Ahmed, "Affective Economies," *Social Text* 22.2 (summer 2004): 119. While emotions are cognitive displays of feelings that move between the individual and the collective, affects are pre-cognitive intensities that precede will and consciousness. Brian Massumi writes, "an affect is a pre-personal intensity corresponding to the passage from one experiential state of the body to another and implying an augmentation or diminution in that body's capacity to act." See Brian Massumi, introduction to Gilles Deleuze and Felix Guattari *A Thousand Plateaus* (University of Minnesota Press, 1997), xvi; and *Parables for the Virtual: Movement, Affect, Sensation* (Durham, NC: Duke University Press, 2003).

17. The Afro-Asian Writers Conference held in Tashkent, Uzbekistan, in October 1958 brought together prominent black, Asian, and South Asian writers, including W.E.B. Du Bois and Shirley Graham. Although this conference was no more a reference point for ANEM than AMSAC, Du Bois was a state guest and followed his visit to Tashkent with a trip to Moscow, where he met with Khrushchev and discussed the funding of the Soviet African Institute and his *Encyclopedia Africana* project. At a time when Du Bois could not find institutional backing in the United States—and when American policy towards Africa focused on taking control out of the hands of Africans—the Soviet response to Du Bois was increasingly positive. Soviet bureaucrats sought to concretize approval among African and Asian intellectuals through the establishment of international conferences and associations that focused attention on the participation of African and Asian scholars and activists. In 1959 Du Bois was awarded the Lenin Peace Prize, for which he received numerous commendations and an outpouring of support in the Soviet press.

18. John A. Davis, *The American Negro Writer and His Roots* (New York: American Society of African Culture, 1960).

19. Washington, *The Other Blacklist*, 240.

20. Catherine Jurca, *White Diaspora: The Suburb and the Twentieth-Century American Novel* (Princeton: Princeton University Press, 2001).

21. "Make New Sounds: Studs Terkel Interview with Lorraine Hansberry," *American Theater* (November 1984): 8.

22. Kenneth Jackson, *Crabgrass Frontier: The Suburbanization of the United States* (New York: Oxford University Press, 1997), 228.

23. Lewis Mumford, *The City in History* (New York, 1961). See also Gwendolyn Wright, *Building the Dream: A Social History of Housing in America* (New York, 1981).

24. Lorraine Hansberry, *A Raisin in the Sun* (New York: Vintage, 1988), 37.

25. In this sense, my engagement with the emotive realm of the domestic is compatible with but very different from Kristin L. Matthews's work on the idea of "home" in *Raisin*. (Matthews investigates what she calls the "psycho-social struggle of mid-century African Americans to attain, secure, and define a sense of place.") "The Politics of 'Home' in Lorraine Hansberry's *A Raisin in the Sun*," *Modern Drama* 51.4 (winter 2008): 578.

26. This exchange occurs on page 79 of the Vintage edition.

27. Ibid., 128.

28. Mama says she wanted "simply to find the nicest house for the least amount of money for my family. . . . Them houses they put up for colored in them areas way out all seem to cost twice as much as other houses" (act 2, scene 1, 93).

29. Hansberry, "Make New Sounds," 8. See the opening pages to Hannah Arendt's *The Human Condition* (Chicago: University of Chicago Press, 1958), for a fuller context for Hansberry's comments about action over escapism. It is worth noting that Arendt also addresses the kitchen, in describing what she terms the "barbaric preconditions" of necessity called the household: "In Greek self-understanding, to force people by violence, to command rather than persuade, were pre-political ways to deal with people characteristic of life outside the polis, of home and family life, where the household head ruled with uncontested, despotic powers, or of life in the barbarian empires of Asia, whose despotism was frequently likened to the organization of the household" (27).

30. Wilkins, "Beyond Bandung: The Critical Nationalism of Lorraine Hansberry, 1950–1965," 199.

31. Becky Nicolaides and Andrew Wiese, eds., *The Suburb Reader* (New York: Routledge, 2006), 321.

32. Ibid., 326–27. See also Dolores Hayden, *Building Suburbia* (New York: Vintage, 2003), especially her discussion of Lakewood, California, titled "We Sell Happiness in Homes," 138.

33. Dianne Harris, "Race, Class, and Privacy in the Ordinary Postwar House, 1945–60," in *Landscape and Race in the United States*, ed. Richard Schein (New York: Routledge, 2006), 127–55. For Harris's expanded argument, see *Little White Houses: How the Postwar Home Constructed Race in America* (Minneapolis: University of Minnesota Press, 2012).

34. "Introduction," *A Raisin in the Sun*, 10.

35. Jurca, *White Diaspora*, 9. Jurca addresses this neglect through a detailed study of the ways white pity comes to stand in for the desire to belong, outlining along the way the oversight of the social and affective geographies of men in domestic fiction of the twentieth century.

36. For a helpful elaboration of "woman's place" in the home and the related architecture of Cold War domestic space, see Dolores Hayden, *Redesigning the American Dream* (New York: Norton, 2002) especially chapter 4, "Nurturing: Home, Mom and Apple Pie." Hayden's account, while immensely instructive in its rethinking of home life in terms of its spatial, technical, cultural, social, and economic dimensions, nonetheless leaves out the constitutive affective component of nurturing as work tied inextricably to the emotions.

37. Ahmed, "Affective Economies," 121.

38. Brown, "Reification, Reanimation: and The American Uncanny," *Critical Inquiry* 32 (winter 2006): 182.

39. Sedgwick writes, "To perceive texture is never only to ask or know What is it like? Nor even just How does it impinge on me? Textural perception always explores two other questions as well: How did it get that way? And What could I do with it?" *Touching Feeling: Affect, Pedagogy, Performativity* (Durham, NC: Duke University Press, 2002), 13.

40. When we meet Mama, the first things she does are cross the room and open the window. She brings in the flower pot, "feels the dirt and puts it back out" (39).

41. See, for example, Jane Jacobs, *The Economy of Cities* (New York: Vintage, 1970); Dianne Harris, ed., *Second Suburb: Levittown, PA* (Pittsburgh: University of Pittsburgh Press, 2010); Joel Foreman, ed., *The Other Fifties: Interrogating American Icons* (Chicago: University of Illinois Press, 1997); and Dianne Harris, "Race, Class, and Privacy in the Ordinary Postwar House, 1945–1960."

42. Isenstadt, *The Modern American House: Spaciousness and Middle Class Identity* (Cambridge: Cambridge University Press, 2006), 252.

43. See Deborah Nelson, *Pursuing Privacy in Cold War America*, and Dianne Harris.

44. Isenstadt, The Modern American House, 206.

45. See John Keats, *The Crack in the Picture Window* (New York: Houghton Mifflin, 1956), a popular sociological condemnation of the suburbs.

46. Harris notes that the picture window also became crass because it threatened individuality ("Race, Class, and Privacy in the Ordinary Postwar House, 1945–1960," 146).

47. Also cited in Cohen, *A Consumer's Republic*, 151.

48. Ibid.

49. "Race, Class, and Privacy in the Ordinary Postwar House, 1945–1960," 132, 148. Harris cites an article by the *House Beautiful* garden editor Joseph Howland, titled "Good Living is NOT Public Living," in which privacy becomes democracy writ large.

50. See, for example, Adrienne Rich, "The Problem with Lorraine Hansberry," *Freedomways: A Quarterly Review of the Freedom Movement* 19 (1979): 252–60; Patricia Hill Collins, *Black Feminist Thought: Knowledge, Consciousness, Empowerment* (New York: Routledge, 1991); and bell hooks, *Ain't I a Woman: Black Women and Feminism* (Boston: South End Press, 1991).

51. Galbraith, *The Affluent Society* (1958; repr., New York: Mariner Books, 1998), 96–97.

52. Hansberry, "The Negro Writer and His Roots," 3.

53. Gwendolyn Brooks, "Maud Martha" (1953) in *Blacks* (New York: Harper and Row, 1987), 168. Emphasis added.

54. Gwendolyn Brooks, *Blacks*, 170.

55. See also Paul Gilroy, who uses epidermalization as a visual politics in which modern self-conception is grounded, noting that it refers to, "a historically specific system for making bodies meaningful by endowing them with quantities of 'color.' It suggests a perceptual regime in which the racialized body is bounded and protected

by its enclosing skin. The observer's gaze does not penetrate that membrane but rests upon it and, in doing so, receives the truths of racial difference from the other body." *Against Race: Imagining Political Culture Beyond the Color Line* (Cambridge: Harvard University Press, 2000), 46.

56. Hortense Spillers, "Mama's Maybe, Papa's Baby: An American Grammar Book," *diacritics* 17.2 (1997): 65–82.

57. John Lewis Gaddis, *Strategies of Containment: A Critical Appraisal of American National Security Policy During the Cold War* (New York: Oxford University Press, 1989); Kate Brown, *Plutopia: Nuclear Families, Atomic Cities and the Great Soviet and American Plutonium Disasters* (New York: Oxford University Press, 2013).

58. See my discussion in *Beyond the Color Line and the Iron Curtain*.

59. Ahmed, "Affective Economies," 127.

60. Here I would argue that the idea of a family (the Youngers) coming together in opposition to a demonized opponent (Lindner) enables this scene to be sentimentalized in its interpretation by contemporary white audiences, such that difference was elided in favor of a familial fantasy of equality and identification across difference, a generic wish for a simple, morally "correct" denouement—no matter the actual structural and material differences between the Youngers and the audience members. In such a fantasy, the Youngers' move to the suburbs would be a blessing, a triumph of moral righteousness over blatant discrimination, and, most importantly, an *ending*— not the messy opening that the play's final scene foreshadows.

61. Kaplan, "Manifest Domesticity," 581.

62. Ibid., 600.

Chapter 5: Selling the Homeland

1. Quoted in Masey and Morgan, *Cold War Confrontations*, 204.

2. Crowther noted that everyone should take a holiday and go see *Silk Stockings* because, "It would sweeten the national disposition, embolden those hesitant towards romance and possibly make us all feel easier about Soviet Russia, the butt of most of the kidding in this film." "'Silk Stockings' Arrives; Fred Astaire and Cyd Charisse Co-Star," *New York Times*, July 19, 1957, 11.

3. David Riesman, *Abundance for What? And Other Essays* (Garden City, NY: Doubleday, 1965), 67.

4. The use of women's undergarments as indicative of Cold War commerce was not uncommon. In 1956, for example, MGM released a non-musical remake of *Ninotchka* titled *The Iron Petticoat*, starring Katherine Hepburn and Bob Hope.

5. A 1952 edition of the U.S. government's *Labor Air Bulletin* claimed that, "in contrast with conditions in communist countries, where the much advertised equality and rights of women means the right to work in coal mines, the United States has shown a growing concern for the health and welfare of working women because of their role as home makers and future bearers of children." Quoted in Laura A. Belmonte, "A Family Affair? Gender, the US Information Agency, and Cold War Ideology, 1945–60," *Culture and International History*, ed. Jessica Gienow-Hecht and Frank Schumacher (New York: Berghahn Books, 2003), 79–93. For more on the use

of gender in U.S. diplomatic discourse, see Belmonte, *Selling the American Way: US Propaganda and the Cold War* (Philadelphia: University of Pennsylvania Press, 2008).

6. Joseph Nye, *Soft Power: The Means to Success in World Politics* (Public Affairs, 2005).

7. See Hixson, *Parting the Curtain* (1997); de Grazia, *Irresistible Empire* (2006); and Castillo, *Cold War on the Home Front* (2010).

8. Helen Laville, "'Our Country Endangered by Underwear': Fashion, Femininity, and the Seduction Narrative in *Ninotchka* and *Silk Stockings*," *Diplomatic History* 30.4 (September 2006): 641.

9. See also Dana Heller, "A Passion for Extremes: Hollywood's Cold War Romance with Russia," *Comparative American Studies* 3.1 (March 2005): 89–110. Both Heller and Laville provide instructive insights about the narrative emplotment of female sexuality in Cold War antagonisms. For related articles, see Choi Chatterjee and Beth Holmgren, eds., *Americans Experience Russia: Encountering the Enigma, 1917 to the Present* (New York: Routledge, 2013); and Tony Shaw and Denise Youngblood, *Cinematic Cold War: The American Struggle for Hearts and Minds* (University Press of Kansas, 2010).

10. See Miriam Bratu Hansen, "The Mass Production of the Senses: Classical Cinema as Vernacular Modernism," *Modernism/Modernity* 6.2 (1999): 71.

11. Rogin, *Blackface, White Noise: Jewish Immigrants in the Hollywood Melting Pot* (Berkeley: University of California Press, 1998), 14.

12. Eric Lott, *Love and Theft: Blackface Minstrelsy and the American Working Class* (New York: Oxford University Press), 49.

13. Ibid., 41.

14. Clover's article has been enormously helpful to me in thinking through the indebtedness of *Silk Stockings* to black cultural forms. "Dancin' in the Rain," *Critical Inquiry* 21.4 (summer 1995): 722–47.

15. Lisa Lowe, "The Liberal Ruses of Freedom," talk delivered at Northwestern University, April 1, 2013.

16. *Ninotchka*, directed by Ernst Lubitsch and starring Greta Garbo, was based on a story by Melchior Lengyel; its screenplay was written by Billy Wilder, Charles Brackett, and Walter Reisch. With the exception of the Astaire numbers, the choreography in *Silk Stockings* was by Eugene Loring.

17. In using the phrase "female masculinity," I am borrowing the title of Judith Halberstam's groundbreaking study, *Female Masculinity* (Durham, NC: Duke University Press, 1998). Unfortunately, the character of Nina Yoshenko eludes the nuanced deployment of Halberstam's ideas. Nina fronts masculinity as a farce, and the audience is clearly intended to recognize this performance of gender as unnatural for her. In fact, the whole point of Nina's character is to demonstrate how masculine traits in women rub nature the wrong way.

18. "It is not an accident that we use the expression 'to see red,' 'to feel blue,' the artist should take advantage of the mental and emotional implications of color and use them upon the screen to increase the power and effectiveness of a scene, situation, or character." Quoted in David Luhrssen, *Mamoulian: Life on Stage and Screen* (Louisville: University Press of Kentucky, 2012), 78.

19. Ibid.

20. Cyd Charisse, "Dancer Had $5 Million Legs," *New York Sun*, June 18, 2008, accessed July 26, 2013.

21. Dana Heller, "Sex and the Series: Paris, New York, and the Postnational Romance," *American Studies* 46.1 (summer 2005): 151.

22. Vanessa Schwartz, *It's So French! Hollywood, Paris, and the Making of Cosmopolitan Film Culture* (Chicago: University of Chicago Press, 2007), 21.

23. See, among other studies, Michel Fabre, *From Harlem to Paris: Black American Writers in France, 1840–1980* (Urbana: University of Illinois Press, 1983); Brent Edwards, *The Practice of Diaspora: Literature, Translation, and the Rise of Black Internationalism* (Cambridge: Harvard University Press, 2003).

24. See especially my chapters on Langston Hughes's collection of short stories, *The Ways of White Folks*, and on Paul Robeson's use of music to establish a soul-based kinship with Soviet Russians.

25. On the Hollywood musical as a genre whose project was the defense of popular entertainment against claims of inferiority launched by proponents of "high" culture, see Jane Feuer, *The Hollywood Musical* (London: British Film Institute, 1982).

26. See Lynn Spigel, *Make Room for TV: Television and the Family Ideal in Postwar America* (Chicago: University of Chicago Press, 1992).

27. Luhrssen, *Mamoulian*, 136.

28. Laville, "Our Country Endangered by Underwear," 640.

29. John Wakeman, ed., *World Film Directors: Volume One, 1890–1945* (New York: The H.W. Wilson Company, 1987), 710–14. *The Scribner Encyclopedia of American Lives: Volume Two, 1986–1990* (New York: Charles Scribner's Sons, 1999), 594–95.

30. Laville, "Our Country Endangered by Underwear," 640.

31. Regarding a different film, Carol Clover identifies the stooge Lina in *Singin' in the Rain*: "she is the scapegoat not only for all the actors, male and female alike, whose voices flunked the shift to sound, *but for all the white performers who danced the art of unseen others—which is to say for the film musical itself*. No wonder her exposure must be so brutal and her humiliation so complete" [emphases added]. Clover, "Dancin' in the Rain," 744.

32. Jean Baudrillard, *Symbolic Exchange and Death*, trans. Iain Hamilton Grant (London: Sage, 1993), 78.

33. Some of these photos are accessible on the Internet. Sochurek's photo essay was published in *Life* on July 6, 1959.

34. "Moscow Missions for Guys and Gals," *Life,* July 6, 1959, 24.

35. Harrison Salisbury, *To Moscow and Beyond: A Reporter's Narrative* (New York: Harpers, 1959), 48.

36. Quoted in Belmonte, "A Family Affair? Gender, the US Information Agency, and Cold War Ideology, 1945–60," 84–85.

37. Catriona Kelly and David Shepherd, "Introduction: Why Cultural Studies?" in Kelly and Shepherd, eds., *Russian Cultural Studies*, 9.

38. Sheila Fitzpatrick, *The Cultural Front: Power and Culture in Revolutionary Russia* (Ithaca: Cornell University Press), 218. See also C. Kelly and V. Volkov, "Directed Desires, Kul'turnost' and Consumption," in Kelly and Shepherd, eds., *Con-*

structing Russian Culture in the Age of Revolution, 291–313; and Vera Dunham, *In Stalin's Time: Middleclass Values in Soviet Fiction* (Cambridge: Cambridge University Press, 1976; repr., Durham: Duke University Press, 1990).

39. A review of the show in *Izvestia* made similar claims. See V. Osipov, "Creature from Another Planet," *Izvestia*, June 22, 1959, 4.

40. These questions were simultaneously present in Soviet critique of Western liberation via consumerism (see chapter 4), and obscured by the desire to keep pace with Western industry in all areas, especially those oriented towards the consumer, who was of course gendered as female. The contradictory nature of these paradoxical impulses, as I explain further, was Soviet to the core.

41. Higgins, *Red Plush and Black Bread: A Famous Reporter's Account of True Conditions in the Forbidden Soviet Countries* (New York: Doubleday, 1955), 180.

42. Ibid., 181.

43. On photography's role in public culture, see Robert Hariman and John Louis Lucaites, *No Caption Needed: Iconic Photographs, Public Culture, and Liberal Democracy* (Chicago: University of Chicago Press, 2007). On the role of "doubleness" in Russian literature, see Dale E. Peterson, *Up From Bondage: The Literatures of Russian and African American Soul* (Durham, NC: Duke University Press, 2000).

44. Salisbury, *To Moscow and Beyond*, 48.

45. Quoted in Larissa Zakharova, "Dior in Moscow: A Taste for Luxury in Soviet Fashion under Khrushchev," in *Pleasures in Socialism: Leisure and Luxury in the Eastern Bloc*, ed. David Crowley and Susan E. Reid (Evanston: Northwestern University Press, 2010), 110.

46. The long-standing relationship between French and Russian aesthetics was not only about Western models of beauty traveling to Russia, but also about intercultural collaboration.

47. Djurdja Bartlett, *FashionEast: The Spectre that Haunted Socialism* (Cambridge: MIT Press, 2010), 123.

48. Two hundred thousand copies of the 1966 edition were printed, with fifteen full-color illustrations. (The previous edition had no color illustrations.) These illustrations were further attempts to mold Soviet taste and create a visual vernacular of modern sophistication. The encyclopedia has suggestions for home interiors as well as family fashions, and offers advice on how to choose and match fabrics by color, pattern, and texture, as well as on how to accessorize the home.

49. Olga Gurova, "The Art of Dressing: Body, Gender, and Discourse on Fashion in the Soviet Union 1950s and 1960s," unpublished ms., 4.

50. Kelly and Volkov, "Directed Desires: *Kul'turnost'* and Consumption," 295.

51. Zakharova, "Dior in Moscow," 100. See also Larissa Zakharova, "Kazhdoi sovetskoi zhenshchine plat'e ot Diora (frantsuzskoe vliianie v sovetskoi mode 1950–60-kh godov)," *Sotsial'naia istoriia; Ezhegodnik* [Yearbook] *2004* (Moscow: Rosspen, 2005), 339–67; and Larissa Zakharova, *S'habiller à la soviétique: la mode et le dégel en URSS* (Paris: CNRS, 2011).

52. See Mikhail Epstein, *After the Future: Paradoxes of Postmodernism and Contemporary Russian Culture* (Amherst: University of Massachusetts Press, 1995); and

Russian Postmodernism: New Perspectives on Late Soviet and Post-Soviet Literature (New York: Berghahn Books, 1999).

53. Zakharova goes on to conclude: "the public repudiation of luxury in Soviet discourse could be construed as an attempt to maintain social consensus in a society where material conditions of ordinary people were defined by shortage. The utopian promise of abundance in the communist future played a similar role by turning people's attention away from the real standards of living" ("Dior in Moscow," 114).

54. See my discussion of Olga in chapter 3. For an illuminating reading of Soviet romance with and incorporation of Westernness, see Yurchak, *Everything Was Forever, Until It Was No More*, 158–206.

55. Salisbury, *To Moscow and Beyond*, 46.

56. Laville points out that, in 1956, Paramount Studios produced a version of *War and Peace* starring Audrey Hepburn; while it wasn't a musical, it was roundly criticized for playing loosely with Tolstoy's novel. She writes, "It is notable that *Silk Stockings* actively mocks the attempts of Hollywood musicals to fuse high classical literature with mass popular culture—the central project of the last fifteen years of Hollywood musicals" ("Our Country Endangered by Underwear," 640).

57. Jane Feuer, *The Hollywood Musical* (Bloomington: Indiana University Press, 1982), 71.

58. See S. Frederick Starr, *Red and Hot: The Fate of Jazz in the Soviet Union* (New York: Oxford University Press, 1983).

59. Todd Decker, *Music Makes Me: Fred Astaire and Jazz* (Berkeley: University of California Press, 2011), 219.

60. Susan Manning, *Modern Dance, Negro Dance: Race in Motion* (Minneapolis: University of Minnesota Press, 2006).

61. Before she gained fame through her performance with Gene Kelley in *Singin' in the Rain* (1952), Cyd Charisse was the resident ballet dancer on the Freed Unit at MGM.

62. Michael Rogin, "'Democracy and Burnt Cork': The End of Blackface, the Beginning of Civil Rights," *Representations* 40 (spring 1994): 10.

63. No friend of the Soviet regime, director Rouben Mamoulian identified as an outsider—as an Armenian raised in Georgia, as a member of the Georgian elite who fled during the nascent days of Soviet rule, and as an émigré in New York who was self-conscious about his heavy accent. "Red Blues" evokes the idea of parallel and overlapping strands of ethnic difference, but it does so through movement, music, and directorial eye. As the original director of *Porgy* and later *Porgy and Bess*, Mamoulian could not have been unaware of the telling absence of African American actors in this scene.

64. Crowther, "'Silk Stockings' Arrives," 11.

65. Luhrssen, *Mamoulian*, 115.

66. Felix Belair, "United States Has Secret Sonic Weapon—Jazz," *New York Times*, August 6, 1955, 1.

67. The phenomenon of the *stilyagi* has been taken up by some of the most influential cultural historians of the Soviet era, including Frederick Starr, Walter Hixson, Timothy Ryback, Yale Richmond, and Artemy Troitsky. See Starr, *Red and Hot: the*

Fate of Jazz in the Soviet Union; Richmond, *Cultural Exchange and the Cold War: Raising the Iron Curtain* (University Park: Penn State Press, 2003); Troitsky, *Back in the USSR: The True Story of Rock in Russia* (London: Omnibus, 1987); and Alexei Yurchak, *Everything Was Forever, Until It Was No More.*

68. See works by Starr, Yurchak, and Troitsky mentioned in note above.

69. Georgy Litvinov, *Stilyagi, Kak Eto Bylo* (St. Petersburg: Amfira, 2009).

70. See Yurchak, *Everything was Forever, Until It Was No More.*

71. Ibid.

72. Higgins, *Red Plush and Black Bread*, 180.

73. Vassily Aksyonov, *In Search of Melancholy Baby* (New York: Random House, 1987), 38; also cited in Timothy Ryback, *Rock Around the Clock: A History of Rock Music in Eastern Europe and the Soviet Union, 1954–1988* (New York: Oxford University Press, 1990), 95.

74. Belyaev, "Stilyiaga," *Krokodil*, March 10, 1949, 10.

75. *Izvestia*, January 6, 1951, 3.

76. Ackerman, "A Theory of Style," *The Journal of Aesthetics and Criticism* 20.3 (spring 1962): 228.

77. Goodman, "The Status of Style," *Critical Inquiry* 1.4 (June 1975): 799–811.

78. In 2008 the Soviet director Valery Todorovsky made a musical film, *Stilyagi*, the first major post-Soviet look at the cultural phenomenon. In addition to the filmic interpretation of these lost youth, see Georgy Litvinov, *Stilyagi, Kak Eto Bylo* (Saint Petersburg: Amfira, 2009).

79. Troitsky, *Back in the USSR*, 7. Also cited in Yurchak, *Everything Was Forever*, 182.

80. This kind of discussion is particularly relevant, I think, for working through the complicated rearticulations of Cold War grievances and animosities appearing in the latter half of the 2010s.

81. Similarly, the temporality of the X-ray record suggests parallels to the "race record," in which the past is part of the present in complicated ways. The moment of X-ray as finite becomes endlessly repeated and respun as a recording, spinning and respinning that imprint into or towards an infinite. Again, a tension between present and future emerges—so long as the music can be played, the futurity of Soviet subjectivity may be heard as infinite. See Robin Kelley, *Freedom Dreams: The Black Radical Imagination* (Boston: Beacon, 2003); Fred Moten, *In the Break: The Aesthetics of the Black Radical Tradition* (Minneapolis: University of Minnesota Press, 2003); and Alexei Yurchak.

82. Walter Hixson, *Parting the Curtain*, 117.

83. A future project involves taking up the apparitional presence of blackness in Soviet jazz—codified in the Soviet vernacular as internationalism or in working-class themes—and tracing it through two films, Grigorii Alexandrov's *Tzirk* (1936), and Valery Todorovsky's *Stilyagi* (2008).

84. See my discussion of Paul Robeson in *Beyond the Color Line and the Iron Curtain.*

85. See Penny Von Eschen, *Satchmo Blows Up the World: Jazz Ambassadors Play the Cold War* (Cambridge: Harvard University Press), 2009.

86. Dana Heller comments about the Hollywood musical's "obsessive need to re-fashion ready-made myths that manipulate relations of nation and history, gender and sexuality, desire and consumption towards the manufacture of a democratic consensus that links the private body with the national body, or the longings of private individuals with the objectives and missions of the democratic sphere"; "A Passion for Extremes," 106.

87. Higgins, *Red Plush and Black Bread*, 183.

88. Quoted in Luhrssen, *Mamoulian*, 135.

89. A lifelong Republican, Astaire was a founding member of the Hollywood Republican Committee and dismayed by the increased emphasis on sexuality and licentiousness in Hollywood film. Joseph Epstein, *Fred Astaire: Icons of America* (New Haven: Yale University Press, 2008), 75.

90. Decker, *Music Makes Me*, 235–36. As Decker points out, by 1957 you certainly couldn't ignore Elvis. In January of that year, his hit "All Shook Up" was at the top of the charts.

91. Although Eugene Loring is credited as the film's choreographer, Astaire insisted on choreographing all of his own pieces himself, along with his friend Dave Robel and longtime collaborator Hermes Pan.

92. Carol Clover notes that Astaire comments in his biography, "I don't know how it all started, and I don't want to know. I have no desire to prove anything by it . . . I just dance" (quoted in Clover, "Dancin' in the Rain," 741).

93. Jill Watts, *Hattie McDaniel: Black Ambition, White Hollywood* (New York: Amistad, 2005), 82.

94. Decker claims that Astaire's "body of consistent if widely spaced work with black musicians, increasing in frequency across the decades, forms another aspect of Astaire's uniqueness among Hollywood musical stars" (273). However, as Decker admits, these musicians were not dancers—Astaire danced with a black dancer only once, in *The Band Wagon*, with LeRoy Daniels in "A Shine on Your Shoes," a number discussed at length by Stanley Cavell. Tom Cripps notes that "Fred Astaire proudly boasted of appearing on the same vaudeville card with Bill Robinson," a point that Clover correlates (I believe correctly) to Astaire's claim of ignorance about the interracialism of dance, a claim that she reads as an admission of knowledge and, beyond that, as a signal of guilt about his denial of this racial history. See Cripps, *Slow Fade to Black: The Negro in American Film, 1900–1942* (New York, 1993), 99.

95. Crowther, "'Silk Stockings' Arrives," *New York Times*, July 19, 1957, 11.

96. Cavell, *Philosophy the Day After Tomorrow* (Cambridge: Harvard University Press, 2006), 69, 76. In sum, Cavell's point is that we cannot praise black dancing without being "compromised by an American scene of mechanical self-praise whose self-forgetfulness the counter-scenes of entertainment" have remembered.

97. While I am in sympathy with Vanessa Schwartz's argument in *It's So French!* about the Frenchness of films like *Silk Stockings*, I rather see the operation of pastness here—to the nineteenth-century Belle Epoque—as a racial screen that serves to occlude the colonial past of France and likewise the policies of the United States with regard to colonialism and slavery. The film seems to me to be as much about racial forgetting as it is about memorializing a rich cultural past that depended upon colonial complicity.

98. The coverage of the Christian Dior show in Moscow highlights this double motion even more aggressively. Attention to haute couture and *défilé* provided a convenient distraction from the brutalization of African bodies in independence movements; fashion was shores away from neocolonial interests, despite the fact that Yves Saint Laurent was a *pied noir* from Oran, Algeria.

Epilogue: A Kitchen in History

1. Roland Barthes, *Camera Lucida* (New York: Macmillan, 1981), 45.

2. "Mrs. Oswald emerges as a woman almost too terrifying to believe," reported *Newsweek* in an article called "Mama Oswald," February 28, 1966, 93–94. An article in *Time* mocked Marguerite Oswald's aspirations to be a writer; "A Mother Who Wants to Write," *Time*, February 21, 1964, 23–24.

3. The piece was originally called "The Strange World of Marguerite Oswald" and appeared in *McCall's* in October 1965. The piece and the book are virtually identical. I discuss *A Mother in History* (1966; repr., New York: Pharos Books, 1992) in detail in "Between Mother and History: Jean Stafford, Marguerite Oswald, and US Cold War Women's Citizenship," *differences* 13.3 (2002): 83–120.

4. Stafford, *A Mother in History* (New York: Pharos, 1992), 25, 54.

5. "My theme is the American way of life," Oswald told Stafford. *A Mother in History*, 6.

6. Ibid., 55.

7. See *Life*, November 29, 1963, 39.

8. Marguerite was indignant that Jackie Kennedy did not send a condolence card for the death of her son, Lee.

9. See Lynn Spigel, "Object Lessons for the Media Home."

INDEX

Note: *page numbers* in italics refer to images.

Ackerman, James, 165
affect aliens, 46–47
Africa, U.S. policy and, xv, 127
African America, as oppressed nation, xv
African American cultural forms, white
    appropriation of, 133–34, 160–62,
    174–77
African American leftists, xiv–xv, 15;
    women and, 89
Ahmed, Sara, 46, 114, 125–26, 216n16
Aksyonov, Vasily, 164
Alcaron, Norma, 74
American exceptionalism: and assumed
    universality of U.S. conceptions, 11;
    Cold War kitchen as lens for
    interrogating, 5; and Cold War
    thinking, 4–5, 178, 191n10; efforts
    to move past, 5; limits of democratic
    state of mind in, 19–20; *Silk
    Stockings* and, 134–35
American National Exhibition in
    Moscow (ANEM): African American
    employees at, xiv, xvii, 36, *37, 38,*
    189n6, 197n18; and black leftists,
    xiv, 107; and communication, 10–11,
    12, 13, 43–44; communication
    theory of, 18–21, 23–24, 49, 196n11,
    197–98n26; consumerist message of,
    1, 2, 20–22, 27; corporate backing
    of, 3; exhibits at, 2–3, 25–29, *30, 31,*
    32–33, 190n4, 191n7; flag raising
    ceremony, xvii; goals of, 20, 22–24,

40–41, 46–47; guest books, 42–45;
    guides at, xiv, xvii, 19, 189n6,
    192n17, 197n18; number of visitors
    to, 13; and occlusion of U.S. issues,
    10, 44; planners of, 2–3; site plan,
    19; Soviet counter exhibition,
    202n80; U.S. press on, xv–xvi, 27,
    28, 36, 37, 38, 47, 49; wedding scene
    at, xiv, xv–xvi, xvii, 35–36, *37, 38,*
    64, 200n53. *See also Glimpses of the
    USA;* kitchen debate; kitchen
    displays at ANEM; Soviet reaction
    to ANEM
*The American Negro writer and His
    Roots* (Davis, ed.), 107
American Society of African Culture
    (AMSAC), 106–7
Anderson, Anne Sonopol, 27, *28, 36*
ANEM. *See* American National
    Exhibition in Moscow
appliances: in Oswald kitchen, 180, *180;*
    and proletarian rise into middle class,
    88; as prosthetic devices for
    emotions, 87–88. *See also* Kitchen
    Aid dishwasher ad
Arendt, Hannah, 106, 217n29
Armstrong, Louis, 39, 162

Baraka, Amiri, 113
Baranskaya, Natalya, 8, 11, 54, 69, 70,
    93. See also *A Week Like Any Other*
    (Baranskaya)